GENTLY WHISPERED

Oral Teachings by the Very Venerable Kalu Rinpoche

Dorje Chang, surrounded by the founding fathers of the Karma Kagyu lineage: Tilopa, Naropa, Marpa Lotsawa, Milarepa, Gampopa, and Dusum Khyenpa (the First Gyalwa Karmapa) (Traditional Tibetan painting with cloth framing by unknown artist, mid-20th century.)

GENTLY WHISPERED

Oral Teachings
by the Very Venerable Kalu Rinpoche

Foreword by His Eminence the XIIth Tai Situpa

Compiled, edited and annotated by
Elizabeth Selandia, O.M.D., C.A.

Station Hill Press

Cover: Kalu Rinpoche leading an assembly of pilgrims in prayer in early 1984 in one of the meditation caves located nearby Bodh-Gaya, India (Photograph by J.G. Sherab Ebin)

Published by Station Hill Press, Inc., Barrytown, New York 12507.

Distributed by the Talman Company, 131 Spring Street, Suite 201 E-N, New York, New York 10012.

Cover and book design by Susan Quasha, assisted by Vicki Hickman.

Library of Congress Cataloging-in-Publication Data
Karma-rań-byuń-kun-khyab-phrin-las, Khenpo Kalu.
    Gently whispered : Oral teachings by the Very Venerable Kalu Rinpoche : foreword by His Eminence the XIIth Tai Situpa / compiled, edited, and annotated by Elizabeth Selandia.
        p.   cm.
    Includes bibliographical references and index.
    ISBN 0-88268-153-2 : $14.95
    1. Spiritual life—Buddhism. 2. Buddhism—China—Tibet-
-Doctrines. I. Selandia, Elizabeth. II. Title.
BQ7775.K38 1994
294.3'42—dc20   93-42823
                                                             CIP

Manufactured in the United States of America

Dedicated to the impeccable perpetuation
of the glorious Kagyu lineage
and to the success of its leaders and followers
in accomplishing their commitment
to bring all sentient beings
to the state of enlightened awareness.

Kalu Rinpoche copying a text while seated in his room at the monastery in Sonada, India, in early 1970 (Photography by J.G. Sherab Ebin)

CONTENTS

Foreword by H.E. the XIIth Tai Situpa		*vii*
Preface		*xi*
Introduction		*xvii*
1	First Reflections	1
	Introduction to the Nature of the Mind	
2	Changing Tides and Times	21
	Examination of Alaya and Karma	
3	Clear Dawning	37
	Explanation of the Vow of Refuge	
4	Gathering Clouds	51
	Resolution of Emotional Subjectivity	
5	Eye of the Storm	67
	Teachings on the Bardos of Death and Dying	
6	Distant Shores	85
	Introduction to the Vajrayana Practices	
7	Rainbow Skies	105
	Insight into the Mantrayana Practices	
8	Lingering Sunset	119
	Commentary on the Bodhisattva Vows	
9	Brilliant Moon	143
	Elucidation of the Mahamudra	
10	Cloud Mountains	161
	Challenges of Samaya and Dharma	

Appendix A: Open Letters to Disciples and Friends of
    The Lord of Refuge, Khyab Je Kalu Rinpoche   181
    From Bokar Tulku Rinpoche, Lama Gyaltsen.,
    and Khenpo Lodrö Dönyo, 15 May 1989
        *Concerning the last moments of Kalu Rinpoche
        and the religious activities following*
    From H.E. the XIIth Tai Situpa
        Concerning the passing of Kalu Rinpoche
Appendix B: Chenrezig Sadhana   195
    Prayers and Practice of Yidam Chenrezig
    With commentary adapted from Kalu Rinpoche's
    teachings
    *A Vajra Melody Imploring the Swift Return of
    the Lord of Refuge, Khyab Je Kalu Rinpoche*
    As translated from the illustrated letter of
    H.E. Jamgon Kongtrul Rinpoche
Appendix C: Glossary of Vajrayana Terminology   227
Bibliography   264
Index   267
Afterword & Prayer for the Continuation of the Kagyu   291
    Tradition

' SHERAB LING '
TITUTE OF BUDDHIST STUDIES

P. O. SANSAL
DIST. KANGRA H. P. INDIA - 176 125

His Eminence the Tai Situpa Rinpoche

The Very Venerable Kalu Rinpoche is one of the most outstanding
teachers of Tibetan Buddhism whose meditative experience and
profound wisdom are appreciated by all that come in contact
with him. It is most appropriate, at this time, that the
opportunity to have his valuable Dharma teachings translated
into English makes the study of the Buddha Dharma more
accessible to a larger group of practitioners and students of
religion and philosophy.

I am very pleased for the time and effort that has been dedicated
to this work. I would like to thank the editors and publisher
for the many hours of time they have spent to bring about this
book.

May this teaching bring happiness to all of those who will read
and study this work. With my humble and sincere dedication for
your well-being.

XIIth TAI SITUPA

PREFACE

It was supposed to be the summertime, but, far away from my California homeland, I was weathering the force of the monsoon, feeling swallowed by dense cloud banks that wholly neglected my presence inside them and that retreated only sometimes in the chill of nights made darker by the distant lightning. The promise of precious initiations into vajrayana had brought me to the monastery known as Samdup Tarjee Chöling, which is located in the Himalayas, an hour's drive down the hill from Darjeeling. Gathered together were more than a thousand followers of Tibetan Buddhism who had come to receive the transmission of *Rinchen Terdzod,* one of the five great treasuries compiled by Jamgon Kongtrul the Great. Together we were to spend six months packed into a shrine room decorated with beautiful murals of deities important to the practice of vajrayana, watching the lineage holders of the Karma Kagyu receive the initiations directly from the vajra master, Kalu Rinpoche. We all awaited the moment that these *tulkus* (recognized reincarnated teachers and *mahasiddhas*) would wind their way through the crowd to bestow the blessing of the day's teachings upon all present.

As I watched Kalu Rinpoche seated for hours on end while he recited the teachings and initiations contained in the collection, I found it easy to admire him for his unending diligence in perpetuation of the Dharma. Truly, in all my travels in search of sacred and occult teachings, I have never met another person quite like him. His tireless efforts to bring benefit to all beings made a strong impression upon me. Needless to say, I hold him in the highest regard, for it is he who has demonstrated to me my potential for enlightenment in this precious human existence.

It was here that a desire arose within me to enable Kalu Rinpoche's teachings to reach a wider range of audiences by offering my skills in communication so that readers might better explore his teachings. And it was here that his quiet whispers and gentle voice encouraged me to firmly believe that faith in the vajrayana, devotion to a genuine lineage, and confidence in the teachings of the Buddha would eventually enlighten anyone who desired such solace.

Drawn from many sources of notes and lectures, from many different translators' versions of Rinpoche's teachings, and from many impromptu talks he has given, this book is an attempt to give a thorough presentation of Kalu Rinpoche's teachings on the important topics of the four veils of obscuration, the bodhisattva vows, the practice of Chenrezig, and the vehicles known as the three yanas. This work has been compiled topic by topic, and, as a result, no one translator is wholly responsible for any one chapter. Further, the chapters are compiled from teachings given over a period of more than two decades, from the late sixties (before Rinpoche had begun his world travels) through the mid-eighties, and the locations where these teachings were given are so widespread as to be worldwide.

The material has been arranged so as to allow the reader to gain a gradual insight into the intricacies of approach and structure of the Tibetan tradition of Buddhadharma. It is, therefore, suggested that the chapters be read in sequence. The first three chapters contain many foundational thoughts, and while these might seem somewhat perplexing to the beginner, they are required for a thorough understanding of the material in the chapters that follow.

It should be noted that Rinpoche tended to repeat various ideas, and to continually refer to ideas already presented by giving brief recollection to those thoughts. At first I considered that these continual references detracted from a smooth flowing, polished style of communication. But, as the process of compilation continued, I came to realize that many of the repeated explanations were not simply rhetorical; rather, they were being given from varying viewpoints. The best example of this insight is reflected in Rinpoche's varying descriptive renditions of the qualities of the nature of mind, which he discusses at varying lengths in three different chapters. Each discussion is flavored with one of the concepts inherent to the differing approaches of the hinayana, the mahayana, and the vajrayana, and, thus, each rendition gives a fresh insight into the most perplexing problem facing the sentient being longing for liberation, namely, what is the true nature of mind?

To assist the reader unfamiliar with Tibetan Buddhism, the technical terms, foreign language terms, and religious terminology are indicated by italics upon first occurrence of mention. Diacritic marking of Sanskrit words is found only in the glossary. Further details specific to the glossary will be found at the beginning of Appendix C.

Permission was granted by His Eminence the XIIth Tai Situpa for the inclusion of a detailed explanation of the visualization and prayers contained in the sadhana of the Yidam Chenrezig. Since devotional practice to this yidam was publicly encouraged by Lord Buddha in the *Surangama Sutra*, the yidam practice is considered to be immediately employable by anyone interested, with no special permission or initiation required. Additionally, a prayer for the swift rebirth of Kalu Rinpoche written by His Eminence Jamgon Kongtrul Rinpoche has been included in this section in response to his personal request to me. Details concerning the sadhana and the commentary will be found at the beginning of Appendix B.

The direct concern and special interest of His Eminence the XIIth Tai Situ in seeing this book reach the public has been most beneficial. Devoting some of his valuable time to the several questions this work presented, he has willingly and openly helped this project reach maturation, indulging the many perplexing considerations of syntax, contracts, and karmic consequences. His blessing to this endeavor is gratefully and most respectfully acknowledged.

Several devoted students with an interest in seeing Rinpoche's teachings reach many peoples and nations have diligently applied themselves to the mastery of either the English language (being Tibetan speaking originally) or the Tibetan language (being of other linguistic backgrounds), and without their translations, Rinpoche's words, while pleasant in their sound, would have no meaning to populations lacking the understanding of the Tibetan language. The indebtedness to all who have assisted in the task of translation during Rinpoche's world tours is incalculable. Specifically, in relation to this collection of teachings, Richard Barron (Chökyi Nyima), J.G. Sherab Ebin, and Jeremy Morrell are gratefully acknowledged for their remarkable translations of Rinpoche's wisdom.

To assure that this compilation of Kalu Rinpoche's teachings has remained true to the Buddhadharma, I requested a few of the original translators (both those who were responsible for a major share of the translation represented in this work and those who have frequently translated for Rinpoche over many years) to read the final draft to make sure that the transmission was not lost. Their extensive training in Dharma helped confirm that this effort of compilation of translations has made the step from Tibetan into English with accuracy.

Still, it was with a joyous relief in seeing a goal accomplished that I received the following secretarial note accompanying the foreword written by His Eminence Tai Situpa Rinpoche. "I am writing to you on behalf of His Eminence Tai Situpa. Thank you for your letter and the main body of the text for *Gently Whispered* by Kalu Rinpoche. Tai Situ Rinpoche was very pleased with all of your efforts and is most happy to send you his foreword for the book. It is composed in the form of a open letter to all those who read the book and has his seal impressed upon it. He would like his foreword to appear as you receive it on his stationery. Rinpoche sends you his blessings and best wishes."

It is with gratitude that the following are acknowledged for personally giving me access to various materials additional to my notes for use in this edited and annotated compilation of Rinpoche's teachings: the translators Richard Barron (Chökyi Nyima), J.G. Sherab Ebin, and Jeremy Morrell; Tsering Lhamo, Tsewang Jurmay, and Tinley Drupa. Additional thanks are due to Phillip Shaw and

Michael Dergosits of Limbach & Limbach of San Francisco for their generous help.

Several people close to the Dharma read the draft and made valuable suggestions according to their expertise. Diane Thygersen added to the contextual perspectives necessary for communicating the Dharma "in a strange land," Wendy Jester provided invaluable support and editorial assistance, and J. G. Sherab Ebin contributed greatly with his ability to communicate in Buddhist Dharma languages as well as his understanding of the historical circumstances in which Buddhism came to both Tibet and the Western world.

Conerning the help received in the physical manifestation of this book, J. G. Sherab Ebin has also made several additional and invaluable contributions. His photographs, taken both recently and many years ago when he lived with Rinpoche in India, have added greatly to the visual format. His understanding of computer installation and software implementation has enabled me to move from archaic parchment copying to illuminating state of the art productions. And, most importantly, his pure devotion to Rinpoche has definitely served as a continual inspiration to me in making *Gently Whispered* become a reality. Michael Ingerman has generously provided the much needed technical support, and Peter Ingerman performed the painstaking task of sorting the text and editing that data to provide the framework upon which the index is based. Many others have been of great personal assistance in questions of grammar, approach, and proper phrasing of polite respect, etc. Rather than my naming some and not others, may they all be gratefully acknowledged for their contribution that has enabled this teaching to reach the general public.

Undoubtedly, this work would not have been possible had it not been for the dauntless efforts of the Very Venerable Kalu Rinpoche. In his bringing the Dharma to the West, in his opening the door of compassionate, loving kindness to all those unaware of the true nature of the mind, and in his lending encouragement to those countless sentient beings anywhere and everywhere along his path, he continually demonstrated the bodhisattva ideal. His willingness to bring immediate and lasting benefit to all with whom he comes in contact, both near and far, has definitely demonstrated his interest in the welfare of sentient beings as a continual and genuine concern.

When I started this book in an effort to help bring this truly wonderful teacher's insights into enlightened awareness to a widening audience, Kalu Rinpoche was still pursuing an active schedule that included world travel to administer to the several centers and three-year retreats he had founded. Some years later, while I was still deeply working on the final draft, I learned from His Eminence the XIIth Tai Situpa that Kalu Rinpoche had passed quietly into his final meditation late one May afternoon in 1989 at his Sonada monastery. Two weeks later I received a personal letter from Kalu Rinpoche's secretary in which he requested that I share with everyone an enclosed open letter concerning the events surrounding Rinpoche's passing. That open letter, plus a letter from His Eminence the XIIth Tai Situpa in which he writes concerning Kalu Rinpoche's passing, form Appendix A.

It is my prayer that the effort that has been put into making this book possible has its truest reward in your own personal realization of Kalu Rinpoche's fondest aspiration: "enlightenment for all sentient beings, our mothers, limitless as space."

Elizabeth Selandia, O.M.D., C.A.
San Simeon
16 March 1992

Introduction

I am very happy to be able to share with you the Buddha's teachings known as Dharma. Your interest in these teachings is a positive sign of the power of a great accumulation of virtuous activity gathered in previous lifetimes coming to fruition at this moment. This is very wonderful, and my greetings to you! I am an old man of eighty-four years now, the first fifty-two of which were spent completely isolated from the rest of the world in the land of Tibet. Several of those years I spent studying and practicing the Dharma and principles of vajrayana in solitary retreat. Since I have left Tibet, I have traveled worldwide to bring the truth of these teachings to all sentient beings ready and capable of receiving them. I welcome you and pray that a continuous rain of benefit comes to you for taking the time and effort to understand that upon which I am discoursing.

For many centuries, the Dharma of the Buddha has been preserved in the snowy, mountainous land of Tibet, where all the pith instructions, traditions of practice, and resultant realizations were widespread. Although this Dharma is often called *Tibetan Buddhism*, it is not originally Tibetan, for it comes directly from the Lord Buddha Shakyamuni. Once a noble prince, Lord Shakyamuni became the historical Buddha of our time when he attained enlightenment in the place called Bodh-Gaya in north-central India. Through his activities during his lifetime and his teachings during the historical occasions of turning the wheel of Dharma, all the vast array of Dharma teachings (numbering eighty-four thousand collections in all) came into existence. This Dharma was originally widespread in the land of India and was later faithfully translated into the Tibetan language by erudite scholars who had endured great hardship to gain these teachings. These translators thus allowed the Dharma to survive in the impenetrable mountains of Tibet long after Buddhism was all but destroyed in the Indian subcontinent.

By virtue of the power and blessings of this faithfully preserved tradition of *Buddhadharma* in Tibet, a great number of practitioners have become realized saints and *siddhas*. They are said to be so numerous that they equal the number of stars in the sky. The efforts and practice that brought realization of the true nature of the mind has allowed this tradition, which is quite profound, to become very advanced.

In Tibet, the teachings of the Dharma include five disciplines, known as the five great branches of learning. These branches incorporate the very important and extensive studies of medicine, astrology, and art, which were brought together as a single unified doctrine. Thus, in our tradition, the basic spiritual teachings of the Buddha also have the enrichment of these other approaches. The branches of learning to which I refer are known as the outer branches of learning, and the many Tibetan traditions present different formats of these outer forms. The basic Dharma taught by the Buddha comprises the inner branch of learning. Within these five great branches of learning are subdivisions called the five lesser subdivisions, which incorporate the traditions of astrology, debate, poetry composition, language, linguistics, and philosophy. Thus, there are ten branches, both the greater and the lesser, which form the whole of Buddhadharma as taught in the Tibetan tradition. Both the inner and outer form comprise what is commonly referred to as *Tibetan Buddhism*.

While in the West, I have noticed Westerners who are very educated and developed in their own particular academic traditions. I feel that many outer traditions with which I have become acquainted are quite similar, either in content or approach, to those taught in the traditions of the five lesser branches of learning in Buddhadharma. In the great libraries and universities of this modern world, several different philosophical discourses are available that are identical in many points with the Buddha's doctrine, and I often feel that these are the same, as though the Buddha himself had taught them.

Buddhadharma is now establishing itself in the West and a process of integration and adaptation has begun. Similar processes of adaptation were made centuries ago in several Asian countries. While traveling, I have observed the practice of Buddhadharma in a number of countries, such as Japan, Thailand, Burma, Sri Lanka, and so on. Each of these Buddhist societies has emphasized and focused on specific aspects of the Buddhadharma, aspects which have become very developed and which are widely practiced within their countries. For example, in Japan the Buddhist tradition relies heavily upon the *Prajna Paramita Sutra*, which teaches the nature of emptiness. The Japanese have developed their practice along that perspective of approach. In China and Taiwan, Buddhism has focused on the pure land sutras, which inspire devotion and reverence to Buddha Amitabha. Although the characters or letters of Japanese and Chinese texts appear somewhat different from Tibetan, I can see from the practice and application of their meaning that, regardless of the language used, the teachings are identical.

Time and time again, I have seen that all the different Dharmas that were preserved in Tibet have appeared in different forms throughout the world. I have observed that, in particular, the Christian and Islamic traditions [of charity] have developed one whole aspect of Buddhadharma and put this widely into practice. I see how wonderful it is that the Buddhadharma has spread throughout the world in many different ways, with various aspects of it being understood and developed through practice, whether it is called Buddhadharma or not. I have great faith in all these traditions and regard this as the flourishing of Buddhadharma.

Those of you who have a great interest and enthusiasm for learning the nature of Dharma and who are trying to understand its meaning by practicing meditation and visualization techniques are definitely doing so because of past karmic endeavors. The result of your previous lifetimes' practice of the ten virtuous actions has created a very powerful development of positive karmic trends, as evidenced by both your presently having a *precious human existence* and your interest in Dharma. This is a theme I will return to many times throughout my discourse, as the fruition of these positive trends and habitual patterns that you established in previous lifetimes is indeed very wonderful. In the same way as the waters of the world flow into rivers which flow into the great oceans, all the teachings of the Buddha were widely spread throughout India, yet they were preserved in whole in the land of the old sea, Tibet. Thus, Buddhists who were so fortunate as to study and practice in Tibet were able to practice the entire doctrine, the whole sea of Buddha's teachings, without having to be limited to any one particular aspect. Therefore, you who are interested in following the practice as taught by the Tibetan lamas will be able to understand the entire meaning of the Buddhadharma. By bringing the entire meaning of Buddhadharma into your practice, you will be able to attain your goal of realizing complete liberation from samsaric suffering very quickly.

Kalu Rinpoche
Los Angeles
29 December 1988

≈ 1 ≈

FIRST REFLECTIONS

Introduction to the Nature of the Mind

Three kinds of mentally projected phenomena are constantly experienced by sentient beings because they believe that these projections are real. One projection is quite familiar. It is called the *fully ripened body,* or *fully ripened corporeal existence,* referring not only to the physical form, but also to the whole world in which sentient beings take rebirth. This world of corporeal existence, which is experienced as a whole environment (with landscape, mountains, etc.), is called fully ripened because it is the ripening of karmic accumulation that gives rise to such an experience.

Another projection is that which is perceived as the dreamer within the dream. During the dream, one believes one has a body that actually experiences the various episodes conceptualized while in the dream state. This dream body is the result of the constant and endless tendency of believing in a self. In believing, "I am," and in constantly clinging to external appearance as being something other than self, one clings to duality. The dream body, or the *body of habitual tendency,* is but a second type of mental manifestation.

Third, there is the *mental body* that arises after death. One's familiar form, or *body of karmic fruition,* is composed of five elements which, at the time of death, dissolve into one another. Finally, the residue of this dissolution again dissolves into a base consciousness which then falls into a kind of oblivion where there is no cognition. This state is like a very thick, heavy sleep, which usually lasts about three days, after which the consciousness re-arises and immediately projects a vast array of illusory images.

These mental projections have a haunting similarity to the way one is in one's dream and waking states. Such projections are, however, very different in that the appearances occur instantaneously and will arise and disappear immediately and very rapidly. Additionally, there is the tendency of the disembodied being that is experiencing this display to believe that it is something real. This, of course, furthers the habitual clinging to a duality of self and other, which complicates the after-death experience. Because the mind is caught into a misbelief of self and other during these illusory, bewildering appearances, such nonrecognition causes the experience of a great deal of fear and suffering.

All three bodies are continually manifesting in *samsara* because of this misconception; in the *death bardo,* or the interval (*bardo*) between dying and being reborn, this habitual misconception eventually compels one to experience rebirth again. However, bardo appearances, just like corporeal and dream appearances, are completely illusory. They have no foundation in *absolute reality.* It is this tendency of clinging to self and other that is inferred when the mental body is mentioned.

To liberate themselves from these delusions of misguided projection that are the source of suffering, the Lord Buddha Shakyamuni and many other realized beings have recognized the true nature of mind as having the quality of empty, unimpeded *clarity.* All sentient beings, without exception, have this same mind. This itself is the seed of buddhahood, the actual buddha nature that is inherent in all sentient beings. However, the ignorance of clinging to a self has obscured this inherent nature, for by clinging to a self, one necessarily defines an other, and therefore one clings to duality. This duality results in the obscuration of emotional reactions and the obscuration of karmic accumulation. This clinging, and these resultant obscurations, is the difference between samsaric existence and enlightened awareness.

According to the teachings of the Lord Buddha, the obscurations that keep us from true liberation are considered to be four in number. First, in the same way as one is unaware of one's facial image without a reflective surface demonstrating it, so the mind also does not see itself and is thus fundamentally ignorant in that it is not directly aware of its own nature. Second, through this ignorance, the mind develops habitual tendencies of dualistic relativeness of a self and an other. Third, unaware in its ignorance and force of habits while confronted by these dualistic projections, the reaction of the mind is that of emotional affliction, producing bewilderment, aversion, and/or attachment. Fourth, this emotional confusion produces accumulative karmic results that manifest in physical, verbal, and mental reactions which, in turn, further the karmic consequences of ignorance.

Despite its having become deluded, this same mind has yet another quality. In its empty, clear, and *unimpeded awareness*, it has a *primordial (or base) wisdom.* This primordial wisdom, and the *primordial consciousness*, are indivisibly mixed together, resulting in the state of sentient beings. Yet, occasionally, in just the same way that the weather produces openings in a thickly clouded sky allowing shafts of sunlight to shine forth, the primordial wisdom (or buddha nature) will somehow shine through the veil of ignorance. At that moment, no matter on what level of existence, sentient beings will experience some kind of feeling of compassion, of faith, or of some altruistic motive. This feeling motivates sentient beings to perform virtuous acts. Such virtuous actions will cause a higher rebirth, which will allow for more opportunity with which to mature Buddhadharma.

All of you who are coming in contact with this discourse have accumulated a great deal of positive karmic trends throughout many previous lifetimes. In these lifetimes, you have definitely developed faith in the *Three Jewels*—Buddha, Dharma, and Sangha. You previously established a connection that is ripening in this lifetime. It is evident that this is true because you are someone who is naturally inclined to acts of virtue and you have an interest in the Dharma. This is a very great attainment. That is what is meant by the *precious human existence*, which is a special type of human existence that has a number of specific conditions. It is extremely difficult to obtain, due to the propensity of the ignorant to cling to ignorance. Thus, by doing that which continues to increase your virtuous accumulation, you can continue to attain a precious human existence and to experience rebirth in higher states of existence, which encourage the flourishing of the Dharma. With such an opportunity, you can liberate yourself from the ocean of samsaric suffering and place yourself in the state of buddhahood. Now that you have this golden opportunity, it would be a shame to waste it or to lose it!

The opportunity of attaining a precious human existence is quite rare. It is often compared to the incalculable chance that a blind sea tortoise, which rises to the surface once every hundred years, would be snared by a single golden yoke afloat on an ocean as vast as space. You might wonder how it is possible for beings in the lower realms to attain a precious human existence when it is not possible for them to understand the Dharma. As well, you might wonder how it is they can ever escape from these lower realms. Since they cannot hear the teachings and are thus unable to put them into practice to free themselves, how is it they are not stuck there forever? I will develop this topic for fuller understanding in a later chapter, but for now I will give a brief answer. Even though sentient beings experience the lower realms as hell denizens, hungry ghosts, and animals, all of which lack the capabilities of understanding the meaning of the Dharma, they can form a connection with the sound of spoken Dharma and with the visible forms of Buddhadharma. These demonstrations of its truth will eventually lead to a rebirth in a higher state of existence in the human realm. Also, the mind of those experiencing the lower realms might feel a kind of virtuous impulse which, at some later stage, will ripen into rebirth in the human realm. Then, as a human being, it is possible to acquire the merit that will allow a rebirth in a precious human existence.

It is therefore possible that you can bring great benefit to all sentient beings through your prayers and good actions. You can be of direct benefit by having contact with beings in the animal realms, especially those that have close contact with the human realm, and you can help these beings progress to a higher rebirth. For example, if you were to explain the Dharma to an animal, or even to groups of animals, the blessing of your action would result in their experiencing a rebirth in a higher realm at some future time, although at the time of your explanation, they would have no understanding of what you had said. You can also speed up their progress by showing them a form or image of the Buddhadharma, or by reciting the sound of sacred *mantra* into their ear. And, of course, by doing these virtuous actions you increase your own positive karmic accumulation which helps assure you of future precious human existences.

There is a wonderful and simple illustration recorded in the *sutras*. Before the era of our historical Buddha, Lord Shakyamuni, there was that of the third Buddha of the present *kalpa*, namely, Buddha Kashyapa. In that epic of time past, there was a shrine, or a *stupa*, which is considered sacred to the Buddhist tradition in that it has many special symbolic meanings. On a leaf hanging from a branch of a tree growing near this stupa were seven insects. During a strong gust of wind, the leaf broke loose and sailed through the air, taking the seven insects with it. As the wind carried the leaf and the insects around the stupa several times, the insects performed the highly meritorious action of circumambulation of a holy place. By this karmic connection, the seven insects were reborn in a celestial realm in their next lifetime.

Yet another example from times past is that of a land tortoise who enjoyed drying off in the sun after a morning of wallowing in the mud of the shore hidden in the shade by the tall tree. The tortoise's sunning spot was on the opposite side of the nearby stupa, which had a crack in its base. Longing for the warmth of the sun, the land tortoise walked daily to his sunning spot, using the stupa as his landmark to guide him there. As his eyesight was not the best, the landmark would all too soon become the stumbling block, causing the tortoise to rub his mud laiden body against the stupa's base. Over time, this caused the mud he had carried to fill in this crack. By the virtue of such a positive karmic action, the land tortoise was reborn in one of the gods' realms. These are not contrived tales to delight an audience; these were taught by the Buddha and were recorded in the Buddhist sutras.

All sentient beings have body, speech, and mind. And, although we think of them all as being important, body and speech are like servants of the mind. Continuing the thought further, they are wholly the manifestations of the mind. Therefore, knowing the nature of the mind is important. Let me take a moment to illustrate how the speech and the body are like servants of the mind. If the mind has a wish to go, the body will move; if the mind has a wish to remain, the body will be still. If the mind has the wish to communicate pleasantly, the speech will convey pleasant sounds; if the mind has the wish to communicate unpleasantly, the speech will reflect this.

In order to benefit all sentient beings, the Lord Buddha Shakyamuni taught the great vastness of the Dharma which is extremely profound. It is said that his reason for doing this was solely to enable sentient beings to realize the nature of mind. Hence the entire corpus of Dharma teachings, numbering eighty-four thousand collections, was given essentially to benefit the mind.

I would now like to clarify what is meant by nature of the mind with an illustration based upon your own experience in a meditative setting. To begin with, completely abandon any preoccupation with things past and any preoccupation with things yet to come. Rest the mind without any distraction, for just a few moments, allowing clarity to become the mind's most apparent quality. Now in this clarity, call to mind cities that are not too far away and not too close (such as New York or Los Angeles), and actually see them with your mind. Were the mind something substantial, something real and existent with the quality of non-interdependence, then, before the mind could visualize a distant city, it would have to cross many mountains, rivers, plains, and so forth. However, because the mind is *emptiness* — insubstantial and interdependent — it is able to call to mind a distant city (like New York) without any arduous effort.

Now, taking our example of these cities further, try calling to mind the vision of New York and Los Angeles simultaneously. If the mind was substantial, something tangible, and self-existent, then in order to see both places the mind would need to cover the distance between New York and Los Angeles, which is many hours by airplane, many months by walking. Fortunately, the mind's insubstantial nature (which is emptiness) allows us to be able to see New York City and Los Angeles in the same instant.

Continuing further in this illustration, consider that the entire sky, or the whole of space, is infinite. Now, let the mind become vast like space. Completely embrace the whole of space, completely fill the whole of space. Let it be so vast. The ability to mix the mind indivisibly with space is also due to the mind's essential nature of emptiness. Emptiness means being completely devoid of any descriptive characteristics, such as size, shape, color, or location. The sky is completely vast, having no limit; and space, like sky, has no boundaries, no periphery, and no limit. Mind, itself, can experience itself as being inseparable and indistinguishable from space itself. This awareness is recognizable during meditation.

However, who recognized this awareness? What is this awareness? What size does it have? What color is it? What can you say about it? Take a moment to consider this. Consider that if formlessness or emptiness itself were the mind, then we would conclude that the whole of space, or the emptiness of this room, or wherever any emptiness existed, would be mind. This is not the case because the emptiness, which is mind, also has clarity. The very ability of being able to call to mind the view of New York or Los Angeles, or whatever, demonstrates this aspect of clarity. Were there no such clarity or luminosity, it would be equivalent to the complete absence of sun, moon, stars, or any kind of light. This, however, is not our situation; our experience of emptiness demonstrates luminosity and clarity.

Were emptiness and luminosity (or clarity) the mind, then, when the sun is shining in the sky, this empty space and light of the sun would be mind. But this is not our experience, because not only does the mind demonstrate emptiness and luminosity, it also has awareness, or consciousness. This awareness is demonstrated in the ability to recognize that when you call New York to mind, you know, "This is New York City." This actual recognition is awareness, or consciousness. Furthermore, this awareness is the same awareness that is able to determine that the mind is empty and has clarity. This fusion of emptiness, clarity, and awareness is what is meant by mind, what has been termed *mind*.

Although the indivisibility of these three qualities of mind has been variously labeled mind, consciousness, awareness, and intellect, whatever name is given, mind is nevertheless the union of emptiness, clarity, and awareness. This is the mind that experiences pleasure; this is the mind that experiences pain. It is the mind that gives rise to thought and notices thought. It is the mind that experiences all phenomenal existence. There is nothing other than that. The Lord Buddha taught that, from beginningless time, sentient beings have taken innumerable, uncountable rebirths, and it is this emptiness, clarity, and awareness that has taken these rebirths, time after time. This is undoubtedly true.

Until the realization of enlightenment, in which the mind's true nature is recognized, this emptiness, clarity, and awareness will continue to take rebirth. There is no need to have any doubt that the mind is insubstantial in its empty, clear awareness. This truth can clearly be illustrated. Consider, for instance, when a child is conceived, nobody actually sees this emptiness, clarity, and unimpededness enter the womb. There is no way that the mother or father can say that a mind of such-and-such a shape or size or substance just entered the womb and has now come into being. There is no form to be seen or measured to demonstrate that a mind has entered the womb at that time.

Right now we all have mind, but we cannot find it. We cannot say that our mind has a particular shape or any particular size or some particular location. The reason we cannot find it and/or define it in this manner is because it simply does not have any characteristics of shape or size, etc. Likewise, when an individual dies, no one actually sees the mind leave the dead person's body. No matter how many people, whether in the hundreds, thousands, or millions, examine a dying or dead person with microscopes, telescopes, or whatever instruments, they are unable to see anything leaving the body. They cannot say that the corpse's mind has gone in any specific direction, neither "up there" nor "out here." This is because the mind is devoid of any form. The fact that nobody can see what another person is thinking is evidence, in and of itself, that the mind is empty. This evening we have a large gathering of people. The lights are on and everybody present can see very clearly. In this room everybody is thinking a great deal and, although there is a vast array of mental discursiveness, nobody can see anybody else's discursive thought.

This non-seeing of the mind's true nature occurs because the mind has no form, no shape, etc.; also, non-recognition occurs as a result of the obscuration of ignorance. Such non-recognition causes one to constantly take rebirth, time and time again. The Lord Buddha has said that because of the non-recognition, sentient beings not only do not recognize the mind's true nature, they also do not perceive the *law of karma* (the law of cause and effect) and they continue to create and accumulate karmic causes for future rebirths without being aware in any way of the effects of their actions.

If you recognize that mind is emptiness, clarity, and unobstructed awareness, then you should recognize that the you that performs an action, that accumulates karma through action, is emptiness, clarity, and unobstructed awareness; and the you that experiences some consequence as a result of that action is also emptiness, clarity, and unobstructed awareness. Additionally, the way that cause is carried to effect is also by means of the empty, clear, and unobstructed awareness. If you can see that, and fully understand that, you will attain the state of buddhahood. In that state, you will be completely free from any further karmic fruition, as buddhahood is completely beyond any further reaping of past action. And, this freedom is still emptiness, clarity, and unobstructed awareness.

The nature of karma and the true nature of the mind are essentially the same. However, what is recognized and experienced by sentient beings is the karmic cause and effect of ignorance, while what is experienced by a buddha, who has completely gone beyond the cause and effect of action, has no karmic fruition. This is why enlightenment is called true liberation.

One characteristic of sentient existence is that the veil of ignorance limits the experience of sentient beings to the samsaric realm then being experienced. As a result, there are many who may believe that there is no such thing as a hell realm experience. Many think that it is impossible that such a realm of suffering exists. Further, this disbelief carries over and becomes an unbelief in the existence of the hungry ghost realm or the gods' realms. People tend to believe only in the human and animal realms because everything they can see is of those realms. However, to exemplify the limits of this perception, let us consider not only the teachings of the Lord Buddha, but also those of such teachers as the third Gyalwa Karmapa, who repeatedly emphasized the illusory nature of all appearance and all the realms. Let us consider the situation of the dream. While dreaming, one conjures up all kinds of seemingly real experiences, and one can seemingly experience a great deal of happiness and/or suffering. All the various emotions and experiences of the dream appear to be real. Yet, although one believes the experience to be something completely real and existent during the dream, it is obvious that this belief is delusional. As insubstantial, arising mental projections, dreams have no reality whatsoever. One recognizes this when one awakens from the dream.

Compare this example of the dream to the perception of the *six realms of samsara*. Sentient beings continually experience one or more of these realms, rebirth after rebirth. Not all of these realms appear to the five human senses, yet this does not validate their lack of existence. In one sense they do exist, in that these are the realms in which the deluded nature of the mind reincarnates. Bound by the ignorance of delusion, sentient beings experience these realms, in one lifetime after another, believing their illusory experience to be real. However great the delusion of sentient beings, this does not ultimately substantiate these realms to be anything more than mere mental projections. From the viewpoint of absolute reality, the six realms of samsara are completely without independent reality.

In a very poetic verse, the Buddha Shakyamuni questioned who made all the hot iron pavement, with its incessant flames and burning fire, in the hell realm. Was there any blacksmith who made that iron pavement? Was there any store of wood that caused the continuous fire? No, it is caused by karmic fruition, by the individual karmic accumulation, which results from misconceived clinging to the illusion of self and other as being substantial. If we are to avoid the suffering of continual reincarnation, we must apply ourselves to practice and recognize, to a degree at least, that the mind's true nature is emptiness, clarity, and unimpeded awareness. Then can we begin to understand and recognize the truth concerning the way in which phenomena are experienced in the realms of samsara. If one does not have the understanding of mind's true nature, then this truth is really difficult to grasp or understand, and one continues to suffer from this delusion of conceptual reality.

All sentient beings have body, speech, and mind, foolishly clinging to these three facets as being the illusory self. If one practices negative actions, then the fruition of these actions takes place in one of the lower realms through the gates of body, speech, and mind. If one practices virtuous action, or positive karmic trends, then it is these same gates that experience the result as rebirth in the superior states of the three higher realms. Also, it is practicing the path of Buddhadharma with body, speech, and mind that allows one to recognize the enlightened nature of body, speech, and mind, for it is these same three gates that are bound in samsara and that are also liberated through enlightenment. In recognizing that the development and experience of all sentient beings are not concurrent or universal, nor even necessarily similar, the Lord Buddha taught broad overviews, termed the *triyanas*, to help open these three gates to liberation.

If one wishes to construct a three-story building, then one must start with the ground floor, continue by adding the next story, then the third, until one has completed the building. If one wishes to practice and understand the full meaning of the Buddhadharma, one can utilize the three yanas — the *hinayana*, the *mahayana*, and the *vajrayana*. By practicing the tradition of Tibetan Buddhism, one can utilize these three vehicles in unison.

One of these three yanas, namely the hinayana, deals with controlling personal behavior and emotionality through the rejection, abandonment, and avoidance of erroneous and mistaken behavior. Erroneous behavior of the body is killing, stealing, or harming others, specifically through sexual misconduct; mistaken behavior of the speech is lying, causing disharmony and/or discord; and so on. One must completely spurn and abandon such behavior. Refusal to practice any form of harmful behavior towards others helps one to maintain the discipline of meditative absorption while employing the practices we term in Tibetan *zhinay* (Skt.: *shamatha*), which stills the mind, and *lhatong* (Skt.: *vipashyana*), which observes the mind's nature. Thus, the whole principle of the hinayana doctrine lies in the abandonment of all harmful actions, and in the maintenance of meditative absorption.

No doubt you have seen that many Tibetan lamas wear robes of maroon and saffron colors, which are similar to the robes that the Lord Buddha once wore. These robes are a sign of their having taken special ordinations. Householders, persons who have a responsibility to their families, will seek less restrictive ordination, which, in Tibetan, are referred to as *genyen*. Depending upon his or her circumstances and the desire to follow ordination, the householder's vows can number three, four, or five. The basic three vows forsake killing, stealing, and lying. Additionally, one can vow abstinence from intoxicating substances, and/or abstinence from sexual activity. The novice monk and nun take vows that are thirty-six in number, which include the basic genyen vows. Beyond this level exists the ordinations of the fully-ordained monk and nun, which number in the several hundreds. Both the novice and the full ordinations are based upon the hinayana approach of practice; a person demonstrates they are observing these ordinations by the wearing of robes.

One's Dharma practice should be based in the hinayana (regardless of whether or not one wishes to take special vows to demonstrate one's practice of the hinayana vehicle), as this is the basis of all practice. It is perfectly alright if one chooses not to be ordained as a monk or nun, because one accomplishes this path not by wearing robes, but by completely abandoning the ten negative actions and by instilling virtuous, wholesome behavior through the practice of the ten virtuous actions of body, speech, and mind. One does this with an understanding of karmic consequences and by knowing why it is better to lead a life based on positive rather than negative action. One actively employs this vehicle as an outer discipline, which equates to having constructed the foundation for one's house. Or, in the case of the three story building, one has completed the lower story. However, even if one were to perfect this practice, the complete realization of buddhahood would still be very distant. One needs to construct the second story of our illustrative dwelling, which in this case is the path of the mahayana.

With a foundation of hinayana purity derived by completely abandoning any harmful activity, one begins upon the path of the mahayana, which is the path of unifying emptiness and compassion. Let us again consider the meaning of emptiness. All sentient beings have mind and all identify with this mind. So, one thinks, "I am this mind," and one thinks, "I am," thereby contributing to the formulations of a variety of likes and dislikes, of aversions and attractions to different phenomena. Although it has absolutely no self whatsoever, this mind has an incidental clinging to a self as being something or someone real. Observing the true nature of mind and discovering that it is devoid of any descriptive characteristics (such as size, shape, color, or location) is to recognize that mind, in essence, is emptiness.

In the hinayana practice, little emphasis is placed upon the recognition of the emptiness of all phenomena; instead, this view of emptiness is attained by seeing the emptiness of personality. It is simply not enough to recognize the emptiness of personality, however, or to recognize that mind itself is empty and devoid of any substantiality. One needs to recognize the void nature of all phenomena, and in so doing, one proceeds to enter the path of the mahayana.

The *Prajna Paramita Sutra*, or the *Perfection of Wisdom Sutra*, is the primary source of the teaching on emptiness in Buddhadharma. Basically, this sutra points out that mind is emptiness in categorically stating that "there is no form; there is no feeling; there is no sensation; there is no taste; there is no touch." In presenting the teaching that all these things are actually empty, this sutra is regarded as the core of elucidation on this topic. Its concept is the basis of the meditative practice that has developed in several schools, most notably in the Buddhist orders in Japan. Emphasis is placed on recognizing the emptiness of form, the emptiness of sound, the emptiness of feeling, the emptiness of smell, and so on. In short, all sensory appearances are recognized as being empty. This realization is achieved by seeing that the mind itself, that all appearances perceived and/or experienced by the mind, are, in fact, mental projections. They are the mind's play; as mind itself is insubstantial, so too are these projections.

The main line from the *Prajna Paramita Sutra* describing this says, "Form is void, void is form; form is no other than void, voidness is no other than form." If someone were to say to you, "There is no sound, no form, no feeling; there is truly nothing real," then you might not believe that. You will reply that you have these definite, real experiences of these sensory sensations: you hear sound; you actually see form, etc. This term *void* does not imply nothingness, but, rather, it infers the interdependence and insubstantiality of all phenomena. In this sense, all phenomena are considered empty or void of any absolute reality. The dream is frequently used as an example of this.

While in the dream state, one can dream up an entire experience with a total environment, and one can experience that as having form, feeling, sound, etc. The dream appears extremely real. Still, there is no reality whatsoever in the dream existence, for with the moment of awakening, it all completely vanishes. The dream experience is believed to be real during the time of the dream, yet it is obviously a projection of the mind. The aim of the practitioner is to recognize that the experience of present phenomena is also merely a projection that has no substantial being.

Let me remind you that the basis of this discourse lies in the teachings of the Buddha Shakyamuni and the third Gyalwa Karmapa [Rangjung Dorje, 1284-1339]. Both taught that all phenomena are insubstantial, like a dream, like a reflection in a mirror, like an illusion, like a rainbow. In seeing that all appearance (not only one's mind and emotions) is luminous, unimpeded suchness, one recognizes that all external appearance, which is also arising from the mind, is only mental projection.

The basis of the mahayana practice differs from the hinayana in that one does not practice abandonment, rejection, etc. Instead, in mahayana, one deals with one's behavior in a manner of transformation. For example, if the desire to harm another sentient being arises on the crest of a wave of great anger, then one immediately applies the antidote of compassion; the energy of the anger is thereby transformed into compassion. One does not deal with an emotion simply by cutting it off; rather, one uses compassion to transform it on the basis of its inherent insubstantiality.

In their ignorance, sentient beings think all that they experience is real, and their misconception entails their experiencing a great deal of suffering. Ones sees that all sentient beings are experiencing the illusory manifestations of the three bodies (the fully ripened, the habitual tendency, and the mental bodies), and that they are completely locked in these illusions. Recognizing the habitual clinging of these three categories of sentient phenomena as being only illusory appearance, then one recognizes emptiness. By recognizing that one's delusion and habitual clinging cause suffering, an intense compassion can arise. The recognition of emptiness itself is referred to as *wisdom*, and the arising compassion is referred to by the term *means*. The path of recognizing the emptiness of these three categories of phenomena, and of developing compassion for all those experiencing such delusion, is the path of mahayana, and this path has its pinnacle in the union of means and wisdom.

Having attained both great compassion and wisdom, one has then finished constructing the second floor of this three story building. The full attainment of buddhahood is still very distant, however, since one must still practice the *six perfections (paramitas)*, (generosity, moral conduct, patience, diligence, meditative contemplation, and wisdom) for many lifetimes, for many kalpas, progressing slowly and steadily through the stages of bodhisattva development, until one finally attains buddhahood. This takes considerable effort and an unimaginable amount of time, yet practicing mahayana is very beneficial. During the great lapse of time before one attains buddhahood, one can benefit a great number of sentient beings, and, of course, oneself. But the only way to achieve rapid progress along the path to enlightenment is to practice vajrayana.

In vajrayana, one goes one step further and does not apply any specific antidote of abandoning or of transforming. Instead, one merely recognizes the true nature of the mind. By recognizing the nature of action, emotion, and so on, there is instantaneous liberation. This is why the vajrayana path is very rapid and is a most powerful method. How does one apply this path of recognition? First, one recognizes that the body is the form of the deity. The form of the deity being the union of void and appearance, one recognizes that this body has the clarity of the rainbow, has the unimpededness of the reflection of the moon in water, and has the insubstantialness of the reflection in a mirror. In this recognition, one has realized the nature of the body as being devoid of form.

Second, one recognizes that all speech and all sound is the sound of mantra. In hearing all sound as being mantra, one recognizes that all sound is devoid of substance, insubstantial like an echo.

Third, one recognizes the mind with all the thought, concepts, cognition, awareness, emotion, etc., as being similar to a wavering mirage in the distance that the deer, thinking it is water, come to drink. One recognizes that all mind, all cognition, is like a mirage which is vacant of consciousness. If one realizes the form void, the sound void, and the consciousness void, then one has completely liberated clinging.

This is the basis of the path of the vajrayana. If one applies oneself to this path in the same way as Jetsün Milarepa and many others, then one can attain complete enlightenment in this very lifetime. Even if one does not realize enlightenment in this lifetime, the blessings of the *yidam* and the power of the mantra enable one to realize liberation in the after-death bardo state. In either case, enlightenment transpires because one has developed and established a good habit in the practice of recognizing all phenomena as having the true nature of the form, mantra, and *samadhi* of the yidam.

This habit can quickly instill one with the ability to realize all visual phenomena as form void, all sound as sound void, and all levels of the *skandas* as being inherently void of causal reality. In the bardo state after death, the mind is exactingly potent and extremely powerful. By applying the vajrayana method, one can instantly accomplish a deep state of meditation and thus gain liberation from suffering in the six realms of samsara. One can end the cycle of karmic rebirth and gain the threshold of mastery of the three yanas, thus enabling one to move in and out of substantial phenomena at will. To illustrate the way vajrayana accomplishment has been demonstrated by a great teacher, I will now tell you a story about Jetsün Milarepa.

One time Jetsün Milarepa, the yogi saint of Tibet, was meditating in an isolated cave, absorbed in samadhi. Some extremely hungry hunters, who had been unsuccessful in their hunt, came to this cave. As they entered, they saw an emaciated Jetsün Milarepa sitting there. Somewhat frightened, they inquired, "Are you a ghost or are you a man?"

Jetsün Milarepa replied quietly, "I am a man."

"If you are a man, give us something to eat. We are all very hungry and our hunt is fruitless."

"But I have nothing to offer you. I have nothing to eat. I am just sitting here absorbed in meditation," replied Milarepa.

"Nonsense," they said, "you must be hiding some kind of food here somewhere. Give us some food!"

They were extremely hungry and became very angry when Jetsün Milarepa again replied that he had absolutely nothing to eat. The hunters decided to torment and abuse the great yogi Milarepa. Firing arrows at him, they were astounded to see that the arrows could not penetrate him. Some of the arrows were deflected straight upwards, some to the left, and some to the right. Some even deflected directly back at the hunters, who became even more infuriated. They then tried to topple him over and injure him by throwing rocks, but somehow Milarepa floated up into the air, like a very light piece of paper. When they threw water on him, the water miraculously vanished. Trying with all their might to throw him into the river nearby, Jetsün Milarepa foiled their efforts by floating in the space above them. No matter what they did to inflict harm, they were totally ineffectual.

This illustrates Milarepa's realization of form void. They had no success because his physical being was form void, his speech and melody were sound void. Additionally, their experience of his unperturbability during this incident demonstrated his being void of karmic fruition. If we have the diligence and the wisdom to apply the skillful means of vajrayana, then we too can realize liberation while we still have the opportunity of this precious human existence.

If one has a precious human existence enabling one to understand mind's true nature, and if one's understanding is of the most excellent degree, the result will be the realization of the *mahamudra.* Even if one does not gain this full level of understanding, the slightest understanding of the nature of mind can give one the ability to meditate with comfort and ease. In fact, even without an average degree of understanding, simply hearing and knowing a little bit about mind's true nature can be extremely beneficial. It enables one to apply oneself to all kinds of worldly activity that benefits many beings.

We have now discussed several different methods (or vehicles) for obtaining buddhahood. But the best method of all is that which leads to the understanding of the meaning of the mahamudra. If the nature of the mind is recognized, one is a buddha. If it is not recognized, one is confused and is a sentient being. Although the basis of mahamudra is easy to understand, putting it into practice can be difficult because one clings to one's obscurations. Due to ignorance, the obscuration of knowledge causes habits of mental afflictions and/or of emotionality to arise, which in turn give rise to karmic action. The presence of these *four veils of obscuration* that cloud our enlightened awareness is similar to the presence of clouds in the sky which prevent the sunlight from brightening the day.

In the *Hevajra Tantra* it is said that sentient beings are buddhas, but, because of their obscurations they do not recognize this. If sentient beings can dispel these obscurations, they will become buddhas. There are two ways to do this. One way is comprised of four practices that are called the *foundational practices* in Tibetan Buddhism. These involve an accumulation of prostrations, refuge vows, purification mantras, *mandala* offerings, and supplications to the *tsaway lama.* Additionally, this way focuses upon bringing the visualization practice through the development and completion stages of vajrayana meditation. The other way was evolved in the hinayana traditions. It involves various methods of meditation that fall into two main categories: zhinay (shamatha), or tranquility meditation, comprised of methods with and without support; and lhatong (vipashyana), or insight meditation, which includes many different methods of meditative approach. Either way, these methods can lead to the realization of mahamudra, or true liberation.

In either approach, it is important to meditate using zhinay, translated into English as tranquility. In defining the two Tibetan words that represent the concept of zhinay, we find the terms pacification and abiding. These refer to the pacifying of the mind of its mental afflictions or emotions, and through this the gaining of the ability to abide with the mind resting one-pointedly. It is considered that without some development of tranquility of mind, one will not be able to perform any other kind of meditation. This is the reason why zhinay is important. According to one tradition, one begins by meditating upon zhinay before one performs the foundational practices of Tibetan Buddhism, while another tradition says that one should begin by performing the foundational practices and there-after meditate upon tranquility and insight. The reasoning upon which both methods are based is equally correct, thus either method may provide results.

The effectiveness of the first tradition lies in one beginning with mastering, or at least experiencing, tranquility before commencing the foundational practices; this procedure allows one to gain control over one's mind so that the objects of meditation appear very clearly. The other tradition states that one will not be able to perform zhinay properly without first dispelling one's obscurations through practices of purification, thus accumulating the merit and wisdom gained from the foundational practices. If one performs the zhinay practice after the foundational practices, then one will be able to perform excellent and effortless zhinay. Both viewpoints are correct.

In introducing these approaches to recognizing the true nature of the mind, it is appropriate to encourage you to strive within your abilities to grasp these concepts and to apply them in your life. Knowing a little of the mind's nature can be very beneficial, even in a worldly sense. You can generally improve any meditation practice you use by recognizing that the intense clinging to a belief in a self (with its emotions, thoughts, etc.) as being something real makes it almost impossible to meditate. If you wish to hold the mind in equipoise and meditate one-pointedly, such clinging prevents this from happening. Even if you wish to give rise to the very clear visualization of the yidam, this clinging also veils your view. If, however, you recognize and see mind's true nature as emptiness, clarity, and unimpeded awareness, then all meditation becomes easy.

Pausing in his meditation, Kalu Rinpoche patiently listens to the question posed by the photographer. (Photograph by J.G. Sherab Ebin)

≈ 2 ≈

CHANGING TIDES AND TIMES

Examination of Alaya and Karma

Throughout the world, there are many religions and spiritual traditions that make the assumption that there is something beyond death. On this basis, they form many teachings. Certainly, there would be no purpose in practicing or propagating their teachings if, in fact, the mind actually died with the body. Regardless of the particular dogma, propagation of their moral code hinges upon the asserted belief that what one does now can influence one's experience in the after-death state.

Indeed, in Buddhism the continuity of the mind is an important point. Mind is not something that comes into being at the beginning of the life of the physical body, nor is it something that ends with the physical body's death. Its continuity, from one state of existence to another, has a great influence on and definite connection with each successive state. In the sense that this empty, clear, and unimpeded nature of mind has always been experienced and always will be experienced, mind itself is eternal. There always will be mind, just as there always has been mind, and, continually, this mind experiences various states of confusion and suffering. This is what the Buddha termed *samsara*, or the cycle of conditioned rebirth, from one state of experience to another.

In samsara, that which is always being experienced is the content of the mind, rather than the nature of mind itself. Such contents are derived from a fundamental confusion or ignorance that projects both the physical body and phenomenal experiences. Far from being permanent, the projections of mind are impermanent and unstable. These projections are always changing, falling apart, and being replaced by some new projection.

For those of you who are longing for something else, it is important to understand that the mind, with its dynamic, empty, and unobstructed luminosity, contains not only the delusion of causal phenomena, but also the potential for liberation. In this empty, clear, and unimpeded nature of mind itself is the very potential or seed for obtaining enlightenment. This inherent quality is referred to as *tathagatagarbha,* or buddha nature. Each and every living being has buddha nature as part of its make-up because this is the inherent nature of its mind. This is true regardless of whatever realm, state, or situation of rebirth a being finds itself experiencing. Although there is no doubt that each being has tathagatagarbha, the mind expresses itself through a fundamental ignorance, in ways which generate more or less merit, and which are positive or negative in terms of the actions one commits physically, verbally, and mentally.

As the mind is "no thing" in and of itself but is essentially empty, it should not be misconstrued to be something tangible, or something limited. It cannot be said that the mind was put together at one point and that it falls apart at some other point. Mind does not behave in that way. There always has been mind; there always will be mind. Because it is not something created at one point and destroyed at another, mind continually expresses itself through an infinite series of rebirths in the different states of samsara in a great many differing and particular ways.

As long as fundamental ignorance remains in the mind, the sources of samsara will continue to exist. Samsara is endless in the sense that the mind will continue to experience its own projections and confusion again, and again, and again, in an endless cycle. This appears to be a rather grim perspective, unless, of course, a means for liberation exists. The situation, however, of a sentient being attaining enlightenment does not imply that this liberation should be interpreted as mind disappearing. It is not as though the mind comes to an end at this point of enlightenment.

Rather, the confusion in the mind comes to an end. Instead of eternally experiencing its own confusion, enlightened mind eternally experiences its own true nature as tathagatagarbha, wholly and without any confusion. In fact, the only reason we can say that samsara is a temporary state that can be ended, is that it is possible to eliminate this primal confusion. Quite literally, samsara is the experiencing of that confusion and, if this confusion is eliminated, then samsara has been eliminated. If, however, that confusion is not eliminated, then samsara remains an endless process. Consequently, it will never exhaust itself.

The whole karmic process has been briefly summed up in a quote from the traditional teachings: "If you wish to understand what has taken place, look at your body; if you wish to see what will take place, look at your actions." This saying is an attempt to indicate that any particular state of rebirth and/or the experiences that currently affect one are due to tendencies that were established at some previous time. Additionally, what the mind will experience in the future is currently being conditioned by how it is expressing itself now in physical, verbal, and mental action. Past, present, or future karmic tendencies are a continuing cycle that, once established, are continually reinforced.

At this time, we all have the common quality of being human, as we share this collective experience of a human rebirth. This is an indication that we share a certain collective karma which has brought us to this particular nature of our experience, instead of to some other form of life experience in some other realm, or to some other human circumstances that proscribe interest in the Dharma. Due to our positive and meritorious physical, verbal, and mental actions, certain meritorious tendencies were reinforced in previous existences that have given us this current result. Such collective experience is easily demonstrable; however, there is another fact that we have to consider. The great variety of ways that human beings experience the human realm is due not to collective karma but to the individual aspects of karma.

For example, in the human realm there are people who die very early, who experience continual poverty, who suffer from the inability to become prosperous, who fail to accomplish their aims, and who suffer from ill health. On a karmic level, all of these frustrations can be traced back to the negative karmic tendencies that were established in previous existences when the mind expressed itself in ways that led to some kind of unskillful action. Perhaps these beings killed many other sentient beings. This action, as complicated or uncomplicated as the circumstances might have been, will give a karmic reaction that will reappear in a retributive way in some future life. Persons who have behaved in such a manner will experience a shortness of life, either through illness or by being killed before their natural time of death. Or, it might be that in a previous time a person may have stolen or robbed a great deal of wealth from others and therefore will experience a resultant poverty in some future time.

Basically, the law of karma describes all causal phenomena as the effective result of previous action, whether this result is positive or negative. Beyond the context of only this lifetime, we are able to trace both positive and negative karmic tendencies that were established in previous existences which directly lead to our present lifetime's experience. If strong positive karmic tendencies were developed through the practice of generosity or cherishing and guarding of life, etc., the result would lead to the experience of longevity, health, prosperity, and the ability to become successful and to obtain one's goals. Consequently, while we indeed share the common experience in being human, our experience of the human realm remains very much a personal one, being individual to each person.

Many people, even those from various spiritual traditions, feel that there is no such thing as previous or future existences. Undoubtedly, they take this opinion because these former or future existences are not apparent and because this truth lacks an empirical basis for substantiation. Their disbelief is very understandable because neither the past nor the future is something that can be seen at the present moment. But then, the mind that experiences the past, the present, and the future cannot be seen either. If karmic fruition propagates this succession of rebirths and is something that originates and arises from the mind, it should not be surprising that it is as intangible as mind itself. Forget about previous and future existences; we do not even see our mind right now! Mind is not some thing that we can take out and examine. It is not some thing we can pin down and say, "This exactly is the mind." In lacking this capability, it should not surprise us that we also lack the potential for validating or verifying the continuity of future or previous existences. Thus, even though we can only see this body right now, our blank memory of having had other bodies should not surprise us. Ultimately speaking, the physical body that we are experiencing at any particular point is only a projection of the mind and, as such, arises from tendencies in the mind, to be experienced by the mind.

Take two people; if one of them goes to sleep and the other observes the sleeper, regardless of how incredible and complicated the dreams of the sleeper are, the other person cannot see them. The observer has no way of seeing what the other person is experiencing because it is intangible. It cannot be seen empirically, nor is it possible from the point of view of the observer to validate empirically any dream with any other sense faculty. This does not mean that the dreamer is not dreaming! For the dreamer, the dream (while lacking tangibility) is perfectly valid. Similarly, any attempt to validate the karmic process empirically is simply a waste of time. Although the dream arises from something intangible, this does not mean that the process of cause and effect does not work. Even though the physical senses do not enable one to validate the law of karma, one can see this truth through spiritual insight. As one's realization develops, one becomes directly aware of cause and effect, which gives an awareness of the process of rebirth. Ordinarily, one is accustomed to verifying the truth or the falsity of something before giving it credence. In the instance of karmic fruition, however, the lack of empirical verification should not be taken as either an indication or absolute proof of its non-existence. Rather, one needs to recognize that one is not necessarily consciously aware of it right now.

Earlier we were discussing the concept of the empty, clear, and unimpeded nature of mind as being the inherent nature of one's self. Due to the several levels of confusion and distortion that take place in the mind, our present unliberated situation manifests. The first of these delusions is a simple lack of direct experience and awareness of the nature of mind. Rather than experiencing the mind's nature in clear awareness, the experience is impregnated with the distortion of a not-knowing, or of an absence, on the most fundamental level, of awareness. This most subtle and most fundamental level of confusion is technically termed *ignorance* or unawareness.

This distortion obscures the direct experience of emptiness of mind so that, rather than the mind directly experiencing its own intangibility, the mind experiences the self. This I, the subject which is taken to be something ultimately real, is, in fact, merely a distortion of the true experience of the emptiness of mind. In a similar manner, the direct experience of the luminosity of mind is distorted or frozen into the experience of being something other. This object, the frozen or distorted other-than-self, is taken to be ultimately real, but, in fact, is a clouding of this direct experience of the luminosity of mind. A dualistic split thereby develops that recognizes subject/object and self/other as seemingly being ultimately separate and independent. In our confusion, we habitually reinforce this dualistic framework.

The picture is further complicated by the unobstructed quality of mind, that awareness which tends to arise only in certain limited ways. If, in this dualistic framework, there arises a positive relationship between subject and object, such experience is usually expressed in terms of an attraction or attachment of subject to object, thereby giving a perception of something good and attractive. When something is perceived as bad, or when the subject takes the object to be something threatening or repulsive, then there arises a negative emotion of aggression or aversion. Ultimately speaking, subject, object, and the emotional response that results are wholly the activity of the mind. It is the mind which conceives of the subject. It is the mind which conceives of the object. It is also the mind which conceives of the split between the two. Although it is the mind which initiates attraction or aversion, somehow this is not perceived by sentient beings. Instead, everything is treated as though it were very solid. Subject is here, object is there, and the relationship between the two is separate and distinct. We believe each is existent in and of itself; we also believe that they are totally independent of mind. This is the delusion caused by the fundamental stupidity (or dullness) of the mind. Basic attachment, aversion, and the quality of stupidity are the three primary emotional responses of sentient beings; they are the source of all suffering.

From these primary delusions spring secondary developments, causing things to become much more complex. Mere attachment can develop into avarice (or greed) and grasping. Stupidity develops into pride and self-aggrandizement. Aversion develops into envy, jealousy, etc. But it does not stop there. With these basic emotions, further developments and ramifications take place until there are literally thousands of emotional responses and emotional situations. To indicate the complexity of this level of confusion and distortion of the mind and emotions, the sutras speak of eighty-four thousand emotional and mental discursive situations. The resolution of these emotions is a topic we will address more at length further on; for now, let us continue to attempt to see the source that affects our emotional response.

Because one has mental and emotional conflicts, one naturally acts in certain physical, verbal, and mental ways. Through such actions, which are again based upon dualistic confusion, one reinforces karmic tendencies, either positive or negative. Generally, however, one tends toward the negative because it is out of this confusion that further confusion reinforces itself. Any overtly negative actions, such as killing and stealing, reinforce this confusion, and these negative karmic patterns will produce even further suffering. This is the fourth level of obscuration which I mentioned when I began this discourse. Actually, the situations we are now experiencing can be described in whole by referring only to those four veils of mind's confusion: fundamental ignorance, dualistic clinging, emotionality, and karmic tendencies.

In the Buddhist tradition, the empty, clear, and dynamic state of awareness (which is the fundamental nature of mind itself), is technically termed the *alaya*, meaning the origin (or source) of all experience and of all transcending or intrinsically pristine awareness. To use a metaphor, take the example of transparently clear, pure water, without any sediment or pollutants, into which a handful of earth or mud is thrown and stirred round until dark clouds of earth particles obscure the water's transparency. The water is still there but there is something that is hiding or masking that transparent clarity. In the same way, what we experience in samsara is rather like this clear water being obscured by pollution, as our inherent, ever-present buddha nature is masked by these four veils of obscuration. This situation of obscuration is also termed alaya. Alaya, then, is not only the fundamental or original state of consciousness, but it is also the discursive consciousness, the confused awareness from which arise all of the illusory or confused perceptions common among sentient beings.

On the one hand, one has the pure alaya, which is the inherent nature of mind itself as pristine awareness, this pure water. On the other hand, one has the practical situation of this impure alaya, which is the fundamental source of confusion and illusion due to the four different veils of confusion of the mind, this impure backwater. At this moment we are unenlightened sentient beings, which means that what we experience is an admixture of both the impure and pure alaya. Simultaneously, samsara is both the inherent (but obscured) buddha nature of mind and also the levels of confusion that result in this impure alaya, or the phenomenal world. *Nirvana*, however, is unobscured awareness having no confusion or karmic fruition to give rise to phenomenal causality.

This concept of pure and impure alaya is important to comprehend. To use another metaphor, take the concept of the sun shining in a cloudless sky, an image of clarity and spaciousness, as the fundamental nature of mind. It is entirely possible that the sky can be obscured by clouds, fog, or mist, all of which can prevent the direct perception of the sun shining in the clear sky. Indeed, these clouds can also give rise to all kinds of other developments, such as lightning, thunder, hail, rain, or snow, which can completely obscure the sky's clear spaciousness. In the same way, these levels of ignorance and confusion of the mind give the result of all of the illusory projections that are ultimately unreal experiences which we, as unenlightened sentient beings, undergo in the belief that *this is real*. Because these delusions obscure true clarity, the result is sentient suffering and pain. In this case, the complication (such as the hail, the rain, and so forth, in our metaphor) is that pain, suffering, and confusion are experienced as a result of this mixture of the pure and the impure alaya.

The fundamental approach of Buddhadharma is to eliminate all of those complications caused by the four veils of ignorance, and so forth, so that the inherent nature of mind can simply shine forth. The aim of Buddhadharma is to allow the mind's nature to manifest itself so that there is nothing hindering or limiting that direct perception. This is what is meant by attaining buddhahood. *Enlightenment* can be understood to be the complete elimination of all that confusion and distortion of impure alaya, so that the pure alaya, that which is already there, can be experienced in its fullest.

It is interesting to examine this admixture we are currently experiencing, this blend of pure and impure alaya that preoccupies our current perceptual existence. When the pure aspect of alaya is predominant, there arise qualities, attitudes, and aspects of our being that we can term positive or virtuous qualities that generate feelings of faith, confidence, compassion, loving kindness, generosity, etc. All the attitudes conducive to spiritual development arise when this pure alaya is making its presence felt most strongly. When the impure alaya is dominant, however, the results expressed are only the emotional confusion of attachment and aversion syndromes; all the complexities of the emotional conflict that develop in the mind are thrown in as well. Because the continual interplay among the pure and impure alaya produces positive and negative karmic patterns that are then reinforced, this is basically the source of the distinction one could make between a positive and a negative (or a virtuous and a non-virtuous) karmic tendency, action, or attitude.

If we are to continue to explore this topic and to examine this concept of virtuous karmic tendency, then this becomes more complex because there are different aspects at play. Most importantly, there are certain karmic tendencies that are virtuous and positive in nature, which arise and are reinforced by simple moral choices. For example, the decisions *not* to kill, steal, commit sexual misconduct, cause disharmony with one's speech, lie, gossip, abuse others with harsh language, develop malevolent or injurious attitudes towards others, covet or grasp at the possessions of others, and entertain confused ideas about the nature of reality are all simple moral choices. These choices, however, are virtues that are temporary in that they are exhaustible. The merit generated by these positive karmic tendencies reinforces a very pleasant but unstable picture, although, in the short term, it is certainly very beneficial. This merit gives rise to rebirth in any of the various gods' and human realms, which are superior states of rebirth within the cycle of samsara, but such rebirth does not, in itself, constitute any ultimate attainment of liberation. Rather, it merely provides the temporary circumstances for a rebirth (or state of experience) which is comfortable and reasonably happy, thereby allowing a certain amount of individual freedom. Such a rebirth is not ultimate or liberated.

On the other hand, there is the kind of virtue or positive tendency established through states of samadhi. *Samadhi* is a deep state of absorption one develops in meditation, or it is the absorption in a transcendental experience, either of which produces a particular state of mind. Samadhi can be of two different kinds. One is a completely mundane samadhi which exhibits a kind of inexhaustible nature in that it is not so unstable and is less likely to break down. This samadhi is defined as mundane because it does not liberate the consciousness from the conditions that produce the cycle of rebirth. Nevertheless, something more significant than mere moral conduct is taking place.

The other kind of samadhi is transcendent samadhi resulting from the culmination of a long spiritual process motivated by faith, compassion, and wisdom. Such progress indicates the deepening of wisdom to the point where the mind can attain liberation. This transcendence is inexhaustible because it remains a stable element of one's experience until the mind attains enlightenment and is thus liberated from the cycle of rebirth.

To examine this question of virtuous actions and attitudes and of positive karma, we therefore need to consider these three distinctions: the practical stage that has a temporary (but not ultimate) benefit, the intermediate stage of mundane states of meditation, and the ultimate state of meditation that is truly inexhaustible in that it leads the mind to a state of experience beyond the cycle of rebirth. What exactly is this transcendental kind of meditation that allows the mind to become totally liberated? I am here referring to the pure practice of zhinay (tranquility and stability of mind) or lhatong (insight into the nature of mind). These practices culminate in what is termed in the *tantras* the mahamudra approach. The term *mahamudra* (supreme symbol) refers to the ultimate and direct experience of the nature of mind and all phenomena, a culmination that results from maturing one's meditation with zhinay and deepening it into lhatong. This topic of mahamudra is the focus of lengthy discussion much later in this discourse. For the time being, we need consider only that there are two stages paramount to experiencing liberated awareness.

Tantric meditation, in the more formal tradition, is considered to have two phases. In Sanskrit, these are termed *utpattiakrama* and *sampannakrama*, and their meanings refer to a stage of creation or development, on the one hand, and one of completion or fulfillment, on the other. We will discuss these in more depth later; now you should know that regardless of the technique being used, the teachings on meditation as presented in vajrayana are essentially concerned with this transcendental aspect of virtuous activity and karma. This transcendental quality itself establishes inexhaustibly stable elements which bring the mind to a state of realization beyond the limited framework of the cycle of rebirth.

In examining the karmic process, then, regardless of whether the activity is positive or negative, virtuous or non-virtuous, the focus is on a process of fruition. Once an action is committed, a tendency is established that remains a latent part of one until such time in the future (however distant) when there is a coming together of circumstances that permit the tendency to mature, ripen, and express itself as an aspect of one's experience. This is primarily a mental process because the physical body and the speech act as the mind's agents for committing actions and accumulating karma. Ultimately speaking, these tendencies are established on the level of mind, even though they may be due to physical and/or verbal action. Although the result might also be experienced on these same physical and/or verbal levels, it is on the mental level that these tendencies are stored and remain latent.

To illustrate, take the analogy of soil into which one plants seeds. These seeds may not germinate for a long time, but as soon as the right conditions are present (such as moisture, warmth, and so forth), they will germinate and mature to fruition. In the same way, committing an action or similar kinds of actions establishes tendencies that remain latent in this fundamental state of awareness, later to emerge as conscious experience. They do not emerge until conditions dictate and conducive circumstances come together, and one's latent karmic tendency becomes one's experience in relative reality.

There is one outstanding characteristic of the karmic process, namely, its infallibility. Not only can karmic fruition take place, it does. Additionally, there is a certain predictability in that certain tendencies will always give rise to certain kinds of experience. Never can it happen that a virtuous action gives rise in some future circumstance to an experience of suffering, nor can a harmful action ever give rise in the future to a personal experience of pleasure.

The distinction between a virtuous and a non-virtuous action is whether the resulting experience of the agent is one of happiness or suffering. The equation is very simple. Virtuous actions result in positive karmic tendencies that emerge as happiness, that give some kind of physical or mental well-being. Non-virtuous actions establish negative karmic tendencies that emerge as the experience of pain and suffering, either physical or mental or both. It may take a lifetime, or several lifetimes, for any given tendency to actually emerge; nonetheless, it is an infallible process.

Suppose we take an example that illustrates a singular, predominant karmic force or tendency in an individual being's makeup. What if a person gave freely of whatever wealth, money, and possessions he or she owned, but was not especially attached to their luxury? No doubt this person would be considered a generous person, but in this instance such giving is not particularly altruistic; it has no spiritual quality. Now, generosity has a basically good moral quality about it. It also has a mundane quality, in that the karmic results it establishes are eventually exhaustible. This does not mean that it is not beneficial, at least on a temporary level, for the law of karma rewards the tendency of generosity with rebirth in the gods' realms, where the enjoyment of wealth is comparatively far greater than that experienced in the human realm.

Temporary rebirth as a god is an incredibly enjoyable, comfortable, and pleasant state of existence and is the result gained from having formerly shared one's wealth. Since such mundane karmic result is not inexhaustible, the resultant tendency will begin to exhaust itself, which usually results in one experiencing yet another rebirth, but in a lower realm of existence. Perhaps the hypothetical person in our example could be reborn in the human realm where there might still be some experience of wealth as evidenced by some prosperity and comfort on a material level. But this, too, will slowly exhaust itself and, eventually, other karmic tendencies will begin to predominate in the general picture of that being's experience. Either in that lifetime or some future lifetime, the merit gained from the original act of generosity will have exhausted itself, and a change will transpire; the whole experience of that hypothetical person will reflect the ripening of other latent tendencies, which will now rise to fruition.

On the other hand, suppose the attitude towards wealth is just the opposite. Our example now is of a person who is very grasping and who is known to be avaricious and miserly. Let us consider that our hypothetical person has gone to the point where wealth has been taken from others by robbing or cheating, and that the person continually grabs and hangs onto this wrongly gained wealth. Such actions establish karmic tendencies that result in the experience of loss and poverty which can lead to a state of rebirth in what is termed the hungry ghost realm. In that realm the beings have an intense hunger, unquenchable thirst, and a sense of deprivation, with such experiences being the main source of suffering in that realm. Even when the negative karma begins to exhaust itself and the mind is perhaps able to attain some slightly higher state of rebirth, possibly even a human one, it will be as a human being experiencing poverty, deprivation, and want. There will be this continual sense of loss, of something lacking that is sorely missed. Gradually that pattern will exhaust itself and, depending upon the ripening of conditions, some other positive or negative tendency will take over, causing the experience of that being to change again.

Things can be different, however. When the correct motivation is present, then any virtuous action performed within the context of that motivation begins to set the mind in a direction from which it does not deviate. Suppose that our person's generosity, rather than merely demonstrating a non-attachment to wealth (however great or small that wealth might be), has instead a spiritual element to it. Suppose that the motivation is truly compassionate and altruistic, thereby giving it a spiritual quality. Such generosity has an inexhaustible result for correct motivation gives much more stability and effectiveness to each action. Not only does correct motivation contribute to a higher state of rebirth, it contributes to the furthering of altruistic qualities and to one's enlightenment eventually! Thus, when one acts from this pure motivation, what is taking place on a karmic level (through the actions that one commits physically, verbally, and mentally) reflects one's altruistic attitude. In this way, karma is no longer unending and self-perpetuating, but rather its refinement through altruism and transcendent samadhi resolves it into its quintessence, that of pure alaya.

This idea of karma and the resulting karmic process as being the basis for our experience is fundamental to Buddhism. *In all of the eighty-four thousand collections of the teachings that the Buddha presented, the most essential is the understanding of the karmic process.* It is important because it elucidates in great detail how what one does and what one experiences have an infallible connection. Yet, this perception is not uniquely Buddhist. It is fundamental to monotheistic traditions as well. The concept of karmic results being experienced in future reincarnations is, however, particular to Eastern traditions.

In the monotheistic traditions, there exists a basic foundation for making moral choices; however, the framework is different from Buddhism in that these traditions are theistic. Such traditions share the idea of a supreme intelligence or a supreme creator, and whatever they call this concept, each dogma has an idea of faithfully acting in accordance with, and not against, its will. Through compliance, a human being experiences the grace and the benevolence of the creator, which results in its essential nature being drawn to a higher state of existence. (A Buddhist would term such a higher state of rebirth as being that of the gods' realms, while in other traditions it is referred to as a kind of heavenly realm.)

Conversely, if a person of these faiths chooses to act contrary to the will of the creator, these traditions insist that such actions incur misfortune. Thus, the essential nature of the person is forced to lower states of rebirth where there is increased suffering, confusion, and pain. Although these traditions do not recognize the Buddha's teachings, nevertheless they have an appreciation that in everything one does (whether physical, verbal, or mental) there is a positive or negative quality that has some kind of causal function that leads to a correspondingly positive or negative effect. While the basis upon which one makes distinctions for moral choice may be very different in theistic and non-theistic traditions, the actual deportment and way in which one goes about enforcing or establishing morality is very similar. Thus, these traditions share with Buddhism the recognition that certain actions are harmful and certain actions are helpful.

Of all the different kinds of actions that one commits with body, speech, and mind, it is the mental action that is the most crucial. From the point of view of one's spiritual development, the most serious action one can commit is to hold a kind of perverted or wrong view concerning the nature of reality. To make basic errors in judgment or to reject certain aspects of the nature of reality that are crucial for one's understanding can render one's spiritual practice ineffective. To doubt that one has tathagatagarbha is a very serious mistake. Even to doubt that the nature of mind itself is empty, clear, and unimpeded in dynamic awareness, that this nature can be realized as complete enlightenment, can be equally serious. Why? The rejection of these ideas means that one has absolutely no basis from which to work. If one rejects the idea of enlightenment, then one has no basis even for attempting to put effort into spiritual practice. Why would one bother doing practices or making efforts in any spiritual tradition if one would not be rewarded?

Thus, the potential for enlightenment must exist for one to

consider going about spiritual practice, let alone for that practice to be effective. So, first and foremost, one needs to come to that conviction; one needs to assure oneself that the potential exists and that it is inherently part of one's makeup. Furthermore, if one were to misunderstand or to reject ideas of causality, then one is actually influencing one's experience and one's development through misguided actions. Such misunderstanding is a fundamental error of judgment and has a very negative effect. With such an attitude, no benefit can be derived from spiritual practice because there would be no process to actualize the potential for enlightenment. Without a fundamental reasoning that allows for a development towards a final goal, there would be no point either in beginning or in continuing spiritual practice. This is why considering the true nature of mind and examining the causality of reality are essential in bringing about the clarity of awareness necessary to end ignorance and suffering.

~ 3 ~

CLEAR DAWNING

Explanation of the Vow of Refuge

When anything and everything that can be experienced in the human realm is compared to the joy, bliss, happiness, and pleasure that comprise experience in the gods' realm, there is no parallel. Take the most intense form of consummate bliss that can be imagined in the human realm: this is only a fraction of what a being normally experiences in the gods' realm. From a spiritual standpoint, however, the human rebirth is far better than a godly rebirth because it is only in the context of human rebirth that one can transcend the cycle of samsara and attain enlightenment.

This does not mean that each and every being currently residing in the human realm is going to become enlightened as a natural consequence of being human. Indeed, while it is true that every human being has such a potential, and certainly every human being has a mind that gives the basis from which to work, some people are not predisposed by nature to do anything at all positive with their lives. In fact, some people are relatively evil by nature and unfortunately spend their whole human existence creating such negative karma through their evil actions that to talk of them becoming enlightened in the present human existence is a joke, something quite impossible. They will have wasted this precious opportunity, for their evil only serves to reinforce their negative karma, which causes their minds to go straight to a lower form of rebirth where even more intense suffering and confusion exist.

From a spiritual standpoint, the vast majority of human beings waste this opportunity and do not make any use of it at all. Either they have no understanding of spiritual development, or, even if they do, they do nothing about it and allow life to pass quietly in a very mediocre way. Nothing very bad happens, but then nothing very good happens either, particularly from the perspective of the opportunity that could be realized if only enlightenment were the goal.

As we have discussed earlier, one's experience in any realm of samsara is a result of positive and negative accumulations of karmic tendencies. One's potential is seemingly dictated by one's own past actions, and when this is recognized, one could possibly become overwhelmed and might even feel guilty or have regrets. But are these feelings of any use on the spiritual path? Actually, regret is a very necessary and mature quality to have, for being able to recognize fault in oneself means that one wants to do something about it. Regret is pure and simple and has a very healthy quality to it. Guilt, however, has the sense of hanging onto a feeling of being a faulty person or of punishing oneself for having a fault, without making any effort to do something about it. Guilt is a bit senseless and is not useful in spiritual development because feeling guilty does nothing to eliminate the cause of the situation.

In some situations, however, it is possible that regret might arise when such a response is not required. This can be a problem. For example, suppose in a particular situation one has feelings of wanting to share and to be helpful by being generous, so one gives and shares a great deal. If one starts regretting this, one might say, "I really should not have been that generous as now I am going to be broke for the next week. That was a really stupid thing to do." Here is a situation where one is really destroying the good of what one has done. Although the recipients still reap the benefit of the generosity, one has turned a very positive act into something that lacks any virtuous quality, because one has regretted one's own goodness. That is a misuse of regret. So, you see, one needs to be careful about how regret is used because although it is an extremely healthy and necessary quality for any kind of spiritual or moral development, it needs to be used in its proper context. Regret brings to light what might be referred to as the one virtue of non-virtue, meaning the potential for non-virtue's possible elimination. If non-virtue were something solid and unworkable, this situation would then be hopeless. Non-virtue can be purified, however, and it can be eliminated; the way one is motivated to eliminate it is by having true regret. There is a story from the lifetime of the Buddha that may illustrate this proper context of regret.

There lived a woman in India who had a son, a young man for whom she had great hopes. She wanted him to marry well, to a girl whose family was in a very good social position and who would include a good dowry along with the bride. This mother watched her son like a hawk, making sure that he would not fall in love with some woman who did not meet with her approval. She was so determined to engineer a perfect marriage for her son that she manipulated his everyday doings and kept a close eye on any and all of his associations.

At a certain point, however, the son became drawn to a girl who was from a lower caste family. He and the girl were both very personable and easily became attracted to each other. One day, as he met his new love in the streets of the village to talk of their many interests, someone else saw their interchange and went directly to the mother. The report went something like this: "You know, you had better watch your son! He has met so-and-so and everybody knows what she is like; you do not want him to fall in love with her!" When the son returned home that evening, the mother insisted on his sleeping in an inner room that had no windows and only one door. With the words, "You are not going anywhere tonight!" she went to sleep right in front of his barred and locked door.

This went on for some while. He was guarded at night and was never out of his mother's sight during the day. Finally, by means of a go-between, the young man was able to arrange a meeting with his girlfriend. As usual, when he went into the inner room that night, his mother shut and bolted the door and then lay down to sleep. Some time passed before he got up, tapped on the door, and said, "Mother, I have to go to the toilet; please open the door." Awaking with a fright, she said, "Stay in your room; I am not going to let you out!" But he kept insisting, "Let me out . . . open the door!" She steadfastly refused, until finally he broke down the door. Undaunted, she skittered about trying to bar his way. By this time he was in such a rage that he struck her with a blow that killed her. He was shocked and upset at what he had done; he had just committed matricide, one of the most serious negative actions. But the only thing he could think of was to go to his girlfriend's house, since, after all, she was expecting him.

When the girlfriend saw him, she was disturbed by his shaken manner and the distressed look in his face. She asked, "Why are you so upset? Are you not happy to see me? What ever could I have done to offend you?"

Her words took him aback slightly and he contemplated quickly: "If I tell her the truth, she will probably be impressed. She would know I cared so much about her that I let nothing prevent me from coming to meet her. If I lie or say nothing, she will be upset when she learns what has happened. No, I must let her know how much I care for her and tell the truth." He took a deep breath, squared his shoulders, and answered, "My dear, I wanted to see you so badly, but when my mother would not let me leave, I became upset and, in my rage, I inadvertently killed her. True, I am shaken by the regrettable loss of my mother, but nothing can stand in the way of my love for you."

When the girlfriend heard this, she was absolutely horrified, and thoughts raced through her mind. "What kind of a monster am I involved with? If he has gone and killed his own mother, what is he going to do to me?" Giving him a reassuring touch on his arm, she modestly begged a moment's leave to go to tend to her toiletry, asking that he await her return. He sat down to wait. His wait continued until the early morning light, for with it dawned the awareness that his girlfriend was long gone. At this point, he was completely remorseful and completely torn Not only had he committed the worst act imaginable in killing his mother, but he had also lost the girl who was the object of his dreams. Not only did he have very negative residue from the karma of his action, but he was also totally bereft of his sweetheart.

His spirit was now so broken that, with a real regret in his heart and mind, he went looking for a spiritual teacher. Eventually he came to stay with Shariputra, who was one of the Buddha's main students. Having taken ordination as a monk and received instruction in meditation, the young man began to practice as Shariputra had suggested. As his intent and regret were sincere, he progressed quite well. His motivation was an essential ingredient in his development, and things appeared to be going better. He was not intent on hiding his past and theretofore nobody at the monastery had ever inquired about his past. But one day, word of his mother's death got out. Being honest, he answered a monk directly and told of the circumstances surrounding his renunciation of worldly life. When the monk heard the tale of matricide, he was horrified that Shariputra would let a murderer into the monastery and proceeded to inform all the other monks. One thing followed another, and before too long the repentant man was ostracized by the monastery and forced to leave.

Going to a distant place where no one knew him, he became a teacher and, because he had gained some realization and had a good understanding of the Dharma, he attracted many students. He was a totally changed man; he had become very pure and was quite a sincere spiritual practitioner. Many of his students attained the level of *arhats*, which is a very significant level of realization, albeit not total enlightenment.

As he approached his last years, this great teacher embarked on a project to heat the buildings of the monastery that had sheltered him for so many years. Located in the shadows of the mountains, the monastery was extremely cold much of the year, which made it very difficult for the monks to practice. Recognizing the difficulty in developing one's meditation under such circumstances, he became completely absorbed in providing a warm, comfortable atmosphere for the monks. He wanted to complete this project before he died, yet he died just before it was finished.

Even though his practice had been quite effective, it had not been totally successful in eliminating the karmic residue from the negative act of killing his mother and this produced a rebirth in a hell realm, where he would have gone anyway had he left his karma untouched. Fortunately, he experienced only a few moments of an intense, hot hell and, interestingly, once there, he made a connection between his experience of intense heat and his desire to heat the monastery. The first conscious thought that emerged from the mind experiencing this karmic reward of hell was, "Gee, it is a little hotter than I expected." At that point, the mental body perceived a denizen of hell walking towards him while saying, "What do you mean; why would it not be hot in hell?" So saying, the denizen immediately clubbed him. The negative residue of matricide, having been dissipated through purification in his recent human life and through this brief visit to hell, vanished; the positive result of his activities as a monk surfaced. This virtue caused him to take rebirth again, this time in one of the gods' realms.

The point of this long story is that recognition of a fault committed, regret over associated actions, and a sincere desire to motivate spiritual practice can, in fact, alter the fault's resultant negative karmic tendency. True regret can be of a very real benefit in bringing one closer to enlightenment!

Returning to the idea of precious human existence, in order for it to be truly precious, one is not only provided with the opportunity and freedom for spiritual development, one must also make use of that opportunity. A person with a precious human existence is someone who, by nature, is not only drawn to spiritual teachings, but who actively gets involved in spiritual practice. Through study and application, one not only recognizes that one indeed has such a spiritual potential, but one is also able to use it and to bring it to some level of realization. Of course, proper development depends on the individual's perspective. One needs to be looking beyond the context of this current life and this present world in order to generate the motivation to best use the opportunity of precious human existence.

A person who is very wise in the ways of the world, for instance, could spend a whole life amassing a huge fortune. It is possible to own millions of square miles, to own enormous palaces, to be worth billions of dollars, and to have hundreds of people at one's command. Everyone might say, "What a wonderful person; what an amazing thing to do with one's life." From a Buddhist point of view, if that person were going to live for a hundred million years, the merit acquired from such activities may be worth the effort, but, in fact, that person is going to live a very short time; all too soon death will approach. When that person dies, the mind is removed from that situation. It is impossible to take any wealth, palaces, land, or servants beyond death's door. Furthermore, the process of gaining wealth and manipulating power is often corrupt, which means that a person in such a position often gets involved in negative activity, reinforcing negative karma, thereby furthering confusion and suffering that, as death dawns, will drag the mind down to a lower state of rebirth. Was that person actually so clever, and was such wonderful use made of that lifetime?

If, instead, that individual sets his or her goal on enlightenment and/or developing the mind through a particular process that would ensure a continual progression towards enlightenment in the future, this would be very beneficial. Or, if this individual had matured *absolute bodhicitta,* actually attaining enlightenment through spiritual practice, then this would have been even better. From this perspective, there are really marvelous and incredible things to do with one's life, with one's precious human existence.

In one of the tantras it says, "Each and every living being is buddha," but as we have already discussed, incidental obscurations of impure alaya prevent direct experience of pure alaya. Once those incidental stains or obscurations are removed, the potential is actualized; enlightenment prevails. One gains the direct experience of enlightenment, rather than simply having the potential for that experience. As unenlightened beings, we lack direct experience of pure alaya. However, once the potential unfolds, we become enlightened. The whole point of the teaching of Buddhadharma is to bring the tathagatagarbha potential to full actualization.

In order to discover this buddha nature through the practice of Buddhadharma, Tibetan Buddhists follow a particular path. The first step or the entrance to this path is known as *taking refuge.* This implies that one understands that in one's present situation one does not see the nature of mind, does not have an existence totally free of all suffering and sorrow, and does not have the direct experience of enlightenment. The Tibetans translate the

Sanskrit term buddha as *sangye,* two syllables that roughly translate as elimination and unfolding, respectively, referring to the
idea that there are presently levels of confusion in the minds of
sentient beings that prevent the direct experience of enlightened
awareness.

As we have previously discussed, sentient beings are obscured
by the four veils. Sentient beings are subject to a fundamental
level of ignorance, dualistic clinging, emotional confusion, and
karmic tendencies which are reinforced through physical and
verbal actions. All of these veils prevent the direct experience of
enlightened mind. By definition, the state of enlightenment of a
buddha or enlightened being is a state which, when attained,
gives that direct experience that sentient beings presently lack. To
proceed with a path of spiritual development is to remove those
layers, which then permits this potential to actualize. Such purification allows the tathagatagarbha to express itself completely, without
any limiting or hindering factors.

In practicing Buddhadharma, one is taking refuge in the
Buddha, confident that the Buddha Shakyamuni attained the state
of direct experience, and confident that one has the ability to
attain this same state. When one takes refuge, one openly
declares that one's spiritual goal is the state of enlightenment.
Now, the state of enlightenment to which one aspires expresses
itself inherently and automatically as supreme compassion. This,
in and of itself, is a source of incredible blessings; but whether or
not one is able to receive such blessings depends upon one's own
particular situation. Specifically, does one have faith in the source
of blessing? Does one have the confidence and faith in Buddha
Shakyamuni? If one does have such faith and confidence, then
this provides a kind of opening and space in which blessings can
enter.

The traditional texts speak of the buddhas' compassion being
like a hook, and the practitioners' faith and confidence being like
a ring which the hook can catch. Once that connection is made,
it is possible for the recipient of the vow of refuge to begin
to experience the benefits of the connection. One receives
actual blessings and begins to develop toward full realization of
enlightenment. If, however, the person's mind remains closed

from lack of faith and confidence, then the ring does not open and the mind can be compared to an iron ball; there is no way for the hook to make its connection. The only way one can definitely experience such blessings is by providing the opening in oneself for the hook to make its connection. In taking refuge, one is creating the open space in one's mind so that the blessings and compassion of all the buddhas, which are inherently there, can be felt.

When one takes refuge in Buddha Shakyamuni, one is additionally taking refuge in his teachings, known as the Dharma, and in the close adherents practicing Buddhadharma, known as the sangha or monastic community. These three sources of refuge Buddha, Dharma, and Sangha — are termed the *Three Jewels*. One takes refuge with the basic confidence that the Three Jewels represent a source of blessing, of inspiration, and of spiritual development. Once the connection has been made and the faith and confidence continues in a person's mind, this connection remains valid. The benefits of the connection are not something limited to the context of this life. It can be said that those who take refuge, acknowledging faith in the Lord Buddha and in their own potential enlightenment, are guaranteed enlightenment at some point, because the first step has been made.

The process of becoming enlightened might be felt as a direction or guidance by some unseen force or principle. However, it is not that one is being led anywhere (in the sense of the hook pulling the ring); rather the individual simply comes to a particular state of attainment. On a practical level, there is a sense of being given guidance and of having found a safe refuge, a source of benefit in helping the practitioner overcome and eliminate the fears, sufferings, and problems in this life and in the future states of existence that the mind will experience. Once a positive connection exists in this life, then the mind can be guarded from lower states of rebirth. There is a sense of being guided towards purity of being, which is, by definition, the attainment of enlightenment.

Once having taken refuge, the whole wealth of the teachings becomes available to the practitioner. Henceforth, a teacher may have confidence when giving teachings to the student. It is understood that through this gesture the student has proved his or her worthiness and regards the teachings as being a source of benefit and blessing. Thus, in taking refuge, one makes oneself accessible to the teachings; or rather, one makes the teachings accessible to oneself.

In each of the three yanas, the principle source of refuge is the Three Jewels. However, if one intends to practice the vehicle of the vajrayana, then one also takes refuge in the *Three Roots*. The root of all blessing is the Tsaway Lama; the root of all accomplishment is the Yidam; and the root of all activity is the *Dharmapalas* (the Dharma protectors).

The person who bestows the vow of refuge is the lama. When one receives the vow of refuge, one visualizes the lama surrounded by innumerable buddhas and *bodhisattvas*, all of whom are giving refuge. There is a mundane aspect, in which one prostrates and recites the vows before a physical spiritual teacher of Buddhadharma. As well, there is a transcendental aspect, in which one connects to the force of blessing and compassion of all the buddha fields and levels of *accomplished bodhisattvas*. If, after having taken this vow, one keeps it unbroken, then, in this very lifetime one will be protected from fear and suffering. Furthermore, throughout all future lifetimes (until one attains complete enlightenment), one is also protected from the fears and suffering of samsara.

The root of keeping the vow of refuge intact is to maintain faith. This is very easily accomplished: by remembering the great blessing, great compassion, and great power of the activity of the Three Jewels and the Three Roots with love, faith, and devotion, one simply recites the refuge prayer seven times each day. This repeated recitation takes less than five minutes of one's busy day, yet the prayer has strong benefits associated with it. The verbal recitation clears away obscurations of the door of speech, while the mental attitude of devotion clears away obscurations of the mind. There are several versions of refuge prayers, some shorter and some longer, but their meaning is all the same. Usually one is encouraged to recite a seven-line refuge prayer; but if this is difficult to remember when beginning, one may also say seven times the simple line, "I take refuge in the Buddha, Dharma, and Sangha until I attain enlightenment."

In the West, when one formally takes vows of refuge with a

lama in the Kagyu tradition, one is usually given a Dharma name. This gift provides a strong memory of the day on which the lama bestowed his blessing. Furthermore, the name itself has a very auspicious meaning and signifies an auspicious connection with the Dharma. Thus, in wholly regarding what takes place on this auspicious occasion of taking the vow of refuge, it can clearly be seen that this simple action is the basis of all one's future Dharma practice and thus is extremely important.

Taking the vow of refuge is not limited by age. Even someone who is very old and incapacitated can still think and come to the conclusion that taking refuge is a beneficial step. But what about a child too young to understand the concept? Due to a number of factors, a certain blessing is imparted to the child taking part in a refuge ceremony. One factor is that parents who bring their child to a refuge ceremony are doing so out of faith. They wish the child to receive some kind of blessing and are acting with a sincere desire to help the child's spiritual development. Further, the teacher has a certain compassionate concern with intent to benefit the child. The child has buddha nature and the potential for enlightenment and thus directly benefits from making this connection with the teacher. Lastly, there is a certain blessing in the transmission of energy that takes place during a refuge ceremony which potentially furthers the child's spiritual progress.

But, if someone misinterprets the concern of parent and teacher for the child's future spiritual pathway and feels this example gives them an authority to go around proselytizing the teachings, or a permission to try and force the teachings on people who, although they have attained the age of reason, have not yet personally indicated a willingness in that direction, then a difficulty is created. Instead of benefiting them spiritually, the teachings may cause a great deal of harm, because the more a person has to resist unwelcome ideas, the more a person is not willing to listen, and the more a negative reaction begins to surface. Such disinclined persons may soon start to reject what is being said and, in so doing, only increase their own confusion and spiritual ignorance. They can end up worse than before, or in an even more acute state of spiritual deprivation.

In taking the vow of refuge, a person is not restricted in his or her actions nor barred from any kind of ordinary worldly activity. Furthermore, there is no conflict in having faith in or practicing another spiritual or religious tradition. Quite the contrary, it is entirely appropriate within the context of taking the vow of refuge to maintain one's association with the faith and belief of one's personal choice. So long as the conviction is held that the Three Jewels are a source of blessing and compassion, the refuge vow remains intact. If, at any point, a person rejects that faith and confidence, then that rejection has terminated the vow of refuge. Such rejection would close that source of benefit; the hook and the ring disengage, so to speak.

When looked at from a more ultimate perspective, while various methods and approaches in different religions and spiritual traditions exist, they all have a common purpose of providing some means of eliminating confusion and suffering. The Buddha himself stated that his followers should consider all religions and spiritual traditions as being none other than emanations of the tathagatagarbha. In presenting eighty-four thousand collections of Dharmas, the Buddha recognized the varying needs of all sentient beings. After all, we are individually stamped with our own personal karmic responsibility. These different expressions of spiritual tradition and religion are also of the same inclination, in that they serve to facilitate the varied spiritual growth of many sentient beings.

The Buddha also stated that one should not make judgments with sectarian bias concerning the truth or falsity of other spiritual approaches, nor reject them out of hand. While these approaches might not work for all people, this does not mean that they do not work for some; while Tibetan Buddhism is known as the quick path to enlightenment and other paths may take longer, there is only one goal. Therefore, taking refuge is the expression and formalization of one's overall faith and confidence in the path of attaining liberation.

I would therefore ask you to fully consider this and the teachings presented herewith. When the opportunity presents itself, I urge you to take refuge formally with a qualified lama. Furthermore, I pray that all mother-like sentient beings benefit by your

The *"Refuge of Enlightenment" Tree:* The Budddha Shakyamuni was not represented iconographically until the second century A.D. Theretofore, only four symbols were used to represent his life and works: the Bodhi Tree, the Wheel of Dharma, the stupa, and his footprints. Lord Buddha described the bodhi tree as "my permanent abode" in the Divyavadana. In vajrayana, the bodhi tree is visualized replete with the lineage holders, with yidams and dharmapalas on the lower branches. (Pen and ink drawing, courtesy of the artist, Diane Thygersen)

decision to set forth on a path that leads to true liberation. Please join me now in reciting the seven line refuge prayer.

Refuge Prayer

From this moment onward, until the heart of enlightenment
is reached, I, and all sentient beings
limitless as the sky,

Go for refuge to all glorious, holy lamas;

We go for refuge to all yidams gathered
in the mandalas;

We go for refuge to all buddhas, conquerors
gone beyond;

We go for refuge to all supreme dharmas;

We go for refuge to all noble sanghas;

We go for refuge to all dakas, dakinis,
protectors and defenders of the Dharma,
who possess the eye of transcending awareness.

Let us dedicate the merit from this recitation to the benefit of all sentient beings that they might attain the true liberation of enlightened awareness.

≈ 4 ≈

GATHERING CLOUDS

Resolution of Emotional Subjectivity

Having been raised in the high remote reaches of a desolately barren country, I find that the Western world has a standard of living and a level of comfort that is quite incredible. The degree to which those born here are well-housed and comforted helps shape their experience, just as ruggedness shaped mine. This incredible standard of living, with all the control over environment (that is, central heating, air conditioning, and so forth), plus the comparative personal wealth that individuals here generally enjoy, makes this Western realm seem like a gods' realm. People abroad look at the West and say, "People there must be laughing night and day, their happiness must be so great." Yet upon closer look, we find that, despite all the modern technology, gadgetry, and luxury, an intense mental suffering exists that can cause equally incredible anguish.

Why is this? Direct observation does not provide a reason for this as, obviously on a material level, everything that is needed, and often more, appears to be provided through this high standard of living. However, underneath this exterior there is a great deal of emotional confusion, which is where the problem lies. In general, the Western mind is subject to the conflicting, confusing aspects of emotionality that give rise to suffering. This is surprising, for it seems that anyone in such a materially abundant environment should be perfectly content. Westerners certainly have few needs that are not answered on a material level. Yet, life in any modern country leaves one highly susceptible to such emotional confusion.

How can we approach this question of emotionality? Can we do away with it completely, impractical though this may seem? Actually, there are a number of ways or approaches that are perfectly valid and lie within the Buddhadharma, allowing various means to overcome emotionality. It is entirely appropriate to adopt an approach that tends to cut off or arrest negative emotions so that they cease to arise. Another method is to transform negative emotional energy into positive emotional energy. The third approach, which is perhaps the most practical and direct, is simply to appreciate the nature of what is taking place when an emotion arises in the mind. Here one is regarding the nature of the experience without especially regarding the content. Understanding the nature of mind itself as being the origin or place from which all emotionality arises is the basis for this approach. Thus, the more one understands about the nature of mind itself as the origin of each emotion, the more one understands emotionality in general, and the more one is effectively able to deal with arising emotions.

To examine emotionality, we start by reducing it to the fundamental, or primary, emotions. In Buddhist theory, we speak of six primary emotions; or even more basically, we consider the emotional tendencies in the mind as being three in number: **desire** *(or attachment)*, **anger** *(or aversion)*, and **ignorance** *(or dull stupidity)*. Within this delineation of emotionality, we are speaking of things that are common to the human condition. They are not emotions upon which any one race or any one country has a particular monopoly, as all human beings suffer from the various effects of these different emotions. For example, it would not be accurate to say that Tibetans have fewer emotions or have less emotionality than Westerners. Nor would it be accurate to state that they have more. If we were to put the emotions of one culture on one pan of a scale, and those of another culture on the other pan, the scale would swing to a more or less even balance. Everybody has problems with emotionality. It is obvious, however, that emotions do express themselves in different ways in the world's various cultures. Whether or not any one emotion is encouraged or discouraged in any culture can create some slight differences, but the emotional raw material, common to everyone, does not differ throughout the world. Part of being alive in the human realm is one's subjection to the three (or six) basic emotions.

It is interesting to distinguish different forms that these emotional tendencies take on the cultural level. For example, the idea of ignorance as an emotion takes into account states of dullness of mind. Furthermore, although it may not seem to be an emotional activity, sleep is in fact part of the emotive quality of mind, for during it, the mind experiences a state of dullness. It is true that some differences in people's sleeping habits exist. Asians generally go to bed about eight o'clock in the evening and arise by five o'clock the next morning. People in the West seem to stay up until quite late at night, often until after midnight, getting up long after the sun has risen, sometimes as late as ten or eleven o'clock in the morning. In the East, our habitual emotional pattern of sleep might well have to do with the fact that we do not have widespread use of electricity or artificial light. When the sun goes down, so does everyone; and when the sun comes up, everyone does the same. On a very superficial level, one can distinguish different patterns that develop in the cultural expression of emotional tendencies, but the amount of emotion does not differ in various cultures in terms of potential.

We each suffer from emotional complexes that confuse the mind. In the case of anger and aggression, there has been a frequent tendency in the Asian cultures to hold up aggressive, fighting behavior as an ideal in proving strength and masculinity. The whole idea of being a warrior, of being an expert in martial arts, of lauding aggression and anger as something praiseworthy, has general cultural implications. It seems, especially nowadays, that Western people actually have fewer of these problems than Eastern world cultures; the tendency to praise physical violence or macho behavior is becoming outmoded in the West. In Eastern world cultures this attitude is still a problem. People continue to have a fixation or fascination with anger and the way it expresses itself in physical violence, in the prowess of one person over another, in defeat or victory in combat, and so forth. From an

Asian's point of view, the culture of the Western world appears to be far more interested in putting down aggression and anger, rather than in reinforcing it, because persons who are very aggressive and pugnacious in killing and fighting are not as highly regarded in that society as they might be in Asian cultures.

In the instance of another basic emotion, namely that of desire or attachment, it appears that by comparison the balance is the other way around. In Asian countries, modesty is encouraged and there exist social restraints in the expression of desires, particularly sexual desire. These cultures tend to be far more modest, by and large, than Western cultures. While there is no real guilt about sexuality, there is a great sense of shame and modesty concerning one's behavior in such matters. One is not very open in the expression of sexual desire. This tends to contribute to sexual fidelity because, on the general cultural level, there is still a strong sense of shame attached to being unfaithful to one's marriage partner. In a country like Tibet, marriages were extremely stable. Even if one of the partners was away for years at a time (as occasionally happened when a man went on a trading excursion to another country or another part of Tibet, or when a wife paid a return visit to her family some distance away), the husband and wife would become celibate for that period of separation. This worked to create a very stable sense of commitment, even if it was only because they were ashamed to consider anything else. The sense of modesty in expressing sexual desire did not mean they did not have it; it is not as though sexuality caused them no problems. People did experience and suffer from sexual desire but, because of social restraints, there was less encouragement of its free expression. Quite simply, there was virtually no cultural support for committing adultery in an expression of this desire. The strictures in Tibetan society allowed few avenues for human sexual expression and deemphasized its importance.

Additionally, a very strong monastic tradition existed in many Asian countries, including Tibet, which prompted large numbers of people to take vows of celibacy. Such a way of life was highly respected in these cultures and was held up as an ideal role model, especially in Tibet. Monks and nuns developed a firm sense of commitment to a modest monastic lifestyle, at times only out of a sense of shame. The cultural morality dictated that it would be extremely embarrassing and shameful for oneself and one's family if a monk or nun were to break or to give back vows. In fact, when a son or daughter had taken vows, parents in Tibet would often be heard to say, "I would rather my child die than break these vows as it would be too shameful to live having broken them." This attitude does not appear as consistently in the West. In comparison there is far more encouragement in Western societies to stimulate an expression of one's sexuality, and/or of personal desires and attachments.

Many of the laws in the West focus upon the control of aggression and in curbing actions committed through aggression and anger. Desire, on the other hand, is not as widely legislated. It remains something that the society not only tolerates but often openly encourages. In the West, one is generally encouraged to stimulate and give rise to all kinds of desire (sexual or otherwise) and to play out these sense-gratifying desires to their fullest. Even among those people who observe in their lives a strict interpretation of the monotheistic traditions, many indulge in satisfying a broad range of desires.

In the current general cultural milieu of the Western world, expression of desire allows emotions to be actively encouraged, actively stimulated, and over-blown, all within the contextual appreciation of this as something healthy. If one has a desire, one is encouraged to fulfill it. If one has an emotion, one is encouraged to stimulate it, to bring it to development by expressing it. Generally, this is seen as a healthy thing to do, while actually, in terms of karmic development, this approach tends to create a disproportionate exaggeration of desire and attachment. In and of itself, desire is one of the least harmful of emotions. It is that to which desire gives rise that is the real problem. It is the breeding ground for all kinds of other, more complicated emotional states. The simple arousal and playing out of desire (whether it is sexuality or any other kind of desire and attachment) will bring other things along with it — greed, jealousy, anger, quarreling, envy, etc. — wherein the problem lies.

In presenting different approaches for dealing with emotionality, Buddha Shakyamuni taught the three yanas or vehicles. The hinayana (or lesser vehicle) emphasizes abandoning or rejecting certain kinds of emotionality that are productive of confusion and suffering. This path places emphasis on the practice of a personal lifestyle and is formulated by various levels of vows or ordinations to be taken by the lay person, the novice, the monk, or the nun. These specific life styles are chosen to allow only certain activities in one's life and to cut off others simply through rejection or abandonment, because these activities are perceived as sources of samsaric suffering. The hinayana idea is to turn off unnecessary, counterproductive parts of one's life: one simply does away with activities that accumulate negative results. In many Eastern countries, where life still goes at a much slower pace and modernization is far from being complete, this path is easier to follow and is still currently in practice. For most Westerners, however, this approach is perhaps too severe, as the modern lifestyle makes it difficult to stop doing things that are considered to be within the social norm. It may not be feasible to exert such an exacting precision in shaping one's own morality without strong social support.

Another path that the Buddha presented was the mahayana, the great vehicle. In this approach, the energy of a negative emotion is rechanneled or transformed into the energy of a positive quality. For example, take a person who is an extremely angry individual, continually giving rise to anger, hatred, and aggression. In the mahayana approach, such a person would be encouraged to develop meditation to channel that negative energy into the development of benevolence, compassion, and loving kindness towards others. Regardless of the emotion, proper use of meditation gives a sense of transmuting and transforming the way in which emotionality expresses itself. Again, this is a fairly involved process. It takes time and commitment, and it may not be the most practical means to solve quickly the problems of emotionality.

There is another option given by the Lord Buddha, that of the vajrayana. This tantric approach seeks to get to the root of emotional experience without worrying about the superficial contents of the situation. In getting right to the root, in seeing directly into the nature of an emotional experience, the liberation from emotion itself is spontaneous and simultaneous with the experience of the emotion. Vajrayana is an extremely direct path, but extremely profound as well. On a practical level, this approach is difficult to explain in so elementary a presentation. In order for it to be beneficial to the general public, an appreciation of the tantric method must necessarily be developed to enable one to understand the truly profound nature of this approach.

What, then, do we have left? We have just eliminated the three basic choices. There is yet another approach that we can try, and this method is not concerned so much with seeing into the nature of the emotion in any profound or mystical sense. Rather, one can automatically gain some understanding, some perspective as to the thoughts, emotions, and so forth, that arise in the mind through understanding the nature of the mind itself. Through examination of the origin of those forces (or those thoughts and emotions), one begins to understand their nature. This approach seems to be reasonable in that we are trying to effect the most benefit in one short lifetime. Additionally, this is an approach that is extremely convenient, very easily explained and understood. Used properly, this method is remarkably effective. It does not require a long term commitment to a learning process or restrictions in life style. Nor does it require any profound insight. It does, of course, require intelligence and understanding of what is being said.

The basic problem is that one believes that everything is *real*, and thus everything is treated as such. "I am real and solid, my body is real and solid, and these emotions I am feeling are real and solid." Given this belief, we have no choice but to play out the emotions and to follow them to their conclusion. We are totally at their mercy. We experience situations where attachment, aversion, anger, stupidity, desire, and jealousy arise. We treat such subjective phenomena as being so very concrete that we automatically surrender to them. We invest this whole concept with such a validity and reality that we fail to recognize these qualities as absolutely false. We feel, "Well, there's no choice, because everywhere I turn, everything is so real; what can I do?"

So, we just play out our delusion. We are totally at the mercy of this projection of the mind.

What is really taking place? As human beings, we experience mind and body, we function in a combination of mind and body. We have a physical form and we have a mind experiencing through that physical form. There is a strong and subtle connection between the two. But, when we experience an emotion, whence is it coming? Does it really have anything to do with the body? Suppose we feel anger. Based upon that anger we might shout at someone, or beat up somebody, or even kill them; but these physical actions occur because we have the mental motivation to enact them. The body acts as an avenue or channel for emotion to be developed and expressed. If we think that emotion is purely and simply a physical manifestation, we should take a look at a corpse, a human body disengaged from its mind. Without a physical form, where is the mind's ability or avenue to express its emotional reality? A corpse is obviously unemotional because the mind no longer uses the physical form to channel its emotional delusions. It can no longer continue to express anger or any other emotion, because the mind does not have the solidity it once had to make this possible.

Understanding this gives one more perspective. It enables the individual to realize that one does not have to give in to the mind's emotional delusions or to surrender to an emotion when it arises. Why? Because ultimately speaking, other than this wave of thought or emotion on the surface of the ocean of mind, nothing is happening. The mind is so fluid, so flexible; these qualities allow any situation to become workable. Mind is emptiness; it has no tangibility. One cannot ascribe any limiting characteristics to mind itself. The only statement we can make is to say that metaphorically mind is essentially empty. Yet, that is not all; we also know that the mind has an illuminating potential and the quality of an unimpeded manifestation of dynamic awareness. Now this is not to say that the emptiness is empty and yet phenomenal things are solid, because the manifestation of *nirmanakaya* is rather like a rainbow. A rainbow, as a whole spectrum of color, is very apparent and very clear, but it is not solid. You can put your hand right through it. This example of an appearance that is essentially empty but not substantial serves to give the idea that all perfectly apparent and clearly present phenomena lack an ascription of true tangibility or any ultimate reality. In a similar manner, the nature of mind, while being intangible, expresses itself as luminosity, as unimpeded dynamism.

What is really taking place when one has a single emotion? The empty, clear, unimpeded, and dynamic awareness is manifesting in a particular emotional form, without there being the necessity to ascribe any reality to that expression beyond the moment in which it arises and then fades away again. Since the emotion has only a very conventional kind of reality, no ultimate, substantial, or tangible reality need be (or even can be) ascribed to it. This makes the situation much more workable. One does not have to feel totally at the mercy of one's emotion. It is only when acquiescing to the emotion, or investing the emotion with the falsehood of reality, that one is forced to play out the consequences. And this is where the trouble really begins, because playing out emotions is an inexhaustible process. As long as one is willing to ascribe reality to emotions, they are continually self-perpetuating. It is like trying to exhaust the Ganges or any other large river; they just keep on coming.

To the extent that one allows desire (or any other emotion) to express itself, one correspondingly finds out how much there is that wants to be expressed. It is such an unending, bottomless well of emotionality that one can spend an infinite amount of time bringing it into expression, which is where the real trouble starts and wherein the real suffering lies. No matter what surfaces into expression as experience, there will be still more emotions and thoughts produced by the mind manifesting essential emptiness in an unimpeded way. In absolute reality there is nothing there. If there were something fixed or solid, you could chip away at it until nothing was left. However, because this is merely a manifestation of an intangible, dynamic state of awareness, it can keep on coming as long as you are willing to allow it. At that point then, the problem is not, "Shall I give up this emotion or not?" "Shall I stop having this emotion or not?" Instead, the question becomes, "Shall I surrender to this emotion or not?" "Do I have to play out this feeling?"

In answer, when an emotion arises in the mind and no relent-less need to play out the whole thing exists, one is then free from having to make crucial decisions of right or wrong. One comes to appreciate what is really happening when an emotion arises in the mind, be it desire, anger, or whatever. One experiences that emotion as a manifestation of mind arising from, and dissolving back into, the mind. It becomes more transparent, and the need to exhibit the emotion becomes less. Getting involved in all of the complications to which emotionality can give rise happens *only* as long as one is willing to ascribe an independent reality to an emotion (or a thought) that arises in the mind.

Emotion and discursive thought are not new to you, yet all this vast array of emotional conflict is not residing in any special place. You cannot store it in a cupboard and bring it in and out at will, for it is of the mind itself; being of the mind, it is insubstan-tial with absolutely no self-existence. As you have had emotional and mental discursiveness in the past, so too will these arise again for you in the future. They are not lost in some drawer or forgotten in last year's move, or even left in your therapist's office. These processes are a part of your being sentient.

I can say, "Emotions arise from the mind and the mind is empty," and you now have an understanding of the meaning of those words. Such comprehension is important, as it is the first step to true understanding. But it is not enough, because nothing of ultimate benefit really comes about exclusively through intellec-tual comprehension. That is only the first step. Comprehension can become a deeper, more intuitive understanding and should ideally be carried through to a stable realization, or to its direct experience. The second step comes when such an understanding is translated into a living and stable experience. It is only then that any true benefit of spiritual teaching can be felt to enhance the practitioner's development, as it allows for the attainment of a greater state of happiness, of balance. Thus, in order for the present discussion to become meaningful, it is important that a process of deepening the understanding of the emptiness of mind begins through meditation and personal experience.

By maintaining a correct and erect posture in meditation, one can reach a point beyond which one does not have to direct the mind in any way. One does not have to look within, one does not have to look without. One does not have to direct the mind in any way but can just let it relax in its own natural state. The authentic experience of this nature of mind is characterized by a spacious, intangible quality, which we term the *emptiness of mind*. It is further characterized by a clarity and a transparency, which is the luminosity of mind. The fact that there is an experience of this emptiness and clarity, that there is a state of awareness at all, is the third aspect of mind — its unimpeded, unobstructed, dynamic manifestation as awareness.

Beyond assuming a correct posture and letting the mind relax naturally, there is no need for the mind to be forced, held, or controlled in any way during this meditation. Quite the opposite, the mind is simply allowed to experience its own true nature without any distraction, without any artifice or contrivance at all, and without this spark of awareness being dulled or lost. This experience, then, is the authentic experience of mind itself. Although the nature of mind is characterized by spacious, intangible, empty essence, it exhibits an extraordinary potential at the same time. The mind could know anything. This potential for experience is none other than its luminosity and its clarity coupled simultaneously with an awareness, or a direct experience, of the intangible, insubstantial nature of mind, which has an omnipotent, transcendental, all-knowing quality. In calling attention to these three different aspects, which in fact are not different things at all, we are able to describe the mind effectively. These three different aspects of the mind are the unique experience of nature of mind itself.

Without wavering from this empty, clear, and unimpeded state of dynamic awareness, let us now try the following. You, no doubt, have emotions. No doubt you feel sexual desire from time to time. Now, allow yourself to think of someone that you find extremely attractive, either romantically or sexually; call the image of that person to mind and watch what happens. Watch the response of the mind to that image as you call it forth. The image called to mind is conditioned by thoughts of things that have happened in the past. There are certain tendencies in the mind, certain habits that dictate the way in which we think. To think of somebody one finds very attractive and appealing is generally a gratifying, pleasing experience. One starts to glow; mind and body begin to warm with that perception. There is a certain blissful quality in that initial experience of calling forth the image of that person, the object one takes to be the source of the emotion. At this point in the exercise, one remains or dwells in the perception of one's individual initial response — without having to indulge further, without having to elaborate, without having to construct anything. Simply experience that first glow of bliss within this empty, clear, and unimpeded spacious state of awareness into which that glow of well-being arises.

Let us now shift the emphasis. Rather than thinking of someone who is attractive to you, think of a person you hate, or who hates you, someone with whom you have a very negative relationship. Call to mind the reason why you are so angry at that person. But instead of playing out the whole range of animosity this evokes, before indulging in it, just be aware of what happens when you call to mind such an image of hostility; simply watch. Take note of the response that occurs when this anger begins to emerge.

What is important here is that regardless of the emotion being experienced — be it desire, anger, pride, jealousy, envy, greed, or whatever — what is really going on is a shift in attention. The mind is expressing itself in a different way. Nothing implicitly requires one to presume that this emotion has any reality in and of itself, that it has any tangibility at all, or even that it has any form, shape, size, location, or any solidity at all. It is just that the mind is expressing itself in a different way than it was a moment ago.

If one does not recognize the mind's true nature, one continues to be completely bewildered by emotional conflict and discursive thought. This can be an endless situation. When I first came to the West in the early seventies, I stopped in Geneva where I met an exotic sheik who had thirty wives; I have since heard that he now has even more. This person obviously has to deal with many conflicting emotions in such a broad-based form of relationship. In recognizing that all this emotional conflict is arising from the mind, one realizes the mind itself is insubstantial and empty. If the force of emotional conflict is removed by one's attaining this recognition, the individual can live peacefully, no matter how many wives or husbands one has.

There is an illustrative incident that occurred between the great saint, Jetsün Milarepa, and one of his students, a young woman referred to as Paldenbum, who had came to him for instruction in meditation. As recorded in *The Hundred Thousand Songs of Milarepa,* Paldenbum's devotion to the Dharma was first tested by Milarepa. Finding she had faith, he proceeded to give her refuge vows. Then he began instructions in meditation. "Meditate on the sky," he said, "and meditate on space which is beyond any limitation, having no center or circumference or limit. Meditate on the ocean; meditate on an ocean so deep that the concepts of surface, depth, and bottom become meaningless. Meditate on your mind; meditate on the nature of mind so that concepts of luminosity or non-luminosity, clarity or lack thereof become irrelevant."

Paldenbum came from a wealthy family where everything was done for her by servants; thus, she was lacking in the physical strength usually required for becoming a student of Milarepa. However, her devotion to Milarepa was extremely great. Courageously, she renounced her worldly life and, with Milarepa's inspirational meditation instructions, went to the rock caves to meditate. Later she returned for clarification. "Milarepa," she said after she had respectfully prostrated several times, "it was fine when I meditated on the sky, but clouds began to fill it and move across it. It was fine when I meditated on the ocean, but waves began to cover the surface. And it was fine when I meditated on the nature of my mind, but thoughts and emotions began to crowd the clarity. I need a way to meditate on the sky, the ocean, and the mind which does not give rise to these problems."

Milarepa replied with a wonderful song, which instructed: If you meditate on space or the sky, clouds are merely a manifestation in space, within the space. Simply concentrate on space rather than on its manifestation. If you meditate upon the ocean, waves are merely a manifestation of the ocean; again there is no problem. Simply be aware of the ocean rather than paying special attention to the waves. When you meditate upon the nature of the mind, thoughts and emotions arise; these are merely a manifestation of mind. Simply be aware of the mind, rather than being caught up in the details of the manifestation.

Encouraged by Milarepa's clarification, Paldenbum continued to practice diligently. At the time of her death, she went to the *dakini* realms without abandoning her physical body because she had been able to resolve all aspects of emotional and mental discursiveness, going beyond the causality of karmic fruition through thoroughly recognizing the true nature of the mind.

This method is quite useful in allowing one to approach meditation in respect to the thoughts and emotions that arise in the mind. Mind, which produces the thought, is essentially empty; therefore, thought is essentially empty. It partakes of the intangibility of mind. The same is true of emotions. This means is that the emotions we experience are completely insubstantial, completely unstable. There is nothing solid or dependable or reliable there at all. Everything is continually changing, precisely because these manifestations are empty and have no independent existence in and of themselves. They are mere momentary manifestations of mind, presently apparent but about to pass away. We see signs of this all the time.

A man falls in love with a woman and has incredible attraction for her until she turns around and goes away with another man. Then all of that attraction becomes anger and hatred. Quite simply, it is the manifestation of mind that has changed. It is not that there was ever anything real that was the attraction, or anything real that was the anger. In one instance the mental energy manifested in one particular way, and later it manifested in another. The emotion the mind presents can change just as quickly and as variedly as the wind changes the pattern of clouds in the sky. In understanding the experience of emotions in this way, one sees that there is very little need to think that they are so important. With this grasp of the situation, there is no need to think of emotional states as being so worthy of our attention that we surrender our mental balance and give in to emotion. There is no need for that at all!

One can continue to employ this approach and then analyze each experience. When something arises in the mind, be it thought or emotion, what is taking place? This can be a perfectly valid pursuit for meditation, especially when it is coupled with a more intuitive approach to the state of bare awareness. On the one hand, the practitioner is spending some time in meditation, consciously analyzing experience and looking for the source of emotion by such analysis, while on the other hand, he or she is employing the approach of just letting the mind rest in the state of bare awareness, of raw experience. This uncontrived state of empty, clear, and unimpeded awareness, is, as I have said many times, the nature of mind itself.

Through this kind of approach, one will find that when experiencing a very strong emotion of desire, anger, or whatever, something does indeed arise strongly in the mind. This can allow for the discovery of the tools to enable one to look into the real nature of that experience. Perhaps one will forge an appreciation of the mind itself, without the particular manifestation being a problem. Perhaps one will focus directly on that thought of desire, anger, pride, or whatever, to see exactly what it is. In either case, the result can be a greater calmness and deeper perspective on what is taking place in the mind when a thought or emotion emerges. The effects of this approach can be dramatic. It is as if one had a pot of furiously boiling water and dashed a cupful of cold water into it. The agitation immediately calms down. Emotions experienced in a solid way make the manner and whole being very coarse, gross, or clumsy. Some people become wrathful or unpleasant simply because there is a barrage of emotional energy. The individual can develop an appreciation for the perspective that allows a seeing of things for what they truly are and not for what one had assumed them to be. This approach calms the clinging of the mind, just as the cold water calms the boiling pot.

In Western society, there are a great many learned psychologists, psychoanalysts, psychiatrists, etc., who profess that the actual expression of emotions encourages those emotions to subside. They believe such expression will alleviate bothersome and perturbing emotional disturbances, and that this can free one from imbalances. But when the true nature of the mind is considered, this viewpoint is extremely erroneous because emotion itself is insubstantial. It arises from insubstantial mind and it continually arises when mind's true nature remains unrecognized. The impossible attitude and approach encouraged by some therapists that attempts to exhaust emotional discharge resembles the misconception of believing the full flowing river will come to a halt given enough time to flow.

Clinging to reality as being something substantial and real is like having a serious illness. The antidote that cures this dilemma is the recognition of its insubstantialness and of its true emptiness. Expressing an emotion cannot stop the flow of karmic consequences, nor does it successfully stem the flow of ignorance that blinds one to the true nature of the mind. The intensity of clinging to oneself as being substantial, of believing one's emotional conflict to be something substantial, can be exaggerated to the point of suicide, a fruitless result of emotional distraction. By recognizing mind's true nature as emptiness and by seeing that emotional conflict, discursive thought, and everything of the mind is indeed illusory and without self-nature, we can transform our constant preoccupation with emotional conflict, bringing about immediate calm. It is the recognition of emptiness that calms and completely removes the power, force, and bewilderment of emotional conflict.

When one experiences the emotions in a much gentler and more transparent way, this awareness really can transform one's entire way of being and the way in which one experiences life and relationships. There evolves a far gentler, more balanced quality of being. A balanced perspective and an equipoise emerge that give a sense of calmness and precision. Even on a very practical level, one's character development and approach to life change. At this point, then, the question is not whether or not one has emotions, or whether or not one should abandon certain emotions. Rather the challenge is to understand the nature of emotional experience more thoroughly, more precisely. The benefits that come about can be quite practical, as evidenced in the general well-being experienced and in the general sense of equipoise and gentle calmness with which one can go about one's life.

⚈ 5 ⚈

EYE OF THE STORM

Teachings on the Bardos of Death and Dying

The idea of rebirth, of the mind's endless continuity from one state of existence to another, rebirth after rebirth in the past, present or future, hinges upon the mind's essential deathlessness. While involved in the six realms of samsara, the mind is continually involved in the varying stages of rebirth, known in Tibetan as the six *bardos* (or intervals). The bardo cycle is said to be endless and is often compared to a wheel that turns unceasingly. This seeming endlessness happens because the mind is not subject to cessation or to being created at any given point, being *no thing* in and of itself. Intrinsic to the Buddhist teachings is the awareness of cyclic samsaric suffering, the desire to end this suffering (not only for oneself, but for all sentient beings), and the assurance of liberation being possible through the attainment of buddhahood.

Consider for a moment one's present rebirth as a human being. How is it that such a rebirth transpired? Try for a moment to think of the state of previous existence. In whatever physical form or realm of experience that had previously transpired, it would seem obvious that death occurred because one no longer takes part in that realm of existence. In between the death of that prior physical embodiment and the birth in this present embodiment several of the six bardo stages fashioned the experiences of dying, death, and rebirth. It is especially interesting for the Dharma student to examine those intermediate stages that transpire in the interim between one lifetime and the next; it also can be quite helpful in understanding the true potential for attaining enlightened awareness.

Following the *bardo of the dying process* (the physical death of a former body), there is a relatively brief period of unconsciousness that is due to the shock of the death experience. This interval is technically termed the *bardo of the ultimate nature of phenomenal reality.* Following this interval, there is a phase known as the *bardo of possibility.* The after-death experience of the bardo is every bit as real as the *bardo between birth and death* we are now experiencing. To elaborate, the projections of mind, the hallucinations, and so forth, that take place in the bardo of possibility are as solid as what we now experience in our daily lives. Additionally, emotional experiences of pleasure, pain, confusion and so forth, that take place in the bardo state are as real as those that we now feel. The only difference is that in the bardo of possibility there is no physical basis for consciousness; it is merely an experience of a mentally projected body without self-existence.

Manifesting in many different ways, the possibilities of all the six bardos, whether of the living, the dying, or the after death, are determined by one's particular karmic tendencies. At the point that the physical body dies, the basis of experience currently employed is removed; the mind experiences in a purely mental way. Nevertheless, this experience has the flavor of embodiment because there is a compulsion (or habitual tendency of the mind) to embody itself in order to experience. Yet this bardo has no physical basis for the consciousness, even though the conditional subject/object clinging weaves a web of myriad forms, all the while believing mind cannot exist without body. Thus, this mental body appears as though there were a physical body, even though there is no physical substantiality.

Despite the delusional qualities of the mental body, the experience is very real to the mind experiencing the after-death state. When the mind is caught up in experience, this *is* the reality, this *is* what is real! At this point, then, this mind (which is essentially clear, dynamic, and unimpeded in its manifestation) is experiencing a disembodied state. There is absolutely no physical basis for consciousness, yet the obscurations that cloud the mind tend to embody themselves as though there were. These obscurations tend to perceive (or to project) this quasi-physical buffer between the mind and the physical outer environment, believing both to be existent. From a subjective point of view, the perceived external embodiment is the receptor for all the pain and pleasure that one's mind can experience in the bardo of possibility.

At a certain point, the karmic tendencies producing the intermediate state begin to fall away, moving the mind to rebirth in any of the six realms, through any of the *twelve links of dependent origination* (*nidanas* in Sanskrit). In our case, our karmic accumulation manifested as an embodiment in the human realm. The mind we once knew as a prior reincarnation has traversed the bardo and has taken rebirth as the human being we now know ourselves to be.

The mind incarnates into a realm of rebirth, wholly dependent upon the karmic tendencies directing that process. Considering all the possibilities, rebirth as a human being is a relatively superior form of existence. On a karmic level, such a rebirth indicates that the positive tendencies (which are reinforced through virtuous or positive actions) tend to be in predominance, and the negative karmic tendencies (which are produced and reinforced through non-virtuous or negative actions) tend to be less dominant. This description is the generalization that can be made about existence in the human realm. This higher realm of human experience has considerably more happiness and fulfillment, and considerably more potential than many other realms of existence.

As human beings, we not only share a collective aspect of karmic existence, we each experience an individual aspect as well. Simply stated, the collective aspect is that predominance of positive tendencies that brings certain individuals together. In addition to shared experience, we share a perception of the human realm, including the physical environment. Activities that go on in the human realm imply a certain shared experience because we share the common karma to pursue those things; we agree on their existence in our world. This collective aspect of karma is reflective of the fact that there exists a certain percentage of shared experience between beings in this human realm.

There is, however, an aspect of karma that remains a completely individual experience. For example, some people live longer than others and may be generally happier throughout life. They may have a more stable or well-balanced personality; they experience physical and mental well-being, good health, and prosperity, with the ability to be successful and fulfill themselves in what they do. Other people, while still taking rebirth in the human realm, may experience something quite different, like a short life and/or a great deal of sickness; they may have considerable unhappiness and instability (mental or physical), and know poverty, want, deprivation, etc. Whether positive or negative, all of these experiences will arise because of habitual tendencies that are the individual aspect to the karmic process.

Even the conception and development of the fetus in the womb will be dependent upon whether or not that being has positive or negative karmic tendencies in his or her makeup. In some cases, for both mother and child, the pregnancy can be a very easy one; it can be a pleasant experience. The birth can be a relatively straightforward, painless affair; the child is born without complications and is healthy, complete with all of its faculties. In the other extreme, it is a miserable experience for the mother and the child. Sometimes the child can be conceived in such a way that deformation, retardation, or any variety of impairment (or lack of normal makeup of a human form or mind) results. The birth process itself can be an extremely painful, traumatic one, and the child takes his or her first step into the world with suffering, complication, and pain. Again, this is an aspect of individual karma.

A good example of how both collective and individual karmic tendencies combine to produce unique experiences is that of the individual's entry into any of the six realms of collective experience. It should be obvious that not every sentient being goes through the same birth process as that of a human being. In fact, there are certain realms in which a kind of miraculous birth takes place, in the sense that the being enters fully developed into that realm of experience, without a gestation period; for such an entity the stages of fetal development are totally unnecessary. The mind simply incarnates in a particular form as a complete entity. This is a characteristic of the hell realms and the gods' realms. In the case of the hell realms, the mind of the being incarnates immediately in a form that experiences the intense heat or cold of any one of the eighteen states that come under the classification of hell realm. In the case of the gods' realms, there is again an immediacy to the mind's incarnating. The mind finds itself in a body surrounded by a pleasant environment in one of the various levels of the heavens. There are descriptive passages in various texts that tell of a being immediately incarnating to a heaven in the center of a flower that immediately opens to reveal the gods' realm to that being.

In the human realm, and in the realm of *pretas* (or hungry ghosts), however, birth has many conditions. It is based upon sexual polarity, upon union between a father and a mother, upon the conception of a child in the womb of the mother, upon the gradual process of development of the physical structure in the womb, and upon the child then being born to become part of that realm. This can often take very strange turns. In the human realm, we are familiar with a woman giving birth to one or two children at the same time, while in certain preta realms, it may be possible for a mother to give birth to hundreds of children, hundreds of pretas, at a single time. As an example of shared or collective karma, these newborn pretas entered into their realm through the same womb door.

In the case of the animal realm, including insect life, there is a variety of possible birthings. There is birth from the womb (as with mammals), birth from eggs (as with birds and insects), and some kinds of immediate birth where the being emerges fully developed into that realm of experience (as with larvae). There are also certain kinds of generation which are based upon the right conditions, such as heat, humidity, etc., that cause life to multiply. In all, there are four basic processes whereby beings come into their respective realms and particular karmic situations; and all four of these are found in the animal realm.

It is interesting to note that prior to conception, while the individual's mind is still experiencing the last stages of the bardo of possibility, a perception (a quirk of karma) is produced that causes a prescience of who the future mother and father will be.

In the case of a sentient being taking rebirth in the human realm, there is an image or experience of seeing the mother and father in sexual union immediately prior to conception. Tied in with the conception process, then, is not only the sperm from the father and the egg cell from the mother joining together to create a physical basis; there is also the consciousness of the bardo being, in its disembodied state, as an involved third element. There are thus two physical elements and one mental element that come together for the complete conception of the human individual.

Furthermore, it is an emotional response of the future child, as part of the propelling force on a psychic level of conception, that determines whether the child will be male or female. If the karmic tendencies are to result in a female rebirth, there will be a positive attraction toward the father, the male energy, in the mind of the disembodied being and a repulsion or aversion to the female energy. This attraction and aversion will be part of the conception process. If the opposite is to occur and the child is to be born male, then an attraction to the mother, with a repulsion or aversion to the masculine energy, will be the emotional component of that conception. In either case, the conception takes place when the physical cells of the two elements from the father and the mother and the consciousness of the being come together. From that point onward, the mind, having gained a physical basis for that consciousness, expresses itself through the growth of the fertilized egg, maturing as a fetus in the womb of the mother until the full term of pregnancy is reached and the child is born with the form and sense faculties of a human individual, as a human baby.

What is significant for us to examine at this point is not so much what takes place during phenomenal life, but that which inevitably happens at the end of it, or death. This is something we are all going to have to face, sooner or later. The very fact that a birth has occurred indicates that a death will occur. Indisputably, they define each other. No one is born who does not die, and nothing comes into being that will not, at a certain point, fall apart. This is as true in the human realm and its phenomena as it is with anything that arises interdependently in any samsaric realm. Our existence as humans, the mind's experience of the human realm, will eventually come to an end.

Death has several phases or intervals. Actually, the whole of life is a process of dying; when the time of surrendering the physical form dawns, there is the interval known as the bardo of the dying process, which begins whenever the particular cause of death strikes. Whenever a fatal disease or accident, or some other element that causes the organism to be afflicted beyond reparation is encountered, the process of dying begins. The bardo of the dying process then continues to the point that a being actually does die, as evidenced by the stoppage of breath, the cessation of heart activity, etc., indicating that the mind and body are separating and their bonding is falling apart. The bardo of the dying process is but another aspect of the concept of bardo, or interval stage, between one state and another.

Regardless of the cause of death, the dying process indicates that the elements that compose one's physical body and one's psycho-physical experience of the body are breaking down. Traditionally, this is viewed as the dissolution of several different essential forces. The *earth element* is not earth as an object hanging in space, but rather pertains to the earth-like quality of the solidity of the body. The fluidity of the body's blood and fluids comprise the *water element*. The biological warmth of the organism is the *fire element*. The respiration and circulation within the channels comprise the *wind (or air) element*. The process by which these various qualities begin to break down is experienced on a psychic and a mental level. There are signs involved with the varying stages of the dying process that happen both subjectively, in that they are purely the experience of the dying individual, and objectively, in that someone else can watch or feel them happening.

When the actual death process begins, the least subtle element, the earth element, dissolves and becomes absorbed into the next most subtle, which is water. When this happens, the person's body appears to become very heavy and is very difficult to move. The dying person is then unable to sit up or to lift the legs and arms; there is a steady loss of bodily movement and control as this element dissolves. As the ability to coordinate and to move the body effectively subsides, the inner subjective experience is that of being crushed by a great weight, as though a mountain were sitting on one's chest. When the breaking down of the earth element reaches the psychic level, there is an experience as though the physical body were being squeezed or crushed, which is very terrifying.

The second stage is the dissolution of water into the next most subtle elemental quality, that of fire. The external sign of this is the inability of the person to control urination, salivation, or mucous discharges. Fluids begin to leak from any and all of the body's orifices, without the person being able to control them through musculature. This sign indicates that the water element is being absorbed into the fire element. On a subjective level, the dying person feels as though he or she were drowning or being inundated with water or carried away by a flood or torrent. Again, this is a very traumatic and terrifying experience.

The third stage of the process is the dissolution of the fire element into the air element, the next most subtle quality. On an inner level, this is experienced as though one were flushed with fire, as though the body was being subjected to incredible heat. To someone watching the process, the objective phenomenon is the gradual loss of bodily warmth from all the extremities. First the fingers and toes begin to become cold, then this cold moves up the legs towards the heart. Overall, there is a gradual loss of body heat. This is a sign that the fire element is dissolving and being absorbed into the air or wind element.

Following this, the wind or air element dissolves into the element of space, which is one's consciousness itself. At this stage, the objective observer would notice the dying person's difficulty with respiration as the most significant symptom. Perhaps there is rapid, shallow panting, or long, sobbing breaths that are hard to hold and are immediately expelled. As soon as the breath has left, the person has great difficulty inhaling the next lungful. Here the process of respiration is being interrupted. The subjective experience is one of being caught in a maelstrom of air, as though a tornado or hurricane were tearing at the fastenings that are binding one, until the process of respiration finally ceases. This cessation indicates that all the elements have broken down and have been absorbed into consciousness itself.

At this point, a rapid three-stage process occurs. You will recall that at conception there are feminine and masculine forces (or energies) present, which were received from the mother and father and were connected with the physical structure of the body. These are technically referred to as the *white and red bindus*. *Bindu* is a Sanskrit word meaning drop or essence, implying something that is concentrated. The white bindu is considered masculine; the red is feminine. Regardless of whether the individual is male or female, the white bindu is the energy received from the father. At the point of dissolution of the element of space, this bindu is considered to be concentrated in the crown of the head. The red bindu is the feminine energy received from the mother and is concentrated at a point below the navel, in the genital region.

Once the elements have completely dissolved into one's consciousness, the death process continues when the polarities of the red and white energies begin to move toward a common center. The first process is that of the white bindu (or force) moving down from the crown of the head to the heart region. For the dying person, this phenomenon is connected with a visual experience of seeing a field of white light. It is as though one were suddenly flooded in moonlight or with clear white light. It is extremely brief, as this happens in just a fraction of a second while the energy is dropping to the heart region.

The white bindu reaching the heart *cakra* implies that the mind is then incapable of experiencing anger or aggression. Emotions having an aggressive or angry quality are temporarily (but not ultimately) blocked, so the mind cannot experience them. The texts say that even if the dying person were to see someone murdering his or her own father at that time, one could not get upset.

Immediately following this (again, very quickly), the red bindu or feminine energy moves up from the genitals to the heart to meet the white energy descending from the crown of the head. The consciousness of the dying person, which at this moment is poised just at the point of death, now experiences a flash of red light. It is as though the sun suddenly rose in front of one's face, directly confronting the individual with a red brilliance. At this stage, all the emotions having a flavor of desire, attachment, or attraction are effectively severed. Even if the most tempting and beautiful goddess, or the most handsome and wonderful god appeared, there would be not the least thought of attraction in the dying consciousness. The mind simply cannot experience those emotions at this point.

It is when these red and white forces meet in the heart region that death truly occurs. At this point the physical body and the mind separate. The energy structure has broken down completely; there is no longer an avenue for that physical basis to maintain consciousness, as it is no longer part of the life experience.

There is a technique in Tibetan Buddhism known as *phowa*, which in Tibetan means consciousness transference, developed to exercise a certain degree of control over the way in which the consciousness leaves the body at the moment of death. The proper time to use the phowa technique is when the white and red bindus come together at the heart. A skillful adept can transfer the consciousness to some higher state of realized awareness, to a realm of pure experience, rather than having the mind plunge into the naturally occurring state of unconsciousness that follows death. Without the use of this powerful technique, the mind will black out; even the coarser levels of ignorance and dullness are blocked, so that the mind experiences a brief but total quality of ignorance.

As you have just seen, the bardo of the process of dying is one in which the elements dissolve into each other in progressive stages and the mind loses contact with the external phenomenal world. Here the senses begin to break down—the eyes dim and are not able to see; the ears cannot hear clearly; additionally, the senses of taste, touch, and feeling are lost. Gradually, as the moment approaches when total oblivion looms, the mind itself loses the ability to think consciously. At this moment, when the mind enters into the total oblivion of complete unconsciousness, the potential also exists for a very different kind of experience, again depending upon whether one has developed advanced spiritual practice during life.

In vajrayana, one of the techniques of the *six yogas of Naropa*, which is termed *radiant light (or luminosity)*, is designed to allow the practitioner to develop a state of clear awareness that can be experienced during this stage of the death process in lieu of the normal experience of unconsciousness. It is also possible to develop this state through the mahamudra meditation approach of directly experiencing the nature of the mind, regardless of content. If, during this lifetime, the practitioner has developed these approaches and techniques in meditation, tendencies have been established that hopefully will appear just at that moment. If these habits carry over beyond the physical death to the ordinary experience of total oblivion, the mind can instead experience a state of awareness that is in direct contact with its own true nature. The attainment of this potential level of direct insight approximates the definition of the realization of the first of the *ten levels of accomplished bodhisattva*. There are ten of these levels or degrees of realization; whatever is beyond the tenth level is the enlightenment of complete buddhahood. In this very subtle experience of bare awareness, it is possible for extremely rapid spiritual progress to take place. One may, in fact, make the transition from the first level to complete enlightenment in that short period of time. Indeed, even a movement from the first to second level, the first to fourth level, or any other leap could produce very dramatic results if this yoga of Naropa has been developed.

The period of unconsciousness after death is generally three and a half days at the most. If one's practice has developed well in this life, the potential exists for one to make dramatic spiritual progress. For the untrained human being, however, dying presents a different reality. We can recognize objectively that once the respiration has stopped and the heart has ceased its activity, the physical body is no longer relevant to the dying person. What we do not see, however, is the subjective experience of intense shock or trauma, the reaction that plunges the mind into a state of unconsciousness. Once the death has occurred, the mind goes blank for a period of time, not unlike ordinary deep sleep. The traditional rule of thumb measures this period as being three and a half days, though it is by no means restricted to that.

Eventually, the consciousness begins to arise and stir anew. As the consciousness begins to become cognizant again, the reawakening individual confronts the projections of the mind. In

the *Tibetan Book of the Dead,* this encounter is termed the experience of the *mandala of the peaceful and wrathful deities* and is experienced in a variety of ways by different beings. The predominant
quality of the experience, however, is that it is misunderstood
and misinterpreted by most mental bodies, for, when a mental
body sees a mandala of deities, it is usually experienced as some
kind of threatening, repulsive external force. The mind shies away,
as though these projections were something actually outside the
mind itself rather than a hallucination taking place in the mind.
One can definitely benefit by receiving empowerment into the
cycle of practices known as the *Bardo Thödol,* of which the *Tibetan
Book of the Dead* is one text. The blessing and the understanding
gained through such practice establish tendencies that can allow
the experience of the bardo hallucinations to be rather attractive,
or at least the confusion can be lessened so that the potential to
progress spiritually might be perceived.

If the consciousness of the deceased person does not perceive
the experience of the peaceful and wrathful deities as being a
pure projection of enlightened mind, but rather draws back from
it, then the mind, in continuing the after-death experience, is
propelled further into another bardo. This next stage is termed
the *bardo of possibility,* because, quite literally, anything can happen in that state. It is a state of immediate experience because
there is absolutely no physical basis for consciousness. This means
that whatever arises in the mind is immediately externalized and
experienced as though it were actually happening. Simply thinking of something is to experience it directly and immediately.

Perhaps this would be like thinking of India and being immediately in India. And with each thought that followed, one would
find oneself instantaneously in that environment, for example,
from India, to America, to Canada, to the family home, to Nepal,
etc. Or one could think of a person one likes and immediately be
in his or her presence, and in the next moment, one can think of
a hated person and poof! be in that presence. We do not now
experience such immediacy of experience because there is a physical
basis for consciousness which slows the process down. In the
bardo of possibility, however, anything can happen, and does.
The mind is tossed from one experience to another, on a second-

by-second basis, or even on a fraction-of-a-second basis. Things jump from place to place, with no coherence and no continuity; whatever pops up is experienced.

Again, in the teaching of the six yogas of Naropa, there is another practice, termed the *bardo yoga,* that specifically relates to the after-death state of the bardo of possibility. Using this technique, one can take advantage of the immediacy of the experience to completely transform it. Given that instability permeates the entire situation, the positive potential exists to enable one completely and instantaneously to transform the experience. If one practices this kind of meditation technique during this life, at the moment the bardo appears, tendencies can arise to permit one to make a complete transformation. For the skilled practitioner, the experience itself can be the antidote to suffering because the tendency established by the practice of bardo yoga can effect a complete transformation, allowing the mandala of deities to be perceived in its true nature.

Even without having perfected this yoga, one can obtain liberation in the bardo of possibility. Any meditation, such as a meditation on Chenrezig (the Bodhisattva of Compassion), in which one identifies with the form of the deity, recites the mantra, and uses the various visualizations, helps develop the ability to recognize the peaceful and wrathful deities because one of the main benefits of such yidam practice is the tendency to recall the practice. If the yidams' images or their mantras arise in the mind strongly enough while in the bardo of possibility, and if one's devotion is sufficient, then a complete transformation of physical, verbal, and mental experience comes about instantaneously upon recognition of the true nature of the bardo experience. If the tendencies developed in daily meditation arise in the mind while there is no longer a gap between the arising and its experience in this bardo, then one will directly experience the purified awareness of *sambhogakaya.*

Development of such potential is the main idea behind the *pure land* practices, which foster the aspiration toward rebirth in a realm of pure bliss, of pure experience. The form given for expressing this motivation is devotion to an enlightened being named Buddha Amitabha. The virtue of devotion to Buddha

Amitabha is that his pure land is directly accessible through faith, motivation, and aspiration. If the aspiration to attain the pure blissful experience of *Dewachen* is strong enough, then during the bardo state where there is no physical body as a hindrance, the process can happen instantaneously. Before the mind is required by karmic patterns to take physical rebirth, the process can be started that will culminate in the experience of the realm of pure awareness. Through the development of faith, motivation, and aspiration to Buddha Amitabha in this life, one can short circuit all established patterns, allowing the mind to break through the individual's enmeshing karma.

With such an approach, one can attain a state equivalent to the realization of the first level of an accomplished bodhisattva. This incredible experience is described in the texts with such phrases as "taking birth in a flower in a beautiful realm of supreme bliss." The eloquent way in which it is presented in several texts has provided a basis for the aspiration and devotion that is the center focus of the pure land school. Practicing Amitabha meditation definitely establishes the tendencies which will allow the transformation to take place in the bardo of possibility. Practice of other yidams can also effect the same result. When the mind is no longer subject to the limitations of the physical embodiment, the complete instability of mental projections provides unusual potential for complete transformation, to the extent that liberation can come about in a very short period of time, even instantaneously, if one's practice is stable enough.

No matter the quality or quantity of one's practice, there is no guarantee that the bardo experience will bring about enlightenment. One complication that can occur is a carry-over of the attachment and clinging from life into the after-death experience. For example, in the bardo of possibility, it is not only possible for the consciousness to recall the home in which the individual had lived, but it is also possible for it to attempt communication with those remaining members of the family, as though those beings were actually present. The limitations of the bardo state, however, do not permit actual communication. There is the appearance of the home and family, but any attempt at communication is ineffectual, as it is wholly the mental body's projection.

It is also possible that the consciousness experiencing the bardo may perceive others speaking about his or her death. In any case, some kind of realization eventually dawns that death has occurred. When the awareness of death becomes conscious, it is too much for the mind to accept, again producing a kind of shock or trauma. The mind can again blank out temporarily; when it subsequently re-arises, another bardo of possibility experience takes over.

It is indeed entirely possible to have an attachment remembered from a previous life, of wealth, possessions, or something similar. Such images emerge in the bardo while recent attachments are still fresh in the mind. The consciousness may similarly perceive that recent wealth or possessions are being taken or divided among other people. Being unable to recapture that wealth, a feeling of pain and suffering arises that can be a real impediment to the aspiration inspired by yidam practice. On the one hand, the individual may be sincerely aspiring to obtain a realm of pure experience through transformation, while, on the other hand, he or she may be holding back due to a sense of all that has been left behind.

With the mind still trying to recapture what happened earlier, the experience can take very strange turns. The mind can perceive, for example, a loved one calling, "Do not go, come back!" This is just a projection of attachment to a person or situation; even though one wishes it, nothing can be recaptured. Thus, instead of aspiring completely, one can be continually looking back. This can be a real problem, a very great obstacle in affecting complete transformation.

The bardo of possibility, this interval in which anything can (and generally does) happen, has an earlier and a later phase. The early phase is more connected with impressions from the recent life, or the immediately preceding state of existence, because these impressions are the freshest in the mind. They play a dominant role in what kinds of impressions and experiences the mental body has. From time to time throughout this phase, situations arise where the mind of the deceased individual understands that death has occurred, again producing the stupor of traumatic shock.

The later phase of the bardo of possibility begins when the impressions from the previous existence begin to fade. Clinging to the past is no longer the object of conscious recollection; the mind begins to forget. What takes predominance at this moment are impressions connected with future destiny and the shaping of whatever physical rebirth the mind will take next. The impressions of the later phase, and the way in which the mind perceives, tend to be conditioned by tendencies of karmic fruition that lead an individual toward a state of rebirth in a particular situation.

The standard length of time traditionally accepted for this whole process of intermediate states between death and rebirth is thought to be roughly forty-nine days. It may be longer or shorter, but this is the standard reference for the amount of time spent by the disembodied consciousness in the three bardos.

If liberation has not been attained, then at a certain moment (regardless of the duration of the bardos) the mind will be propelled by the forces of karmic fruition into a state of rebirth. The circumstances of all rebirths will be individual, for this is the process of samsara. The term samsara implies "going around and around and around," referring to the cyclic state of birth and death, from one form to another, from one realm to another. It is not a cycle in the sense of coming back to the same place each time; rather, it suggests moving continually from one state of limited existence to another, with the experiences of disembodied consciousness of the bardo filling the gap between rebirths. The process is that of the mind experiencing one state after another, and/or one realm after another, with varying successive karmic accumulations. As long as the individual does not attain enlightenment, the process is endless. Samsara does not exhaust itself of its own accord. It does not run out of bodies, nor does it run out of possibilities of confused awareness. It goes on and on and on, continually renewing itself as it exhausts itself.

Only one context provides the opportunity to transcend all this ceaseless suffering and to step out of the whole vicious cycle. That is the opportunity of the precious human existence. What is most significant about having such an existence is the karmic fruition that allows one to encounter spiritual teachings, have an interest in them, and to develop the faith and confidence to employ them.

When such opportunities are activated, the individual can actually make the necessary steps to become free of the endless and relentless cycle of rebirth.

In the courtyard of Rumtek Monastery, Kalu Rinpoche poses before going into the shrine room for the Mahakala puja. (Photograph by J.G. Sherab Ebin)

≈ 6 ≈

DISTANT SHORES

Introduction to the Vajrayana Practices

As living beings, our experience of existence occurs through means of five (or six) elements. Furthermore, *all* sentient beings, not only human beings, have variable concentrations of the elements of earth, water, fire, wind, and space, each of which contributes towards the substantiation of physical form. As you may recall from our earlier discussion, the element of earth, or the sphere of earth, manifests as the solidity of bodily existence. The sphere of water is present in the body as its fluids. The sphere of fire is its warmth. The sphere of wind is associated with the breath. The orifices and spatiality of the body are representative of the sphere of space. Additionally, all sentient beings have the sphere of wisdom. In all the realms except human, however, this wisdom element is likened to one of the other five, such as fire or water. This similarity obscures the essential quality of wisdom, making wisdom an indistinct and unrevealed quality for the beings manifesting in those realms. These beings function as though they have only five essential elements. It is extremely fortunate that human beings have the separate and distinct element of wisdom in addition to their quintessential physical being.

The element of wisdom is one's inherent buddha nature, and, as we have discussed, is present within all sentient beings. As you may recall, this buddha nature may be likened to perfectly pure water, and the obscurations of ignorance and stupidity may be likened to mud. The nature of the water is undiminished when it becomes mixed with the impurity of the mud. Similarly, insubstantial obscurations veil our innate, inherent buddha nature, yet it is the wisdom element that enables one to recognize the mind's true nature. Unfortunately, sentient beings in the three lower realms are so heavily obscured, mostly by ignorance and stupidity, that they have no recognition or experience of the wisdom element or buddha nature.

Within the human realm of our experience, the wisdom element makes its presence known to varying degrees. The degree of revelation is a result of one's previous positive accumulations that allows partial purification of the obscurations veiling the mind's true nature. The unveiling of this awareness is known as "the dawning of our innate wisdom element." Such awareness distinguishes itself in our recognition that the human ability to understand certain things differs from that of beings in the other realms, most notably and observably from the capabilities of those beings in the animal realm.

Further, this wisdom can be developed and increased, especially if one uses the path of Dharma. To illustrate this, remember that in the middle of the night there is such total darkness that it is impossible to see or to discern anything except the state of darkness. But, come the earliest part of dawn, the outlines of mountains and different landscapes can be vaguely perceived, and as the sun continues to rise, the details of the environment become clearer. This comparison illustrates the character of the wisdom element which awaits the clarity of perception, the dawning recognition of mind's true nature. With the practice of Dharma, this wisdom element increases, flourishes, and becomes fully illuminated; much like the sun's gradual rise into full daylight, it allows all phenomena to be seen with great clarity.

Although the wisdom element is a sixth and separate element in the human realm, still it is obscured by the discursive consciousness, the element of consciousness. Even though one may hear the Buddha's teachings on the nature of mind and of all phenomena, the obscuration of discursive consciousness prevents the element of wisdom from fully manifesting and, without this full wisdom, one is unable to recognize fully the true nature of the mind. With meditation practice, however, the obscuration of discursive consciousness decreases and the sphere of wisdom increases, becoming more apparent, and thus more powerful. This is the process of the path of Dharma.

As we have discussed, the discursive element of consciousness is thought of as being of four types. These are the obscurations of primordial ignorance, dualistic clinging, emotional distraction, and karmic accumulations; all four obscure the element of wisdom. Fortunately, through the practice of Dharma, these four veils may be completely purified. When the clouds that obscure the light at noon have vanished, the sun appears completely brilliant in the mid-heaven; similarly when the four mental obscurations are eliminated, primordial wisdom is completely present and shining. This is what is meant by the Tibetan word *sangye*, meaning completely purified, opened, and accomplished. This is the Tibetan term for *buddha*.

Once a sentient being has purified the four obscurations and has attained the state of sangye or buddhahood, then his or her wisdom is completely developed and open. At that point, tremendous power and qualities of great compassion, great wisdom, etc., spontaneously arise. Such qualities are totally beyond any similar mental qualities that are ordinarily attainable by gods or human beings. Traditionally, it is recognized that there are thirty-two great qualities of enlightened mind ascribable to the historical Buddhas.

The speech of a buddha also has immaculate qualities that are totally beyond any qualities of speech available or attainable by gods or men. For example, if a buddha is speaking to a large audience with several different language backgrounds, all present understand the meaning perfectly. Furthermore, all present are able to hear the words carried over great distances without a buddha ever raising his or her voice. In all, a buddha has sixty such immaculate qualities of speech.

The body of the historical Buddha possessed thirty-two major and eighty minor signs of perfection that are totally beyond the marks of perfection attainable by any gods or humans. A historical buddha's being is completely free from any kind of physical faults and is able to manifest in a dazzling and wondrous form, which is incredibly beautiful by anyone's standards and has one hundred twelve immaculate qualities.

Through the perspective gained by having these truly amazing qualities, a historical Buddha displays remarkable compassion. Seeing all sentient beings in the same way that a mother looks at her only child, the Buddha Shakyamuni gave teachings on each of the different paths of the Dharma, compassionately designed according to the various predispositions of karmic capacities of each individual sentient being. Of these several different paths, such as the path of the bodhisattva, the *pratyekabuddha,* or the arhat (to name but a few), *all* were manifested by the generosity of Lord Buddha's compassion towards sentient beings.

While all sentient beings differ in the degree of their positive and negative accumulations, in general they may be grouped into three categories: excellent, average, and inferior. For sentient beings of the excellent or average type, the Buddha Shakyamuni taught the path of the yidam. The yidam practice allows those of excellent capacities and of great meritorious accumulations to attain complete realization in this very lifetime. Through the practice of this same yidam path, those of mediocre or average capacities and moderate merit accumulations may attain complete liberation at the time of death, or in the period after death. Designed especially for those beings having the qualities to practice it, this path comprises the pith teachings. The yidam deities are called transcendent deities. This means that they are deities through whom one may attain the ten levels of accomplished bodhisattva and the ultimate level of buddhahood. They were emanated by the Buddha Shakyamuni to help speed those of excellent capacity towards the goal of final liberation.

The fact that all the yidams are emanated by Buddha Shakyamuni does not mean they are all identical. Instead, they have different appearances, physical characteristics, ornamentations, colors, and attributes. There is a reason for this. In much the same way that a restaurant menu has a wide variety of choices because not everybody eats the same thing, sentient beings have many differing desires or requirements. Each person discriminates and has obvious preferences, be it food, clothes, music, or approach to spirituality. Acknowledging varying types of sentient discrimination, the Buddha Shakyamuni emanated myriad yidam deities.

To understand why the path of yidam practice is important, let me now refresh the discussion of the nature and function of the three yanas. As you recall, the three yanas are the hinayana (or the lesser vehicle), the mahayana (or the greater vehicle) and thirdly, the secret vajrayana (or supreme vehicle). We can think of these three as being a process, in that one starts with the lesser vehicle, increases gradually by attaining more superior levels, and finally reaches the secret mantra vehicle. These can also be considered three different vehicles, each of which may be approached in its own right.

A fuller explanation of the nature of the three yanas has already been given, but let us now briefly review them. Basically, the hinayana is that path which emphasizes outer activity, wherein one completely abandons all manner of causing harm to others. With the development of pure conduct underway, one absorbs the mind into one-pointed samadhi in which one can recognize the emptiness of self and, thus, come to realize the state of an arhat.

The recognition that not only the self but all phenomena are empty is the basis for the path of mahayana. This path views all phenomenal appearances as mental projections that are empty of any independently existent characteristics. Furthermore, one recognizes this emptiness and sees that all sentient beings are foolishly clinging to that which is emptiness as though it were something real. They cling to that which is suffering as being pleasure, and cling to that which is impermanent as being something permanent. Aware of the totally erroneous viewpoint to which sentient beings cling, those practicing the mahayana path experience very intense compassion. The development of compassion and emptiness based on the practice of the path of the six perfections (the six paramitas) is said to be the *two wings* of this path. By using these wings, those practicing mahayana will attain the fully enlightened state, having passed successfully through all the bodhisattva stages. This is the path of mahayana.

In the vajrayana, or the secret mantrayana, the view held is that the mind itself is emptiness, and that all appearance is emptiness.

This recognition of mind and all appearance as being innately empty is termed *wisdom*. All appearance of form, sight, sound, and all kinds of sensory appearances are termed *skillful means*. Thus, in vajrayana, the whole of samsara and nirvana is recognized as being the union of wisdom and skillful means.

For example, consider the use of the organ of the eye to see. With our eyes we see the realm of form; we perceive form and actually believe that there is something that we are seeing. This demonstrates the quality of unimpeded luminosity, which is, again, termed *skillful means*. However, the mind that sees is emptiness. And thus, these two — the emptiness of mind itself, and the actual manifestation of appearance that we think we are seeing — are totally the union of means and wisdom.

Similarly, when we hear sound with the organ of the ear, we seem to be hearing something. It is as though there is really something that is being heard. This is also considered to be skillful means. At the same time, however, the one that is hearing and the sound itself are completely empty and have no substantial existence. This phenomenon is the union of means and wisdom, as well.

When considering the total of all the five sense organs and their objects of sensory consciousness — such as eye consciousness, the eye itself, and the vision of form (and similarly throughout the remaining senses of hearing, smelling, tasting, feeling) — know that these are none other than *dharmata* itself.

Remembering that the basis of all this is the nature of mind itself, if we call to mind the view or imagination of perhaps a mountain, possibly a lake, or something less distant like the physical appearance of our parents, can we not recognize our ability to do so instantaneously? Being able to see anything instantly and having the ability to call such images to mind is again what is referred to as means. Recognizing that these images themselves are emptiness — that there is actually nothing there, that there is no substantial existence, and that mind itself is devoid of any substantial existence — is what is referred to as wisdom. Thus, quite simply, all appearances, all phenomena are the union of means and wisdom. Even in a single lifetime, one is able to manifest completely as an enlightened being and attain true liberation without any obstacle on the path when one real-izes the actuality of the union of skillful means and wisdom.

In order to attain this realization, one performs the yidam practice; therein lies an easy method to recognize all appearances as the union of skillful means and wisdom. It is the yidam itself that has the power and blessing to bring about this very realiza-tion. In previous times, this approach to practice, this tradition of mantrayana, was extremely secret. The practices of the yidam were very closely guarded and were not generally available. Rather, only those with a certain degree of understanding and with the good quality of capacity actually received these teachings. Nowa-days, we lamas give these secret precepts and yidam practices to whomever attends the teaching or initiation. We understand that without the karmic accumulation to be initiated into such prac-tices, then you would not be reading this book or hearing this lecture, or even be fascinated enough to inquire about this path.

In this kalpa of one thousand historical Buddhas, only three will publicly teach this vehicle of secret mantrayana, which is also known as vajrayana. Buddha Shakyamuni, our historical Buddha who is the fourth of this kalpa, is one of these three. This is essentially why vajrayana teachings are being offered to the gen-eral public without there first being an extremely long association between the teacher and the student. In the lifetimes of historical Buddhas who will not give vajrayana teachings to the public, these teachings will be given only to a few close and selected students. Therefore, it is extremely auspicious that you have the karma to receive these teachings and that you are instilled with the desire to use the insights of vajrayana to gain the liberated awareness of mind's true nature.

Let me return for a moment to continue an earlier discussion on the various capabilities of sentient beings, namely, that within the human realm there are inferior, average, and excellent types of human beings. Such distinctions have nothing to do with any sexual gender, racial, religious, or economic considerations; rather, these are levels of positive and negative accumulations. We find that the inferior type of human rebirth, which consists of those who have a natural inclination to cause harm and to destroy, etc., is extremely abundant. Such beings have no actual faith in the

Dharma or any type of morality, and furthermore lack the ability to gain faith in the Dharma. This is called an inferior human existence, because once these humans die, they are again subjected to the experience of constant suffering in the painful lower realms.

Average human existence refers to those beings who are not particularly moved by any type of inspiration and who spend their human lifespan in distraction, doing various things of little account. They are not developing positive trends. As a result, their next rebirth will not be in any way superior to that experienced in this lifetime.

The excellent human existence is also called the precious human existence. It belongs to those beings who have interest in the Dharma, who listen to the Dharma, and who, in gaining an inspiration from it, wish to establish positive karmic trends. In comparison to the other kinds of human existence, the level of precious human existence is extremely rare. In illustration, if you were to take a great number of people, perhaps more than a thousand, in that number there may be only a handful, perhaps five at most, who have this preciousness.

Primary to having a human body are the bases of consciousnesses associated with the organs of sense, i.e., eye consciousness, ear consciousness, nose consciousness, etc. In the Tibetan tradition, the consciousnesses are seen as subtle organs shaped as described. The basis of visual consciousness is like a flower. That of the olfactory consciousness is like two copper tubes. The basis of auditory consciousness is like the rolled bark of a tree. The basis of the gustatory consciousness is like a crescent moon. The basis of tactile consciousness is like the very fine down of a baby bird. And, the organ of mind is like a clear mirror. We Tibetans also liken the five or six sense functions as similar to windows in a house. Here the consciousness associated with each organ is thought of as being an individual, making five or six beings in that house, each with its individual sense consciousness. It is by the means of the sense organs, each with its associated consciousness, that the sphere of sensation is experienced. It is from the eye organ and visual consciousness that the experience of the realm of form is derived. Similarly, the other organs and their associated consciousnesses allow the experience of the sensation of phenomenal existence. Perhaps it would be possible to consider that the six consciousnesses experiencing this realm through the six sense organs are indeed separate consciousnesses, in that each has some degree of distinction or separation because each has a different function. In essence and in meaning, however, together these comprise one consciousness, that of our human experience.

That which is perceiving the realm of form through the sensory organs is the base consciousness of pure and impure alaya. With a constant, habitual tendency of clinging to the experience of the sense consciousnesses as being something real, one could well believe that, without the eye organ, there can be no perception of form (and so on, with each of the other organs). In fact, this is not the case. The view that leads us to this conclusion is illustrated by examining the mind's experience of the state of dreams while asleep. During the dream time, the mind will project all the different consciousnesses very clearly, so that one will perceive form, will hear sounds, and will experience pleasure, pain, and a whole array of phenomenal concepts, including the whole environment contained in the dream. At the time of the dream, these are perceived as being absolutely real. When one wakes up, however, they have completely vanished.

You will recall that this very moment (in which you are open to the entire possible range of human sensory experience) is the experience of the body of karmic fruition. During the dream state, by means of the body of habitual tendencies, you are open to the realm of the dream's sensory experiences. Further, in the after-death bardo state, you will undergo the realm of bardo's sensory experiences by means of the mental body. In cycles of one following the other, you (and every other sentient being) have these bodies going through these various states. With the various bodies, every sentient being endlessly wanders in samsara. Certainly, this is a dilemma; but it is one that is resolved in recognizing the mahayana view as valid and useful. Resolving the issue of duality — of self and other, and of self-phenomena and the totality of other phenomena — one employs emptiness to gain liberation. Through meditating, one gains some experience of the emptiness (or non-self) of the individual personality, and the non-self (or emptiness) of phenomena, and by actually seeing the indivisibility of these two non-selves, one attains great realization. Then, just like Jetsün Milarepa, one can manifest many miracles, similar to those given in various examples in the book of his one hundred thousand songs.

Taking this step towards liberation, one encounters the experience of the mahamudra, a Sanskrit word meaning great gesture, which has been translated into Tibetan as *chakja chenpo*. The nature of emptiness that comprises the whole of samsara and nirvana, this entire sphere of becoming which contains the entire universe and all possibility of experience, is represented by the first syllable, *chak* (the honorary prefix to *ja*). The fact that all of samsara and nirvana, and all possibility of experience throughout the whole universe, does not go beyond this emptiness is represented by the second syllable, *ja* (literally, seal). *Chakja* indicates that in meditating upon this seal of voidness, one attains the wonderful perfection of complete liberation as a fully realized buddha. By traveling on the path of refinement and employing the recognition of this seal of emptiness, one attains what is called in Tibetan *chenpo* (literally, greatness). So, this is what is meant by mahamudra in Sanskrit or chakja chenpo in Tibetan.

In order to recognize this seal of voidness, this mahamudra, the student must first meditate to recognize the nature of mind. Then, when a certain amount of development in meditation is plainly evident, the tsaway lama, out of his great kindness and blessings, will give the student the explanation of the nature of mahamudra. If the student is of the most excellent capacity or acumen, then simultaneous with the very moment of this nature being pointed out, instantaneous liberation can occur. Literally, the whole path of purifying obscurations, of great accumulations of merit and wisdom, and of the blessing of wisdom occurs right at that very moment of revelation between teacher and student. The great leap from samsara to nirvana is covered completely and spontaneously, right then, right there! However, a student of such excellent capabilities is extremely rare; most students who hear this explanation must first apply the methods of purification, of accumulation of wisdom, and of supplications to the tsaway lama in order to realize the fruition of the mahamudra.

On the other end of the scale is the inferior student who simply cannot understand the nature of the Dharma. However it is explained, it really makes no sense in his or her mind. Within the range of contact I have had in the Western nations that I have visited, I have seen very, very few inferior students, as just about every one seems to fall into the category of average, an assessment based on apparent intelligence, insight, application, and so forth. Average students progress naturally along the path, but they need to supplicate their tsaway lama with devotion, so that they might receive the blessings of the lama. Further, they need to do the practices to purify obscurations and develop an accumulation of merit and wisdom in order to attain liberation from samsara through the mahamudra.

How is it known for certain that the efforts just detailed will lead one to the fruition of mahamudra? The Lord Buddha himself, in referring to it, said that the absolute truth of co-emergent wisdom (meaning mahamudra) is only attained through the accumulation of merit and the purification of obscurations, combined with intense longing and devotion for the tsaway lama. The coming together of these two qualities (that is, one of accumulation and purification, the other of devotion) gives rise to the mahamudra experience; there is no other possibility for such occurrence. In accordance with this teaching of the Buddha, the whole approach of Tibetan Buddhism (under the guidance of one's tsaway lama) is based upon purifying obscurations and developing accumulations of merit and wisdom. Once beginning this path by taking refuge, one can quickly proceed through what are termed the foundation practices, or one can do yidam practice directly.

First, let us consider the benefit of doing the foundation practices. These are powerful practices designed to eliminate obscurations and defilements, plus they are useful in developing an accumulation of merit and wisdom. Inwardly, these practices work by primarily developing faith and devotion in the Three Jewels — Buddha, Dharma, and Sangha. With this faith firmly established, through the power of the blessing of the Buddha Shakyamuni, the root of all blessings manifests as the tsaway lama, the root of all accomplishments manifests as the yidam, and the root of all buddha activity manifests as the dharmapalas, or Dharma protectors. Thus, one has faith in the Three Jewels — Buddha, Dharma, and Sangha — and in the Three Roots — Lama, Yidam, and Dharmapalas — which are visualized with great devotion, resting in the blue expanse of sky in front of one. Keeping this visualization stable, one then offers prostrations so that the body and speech, acting as servants of the mind, fulfill the intention of paying homage to the visualization of the enlightened sources of refuge. By reciting the refuge prayer while performing prostrations, one is developing faith in the Three Jewels and the Three Roots visualized before one.

A prostration is a wonderful action that allows one to offer faith by means of the body. By joining the two palms together and placing them on the forehead, one offers the world of form. To offer devotion by means of speech, next the joined hands touch the throat; and to offer devotion with the mind itself, the hands then touch the sternum of the chest, directly over the heart. Then, with the thought, "I offer devotion with this body, speech, and mind," one offers a whole prostration by lowering oneself flat on the ground. The Buddha said that even a single prostration will give benefits, such as robust health, good complexion, and handsome features, an influential position with the quality of affection from gods and men, and influential speech and a goodly accumulation of wealth, a higher rebirth having the companionship of holy men, and most importantly, liberation. By performing even. a single prostration, one gains the amount of merit equal to the number of atoms in the piece of ground over which the five limbs are extended, from the surface straight down to the *golden ground of the universe.* By offering this simple physical action, the effects of negative actions accumulated through the body, speech, and mind are purified and eliminated, so that instead one realizes the qualities of the body, speech, and mind of the historical Buddha. By this foundation practice, a deep and profound accumulation of merit and wisdom is thus developed and realized.

If there were no such thing as the Three Jewels or the Three Roots, then there would be absolutely no benefit in having faith and devotion in them, and absolutely no benefit in doing this practice. But have no doubts, because the Three Jewels and the

Three Roots are the essence of buddha activity to benefit all sentient beings. In having the very powerful qualities of blessing and compassion, the Three Jewels and Three Roots act just like a hook. Because a hook can not catch anything if there is no ring, one's devotion and faith are like putting up a ring. Thus, the blessings and compassion of the sources of refuge catches one's ring of devotion and faith, turning one away from the bewildering confusion of the lower realms and towards liberation.

Despite my assurances, you may well doubt this because you cannot see the compassion and blessings that emanate from the Three Jewels and Three Roots at work. While it is true that there is no actual way to see this, such doubt is unnecessary because the visualization practice works by *interdependent arising*. To illustrate what is meant by interdependent arising, the technology of the Western world offers some useful examples. An especially good illustration is that of remote control TV, whereby one can alter the picture on the screen simply by pushing a button. Similar devices have a wide range of exact usage (e.g., garage door openers, [cordless telephones, etc.]), yet all have the quality of affecting an action for no apparent reason. There being no connecting wire, one cannot see a direct connection between the remote control device and the mechanism the device triggers. But this makes no difference; such devices definitely work.

To carry this illustration further, given a remote control TV, one can not operate it from a distance unless one has the control device. Given an incompatible brand of device buttons, the TV cannot be switched on remotely, no matter how many buttons one pushes. Given only a remote control device, pushing all the buttons does not allow one to bring about a TV image if there is no TV present. It is the interdependent arising of this device and the TV that enables such phenomenal expression to take place. In the same way, interdependent arising enhances the connection to the Three Jewels and Three Roots through the visualization practice.

Most of you receiving this teaching have adequate possessions and can provide your physical comforts, and so forth. By means of this wealth, you can be generous and, for instance, can buy butter lamps as an offering of devotion, or can give support to the poor and needy. These acts are exemplary of the means by which generosity can actually help in the elimination of negative accumulations and can aid in the acquisition of accumulated merit. In the foundation practice termed mandala offerings, one conceptualizes and visualizes a mandala (or arrangement) of great iron mountains ringing a vast sea containing an even higher Mt. Sumeru, itself surrounded by four major continents and eight minor islands. Together, these represent our universe. By mentally arranging these into a beautiful mandala, and by mentally offering all the wealth and possessions of the whole universe of gods and men, time and time again, one develops a very great accumulation of merit.

In the foundation practice known as Dorje Sempa (Sanskrit: Vajrasattva), one does the practice of purification. Consider for a moment an item, perhaps some clothing or a piece of cloth, that is stained and dirty. To cleanse it, one employs soap and water, scrubbing and rinsing it in many different ways until the blackness or stain has been removed. Consider that from beginningless time until present, each sentient being has a vast accumulation of negative trends and tendencies. The easiest and best way to purify such negativity is the cleansing process in which Tibetan Buddhism specializes, namely the meditation of Vajrasattva. By meditating that Vajrasattva rests upon the crown of one's head as the essence of the tsaway lama, and by reciting his one-hundred syllable mantra, all the while visualizing the descent of his purifying blessings washing away negative accumulations, one actually uses this process of karmic washing to purify and cleanse stains of one's faults, broken vows, transgressions, etc. In a manner similar to rinsing the dirt and soap from a dirty cloth, by reciting the one-hundred syllable mantra while visualizing this nectar-like blessing rinsing away karmic accumulations, one is illuminated and purified. This practice successfully removes all previously accumulated negative karma.

I should note here that one usually begins the foundation practices by first taking refuge and doing prostrations. Then one does the purification of Dorje Sempa, followed by mandala offerings, before one supplicates the tsaway lama in guru yoga. However, one may begin with the purification practice of Dorje Sempa, especially if one is having a problem with the visualization technique.

In the fourth foundation practice, one does guru yoga, whereby one develops unshakable devotion to all the buddhas and bodhisattvas, lamas, yidams, and dharmapalas, plus one supplicates their great blessings, great compassion, and great power. In the actual practice, one visualizes and thinks that the tsaway lama is the united essence of all buddhas and bodhisattvas, to whom one prays with great faith and devotional homage. By means of the merit thus accumulated, and by having purified one's negative karmic accumulations in doing the first three foundation practices, the great wisdom of the mahamudra is then quickened by guru yoga. Now, you might well wonder, "Who is the guru?" In inner essence, the guru, or tsaway lama, is none other than Dorje Chang (Sanskrit: Vajradhara), the primordial buddha. However, in external phenomena, the nirmanakaya body of the guru for those associated with the Karma Kagyu lineage is most likely that of His Holiness the Gyalwa Karmapa, or one of his four spiritual sons, Their Eminences Tai Situpa Rinpoche, Sharmarpa Rinpoche, Jamgon Kongtrul Rinpoche, and Gyaltshap Rinpoche.

Actually, whatever well-known and recognized lama of any lineage one chooses as one's tsaway lama is the person from whom blessings and teachings will be received. Additionally, one's tsaway lama is that being who clarifies and demonstrates the true nature of mind, so that one rests assured not only in the qualities, but also in the capabilities of one's tsaway lama. To make a comparison, if there is a very large deposit of gold above ground that gives off a light that shines into the sky, then any one who is interested knows exactly where to locate that deposit of gold. In the same way, the great qualities of the spiritual sons of the Kagyu lineage and of its great lamas have a similar light that shines forth proclaiming the great qualities of these realized ones. This field of attraction is the activity or work of the dakinis who want to benefit beings by illuminating the Dharma to allow all to see its essential nature. Obviously, there are many other qualities apart from fame that connote great lamas; however, the most important quality is the teacher's having an unbroken lineage.

Dorje Chang (Skt: Vajradhara) is traditionally visualized as a rich dark blue in color, seated in vajrasana on a lotus and moon disk, adorned with silken garments, with his hands crossed over his chest, holding a bell and dorje (the symbols of wisdom and skillful means, respectively), and crowned with the five-jeweled crown (symbolizing the transcendence of the five skandhas). He is also visualized resting in the center of the foliage of the Karma Kagyu Refuge tree. (Pen and ink drawing by unknown artist, 20th century)

From the primordial buddha Vajradhara, the realization of blessings, of empowerments and instructions, and of spiritual authority should be transmitted in an unbroken manner through the succession of realized masters, generation by generation, until it currently rests with the tsaway lama you have chosen. With this assurance, one can rest steadfastly in the belief that the tsaway lama's power of realization and transcendence goes directly to the source of the buddha fields, that of *dharmakaya* itself.

If, however, one does not have the time, the ability, or the inclination to do the foundation practices at this moment, then the other method to accumulate very great merit and wisdom, to purify negative obscurations, is to regularly perform yidam practice. In the various Dharma centers scattered around the world, one can become familiar and comfortable with the yidam recitation and visualization practices, especially the practice of visualizing one's body as the deity, one's speech as the mantra, and recognizing mind's nature as the profound samadhi of the deity. Doing these yidam practices is extremely beneficial and, in the beginning, one can develop this habit by frequenting a nearby Dharma center, taking visualization instruction, and doing this practice together with others as a group.

Meditating with visualization, whether employed in the yidam or the foundation practices, can present some stages of development that are important to recognize. Within one's daily experience, one constantly experiences many emotions, discursive thoughts, and so forth. These, however, are constantly dissolving into emptiness; actually, they are as much non-existent as they are existent. Just imagine the amount of discursive thought or emotional types of experience that happen during a conversation lasting six hours. Yet for half that time, the mind is totally at rest, although the individual does not see that because the mind is obscured by ignorance.

When one is asleep and not dreaming, the constant arising of discursive thought and emotions does not occur, for in sleep one is meditating in some kind of thick, unconscious type of samadhi where the mind is quite still. One does not recognize this natural meditation because of the obscuration of ignorance. Actually, half the lifespan is normally spent developing emotional conflicts and discursive thoughts, and the other half is spent wallowing in ignorance. Were one aware of the natural meditation, however, one's life could be spent in the realization of enlightened awareness.

Immediately after death, the mind is usually absorbed in a state of total oblivion without any consciousness, any thought, or any type of awareness for three days. This type of oblivion is, however, even more overwhelming than that experienced during sleep or during one's active life because it is the experience of ignorance itself.

The antidote to this state of affairs is known in Tibetan as *kyirim* (Sanskrit: utpattiakrama), which is the generation stage of visualization. This arising yoga stage deals directly with the individual's deeply rooted clinging to the world of form, sound, and all sensory experiences in one's daily experience. One's tendency as a sentient being is to cling to these as being completely real, and to have a great attachment to all these sensations. So, the antidote of kyirim is to visualize all experiences as being the bliss realm of Dewachen, or the pure realm of the yidam, and to understand all sound as being mantra. Additionally, in recognizing that all phenomena are like a reflection in a mirror, like an illusion, like a cloud, like an echo, then one actually transfers one's clinging to something that is insubstantial, thus allowing such clinging to be overcome. This is the function and reason for kyirim and, when one attains this realization, one can practice meditation clearly and can awaken from ignorance. Such awakening leads to the realization of the mahamudra itself.

As an example, let us suppose that half of one's life is spent in a state of stupor, and let us compare that stupidity to the empty space in a room. When the lights in the room are out, it is totally dark and one is unable to see anything. Liken this darkness to one's ignorance. The completion stage of meditation, termed in Tibetan *dzogrim* (Sanskrit: sampannakrama) is the further antidote that leads to the accomplishment of meditation. In our example, this is comparable to one's switching on the lights, where everything can be seen in absolute clarity; here the first stage of mahamudra can be obtained.

In bygone times, when beings in the human realm were not experiencing emotional bewilderment to the degree being experienced now, the practice of hinayana (or the lesser vehicle) was very applicable. Practitioners were able to perform the hinayana practice of meditating one-pointedly (termed zhinay) and were able, even as beginners, to meditate one-pointedly for a day, a month, or a year. With less emotional bewilderment, they were able easily to attain a level of mental stability and find that whatever meditation practice was attempted became easy. In the past, the practice of the hinayana method was indeed most suitable.

In these current times, however, there is a pervasive and powerful emotional bewilderment, with its very strong reactions. The practice of the zhinay is difficult to develop and turn into something beneficial. For this reason, there exists a method that is very useful in overcoming emotional conflict: develop the bodhisattva attitude of emptiness and compassion, and practice the six paramitas (or six perfections) of giving generously, guarding one's morality, developing patience, applying energy, attaining samadhi, and reflecting on wisdom. Although the mahayana path is suitable even to this present day, it is becoming more and more difficult as time goes by to be successful with it, because the emotional conflict and discursive thinking have reached an intense and pervasive state. As a result, even though someone might claim to be a great meditator and will meditate on emptiness perhaps one whole day, actually only a few moments of true meditation will be experienced.

This state of emotional and discursive darkness weighs heavily upon us all at this particular time in our kalpa. In the encroaching darkness, there remains but one sure path — that of vajrayana. Because the Lord Buddha Shakyamuni publicly demonstrated the power of this vehicle on different occasions (and is thereby considered to be one of the three Buddhas of our kalpa that will do so), the Indian *panditas*, the first Tibetan translators, and the successive generation of enlightened masters in Tibet were thus enabled to transmit the invaluable vajrayana insights, empowerments, and teachings. The rarity of this occurrence should not be overlooked; the vajrayana is a path so sacred, so revered, and so secret that in the future only the closest and well-chosen students of the coming nine hundred and ninety-six historical Buddhas of this kalpa will receive the teachings and have this powerful path demonstrated to them. We are indeed extremely fortunate to be living in the time of such accessibility to this valuable vehicle. We must not waste this precious opportunity, this precious human existence; instead we must take it upon ourselves to gain true liberation through practicing the vajrayana.

≋ 7 ≋

RAINBOW SKIES

Insight into the Mantrayana Practices

From our previous discussions, you should now understand what is meant when it is stated that mind in essence is emptiness, in its fundamental characteristic is clarity, and in its manifestation is unimpeded. In the conscious awareness of sentient beings, however, this whole essence is obscured (somewhat like wallowing in some kind of thick sleep), which causes sentient beings to be ignorant of the mind's true nature. Consequently, in these dark times, we are extremely fortunate that we have available a powerful and rapid path to help speed our accomplishment of buddhahood. The quick path of vajrayana has its success because it encourages meditation on the human body and all substantial phenomena as being the body of the deity, all sound as being its mantra, and all mental phenomena as being the samadhi of the deity. Meditating in this way, the individual is dealing effectively with obscuring emotionality and discursive thought by recognizing their truer nature. Simply recognizing mind's true nature as emptiness, clarity, and unimpededness can completely and instantaneously destroy emotional distraction, mental discursiveness, and so on. This kind of instantaneous power of recognition completely crushes one's emotional and mental imbalances.

The vajrayana path is undoubtedly the most suitable, the most applicable, and the most powerful for this day and age. One may compare it to getting all one's belongings together, putting them in a great ship, and traversing the great ocean in comfort and ease, all without having to leave anything behind. With this path, there is no abandoning as there is in hinayana; instead, this is the path of transformation by recognition of the inherence of dharmakaya in sambhogakaya, and of sambhogakaya in nirmanakaya.

In employing the techniques of vajrayana, one will use the visualization techniques according to the particulars of each sadhana while one recites the mantra of that deity. It is important to note that such a mantra has not only a very great blessing, but also a profound and beneficial effect, having been blessed with the power of all the buddhas and bodhisattvas. Before I go further into the topic of liberation through mantrayana, I would like to discuss the nature of mantra as it relates to our present state of existence.

Right now, we all have a human physical body that belongs to a higher samsaric realm. Within this body, there are three principal *channels*, or pathways, of both pure and impure alaya as it is connected with the physical body. These course from below the navel to the crown of the head. They are known as *tsa-u-ma*, (which is the central channel), *ro-ma*, and *kyang-ma* (which are to the right and left, respectively, of the central channel). Situated along the length of these three main channels are five *cakras* (a Sanskrit term meaning wheel, referring to the spinning vortexes of energy situated along the channels, with their location in ascending order being genital region, navel, heart, throat, and crown of one's head). In turn, spreading out from these five cakras are other channels (or *nadis* in Sanskrit) that support twelve minor cakras, which are primarily located in the body's extremities. Altogether, the human body has seventy-two thousand energy pathways, or channels, in which one's vital energies course, a phenomena that, if properly cultivated, can serve to lengthen to one's life, health, and state of well-being.

In closely examining these nadis, we will find that, exactly at their needle-point openings, there appear sacred letters, which arise due to the power and potential of the wisdom element flowing within these channels. Unbelievable as this may sound, the power of the wisdom element manifests itself as these very small letters within the nadis. Additionally, we find that the energies (or winds) of the wisdom element and the winds of discursive consciousness blow (or flow) within and throughout the nadis. This movement causes the creation of the experience of sound. We, as humans, experience sound and are able to make sound; as well, we are able to express whatever thought may cross our mind by the use of sound, all because the wisdom element as sacred letters (or sounds) is present at the tips of the nadis. Furthermore, the potential of the many sounds of our everyday life are heard due only to the presence of the energy potential of the wisdom element within the nadis.

Although it might seem a bit beyond our daily thinking, nevertheless, each level of the ten levels or *bhumis* of an accomplished bodhisattva has special powers associated with its degree of development. Let us consider a moment the first level of attainment, which results from the complete and total eradication of the grossest of the four veils, that of the obscuration of karma itself. Once a being has attained the complete eradication of the obscuration of karma, the ability is gained to delve instantaneously into the depths of a hundred different samadhis and to manifest in a hundred different forms to benefit beings. Actually, a first of the ten bhumis of accomplished bodhisattva attains twelve such amazing qualities. Even so, the ability to perceive the power of the *dharanis* and mantras has not yet arisen.

An accomplished bodhisattva of the second level has a much more profound realization than a bodhisattva of the first bhumi. For instance, here an evolved being is able to see clearly into the past for one thousand previous lifetimes and to see into the future for one thousand lifetimes, plus he or she is able to manifest one thousand bodies and experience one thousand samadhis. Likewise, on each of the third through sixth levels of an accomplished bodhisattva, the different powerful qualities that these evolved beings possess increase tenfold. Then, at the seventh bhumi of accomplished bodhisattva, the last vestige of the obscuration of emotional distraction is completely eradicated. Despite such accomplishment, however, even seventh level bodhisattvas are not able to see the mantras and dharanis.

It is only when a bodhisattva attains the eighth bhumi that these amazing qualities result in the ability to begin to perceive and to recognize the mantras, the dharanis, and the power of these sounds. At that time of recognition on this eighth level, such a being would attain what are called the *ten powers*. One such power is the ability to see into the stream of consciousness of immeasurable sentient beings and to be able to recognize clearly and to sense accurately what is going on with any individual. Another such power is being able to completely control the environment, so as to control the weather and to thus bring about whatever weather is required to benefit the land, the people, or whatever. Or, there is the power of being able to have complete control over the life force itself; thus such beings have the ability to extend their life, and that of other beings, completely at will.

On the ninth bhumi, these powers are even more developed than at the eighth level, and it is on this level that the obscuration of dualistic clinging is totally eliminated. Finally, on the tenth bhumi, all that remains are the subtle remnants of the veil of ignorance itself, or the remaining obscuration preventing full knowledge of the nature of mind. Throughout the path of completion of the tenth level, this veil of remaining ignorance is gradually purified until it is eventually and completely eradicated. At that time, there occurs the realization of the state of buddhahood where there is absolutely no obstruction; rather there is total knowledge of the true nature of reality.

Because buddhas and high level bodhisattvas have imbued mantras with unique and individual power, certain mantras have powers to do specific things. For instance, some mantras have the power to extend life. Other mantras have the power to provide different kinds of accomplishments, such as health, wealth, protection, success in study or learning languages, and so on. Thus, different mantras have different kinds of powerful impact on the individual's being and existence. There are some mantras that convey several different powers that can be used by one and all, such as the mantra *Om Mani Padme Hung*. And, there are some mantras that are so specifically designed that they are suitable only to certain types of beings.

The mantras and dharanis that originated from Buddha Shakyamuni's completely unobstructed and completely unveiled state of perfect enlightenment were transmitted over the generations in India by the great saints and great learned pandits of old, who carefully kept them in perfect condition. Later, during the time of translation of Buddhist works into the Tibetan language, a great number of extremely erudite Tibetans gathered together to work on the various translations and wrote with great accuracy the sound of these mantras and dharanis. To this day, the sounds of the various mantras, such as the six-syllable mantra of Chenrezig, the hundred-syllable mantra, etc., have been kept in perfectly accurate and original form in Tibet. There is no need to have any doubt that these mantras are indeed those that originated from this completely perfect state of buddhahood.

As you have a precious human body endowed with all the great qualities, such as great inner intelligence, etc., the whole path of mantrayana (or vajrayana) is available and open to you. From this vantage, you are able to practice several techniques to further your understanding. This is very wonderful! However, it is important not to allow yourselves to develop any kind of erroneous view about this path. In performing the practice of any yidam, there are three essential requirements of meditation skill, termed the *three characteristics*. Firstly, there is the characteristic of *clarity;* secondly, there is the characteristic of recognition of *mudra;* and thirdly, there is the characteristic of *vajra pride*. In referring to the first characteristic, during the meditation practice one visualizes the deity's form very clearly as being radiantly brilliant and complete, with the correct colors and the correct ornaments; one develops this visualization in stabilized clarity. In vajrayana meditation practice, this is the first important principle of visualization.

The second characteristic of vajrayana practice is that of recognition of mudra, or symbolism. This characteristic requires that one is able to call to mind the various meanings of the deity's form during the meditation. Please understand that the form of Chenrezig (or any other yidam) is not something that appears due to some kind of karmic accumulation. Clearly, the yidam's manifestations, such as beauty, clarity, etc., have nothing to do with karmic fruition. While meditating on Chenrezig, for example, in remembering the symbolic meaning of Chenrezig's one face, recall that this represents samsara and nirvana as having one taste. Additionally, his white color symbolizes his complete purity and absence of any kind of stain or defilement. His different ornaments (jewels, silks, etc.) symbolize the complete realization of all the Dharma qualities, both worldly and other-worldly; etc. [See Appendix B for further symbolism.] Thus, all the numerous and differing aspects of the deity's form have a very important symbolic meaning that one needs to hold in mind during the visualization practice.

The third characteristic is that of vajra pride, which means that in clearly visualizing the yidam form, and in effortlessly remaining cognizant of the yidam's symbolism (as in the first and second characteristics explained above), one takes wholesome pride in perfectly performing vajrayana visualization practice. I will speak more of this later.

Most *tantrayana* or vajrayana visualization and mantra practices require that an initiation and subsequent authorization and instruction be given by a qualified lama before the sadhana, or ritual practice, can begin. However, a few practices, those that were given publicly by Lord Buddha Shakyamuni, do not fall under such restrictions. Very definitely, all the practices given in the sutras have the full blessing of the Buddha and therefore can be practiced if one has the aspiration to do so. Such practices include those of the noble Chenrezig and of the mother of the buddhas, Green Tara.

Naturally, whenever it becomes possible for you to take the vajrayana initiation of Chenrezig or Green Tara, you are encouraged to do so. Right now, however, the practice in which I am giving you instruction can be practiced straight away, due wholly to the blessing of Buddha Shakyamuni. When you finally do get around to receiving the Chenrezig initiation, it will deepen your practice and strengthen your connection with your tsaway lama and with Yidam Chenrezig.

Prior to sitting down to meditate, a vajrayana practitioner has usually taken the time to arrange a shrine to give a special, distinct wholeness of presence of the Three Jewels and the Three Roots. Generally, ritual objects are arranged above waist level. The variety of ritual items that can be arranged on a shrine is virtually endless, but an adequate shrine includes a picture of the lineage lamas, and/or a representation of Chenrezig (either on paper or canvas, or in metal), and the seven offerings of water, fruit, lights, incense, and so on. The practitioner is mindful and respectful of this part of the ritual, so one keeps the shrine area clean and is respectful of this area during any activity that might occur. Also, one regularly offers incense and flowers; in behaving in this way, one thus increases positive accumulations.

One begins meditation by first lighting fresh incense, making three prostrations in front of the shrine, and sitting comfortably in a cross-legged position. The hands rest either together with palms upwards at the navel, or covering each knee, palms downward.

Giving rise to the supreme motivation to establish all sentient beings (as vast as space, all of whom have been my mothers in the three times of past, present, and future) in the supreme state of buddhahood, which is free from all suffering, I now wish to offer you this teaching on the sadhana of Chenrezig. Through practicing and realizing the fruition of the practice, one may realize the essence of all practices, of all the yidams, thereby fulfilling the vajrayana commitments. This practice is very easy and of great blessing in that it can liberate you from the endless cycle of samsaric suffering. Adapting yourself to doing this practice is not difficult.

Now, who or what is Chenrezig? In Sanskrit, the name of Chenrezig is Avalokiteshvara, which means the one who sees with compassionate eyes. The name indicates that the mind of Chenrezig is supreme, all-embracing compassion, and that his greatest wish is one of loving kindness and compassion in establishing all sentient beings in the state of buddhahood. The Tibetan expression for the qualities of loving kindness and compassion is termed chenrezig. Coincidently, there are many forms of Chenrezig; there is Buddha Chenrezig, Bodhisattva Chenrezig, and Yidam Chenrezig. Furthermore, many different emanations of Yidam Chenrezig (the white, yellow, red, etc.) can appear, each with a differing appearance, some with many faces or arms, some only in conventional appearance, and so forth. All these differing aspects are different emanations of this deity. The teaching I am offering here is the practice of visualizing white Chenrezig with

ABOVE: *The sacred symbol HRI.* (Courtesy of Tinley Drupa)
BELOW: *Four-armed Chenrezig* (Woodblock print from Nepal, 20th century)

one face and four arms, which is the essential practice of all Tibetan Buddhists.

One of the most important features of this practice is that the mantra employed in the sadhana is extremely powerful. So powerful, in fact, that merely by hearing its words, *"Om Mani Padme Hung,"* a beginning has been formed, the connection and continuation of which will result in the eventual realization of buddhahood, if not in this current lifetime, then in a future existence. In taking the empowerment of Chenrezig and practicing the appropriate sadhana, the practitioner will have great aid and assistance in the process of realizing the true nature of the mind and may thus transcend this cycle of samsaric suffering. Such transcendence is possible in this very lifetime, or at the time of death or thereafter, especially in the bardo of possibility. Therefore, I urge you to consider this teaching very intently and to recall that the most beneficial thing you can do with this precious human existence is to become enlightened. You should be thankful that, in this age of darkness, one of the easiest ways to become enlightened is to practice the sadhana of the Yidam Chenrezig.

To begin any vajrayana practice, we begin by visualizing that in the sky in front of you is a great cloud filled with all the sources of refuge, in the center of which is the yidam, in this instance Yidam Chenrezig, surrounded by all the buddhas and bodhisattvas. Develop the thought that we are taking refuge in order to establish all sentient beings, without exception, in the perfect state of buddhahood. Give rise to this thought of enlightenment while reciting the liturgy of refuge and bodhicitta that accompanies this refuge visualization. [The liturgy or sadhana is given in entirety in Appendix B.]

The actual practice of Chenrezig begins by visualizing that upon your own head and upon the heads of all sentient beings without exception, there appears a white lotus blossom upon which a white moon disk rests. Upon this moon disk is a white letter *"HRI,"* [refer to illustration, figure 1], which instantaneously transforms into the form of Chenrezig, who is white, with one face and four arms. He rests on the moon disk, and his back is also supported by a moon disk. He is replete with all qualities, all the ornaments, and so on, of a sambhogakaya buddha. This form being insubstantial, it has an empty, translucent appearance, like a rainbow in the sky or the image of the moon reflected on water. It is very clear, apparent, and present, yet there is no tangibility, solidity, or reality to this appearance. [For additional explanation of this and other visualizations of this practice, see the commentary in Appendix B.]

Visualize very clearly the Lama Chenrezig seated upon not only your head, but that of all sentient beings. As you see this completely clear and luminous visualization, recite the prayer requesting that great, immeasurable love and compassion may arise in the stream of your being, and that all sentient beings may recognize the true nature of mind to be that of mahamudra.

Prayer

Lord, whose white body is not clothed by fault,
And whose head is adorned by a perfect Buddha,
You look upon all beings with the eyes of compassion.
To you, Chenrezig, I offer homage.

Now visualize that an immeasurable number of offering goddesses emanate from your heart, all of whom make offerings to Chenrezig and to all the buddhas and bodhisattvas. Visualize them offering homage, prayers, etc, while you yourself also offer homage by reciting the seven branch offering prayer.

After you have recited the seven branch offering prayer and the prayer of aspiration composed by the nun named Palmo, next you visualize that a five-colored light radiates from the Chenrezig resting on the top of your head and from those resting on the heads of all sentient beings. This light serves to eradicate negative accumulations in the whole of sentient existence, causing the outer world to be transformed into the pure land of Dewachen. Now, you and all beings become undifferentiated from Chenrezig's three doors of body, speech, and mind.

Visualization

Through this one-pointed prayer, light radiates
from the body of the sublime one, purifying
impure karma, impure appearances,
and the deluded mind.

The outer realm is the pure land of Dewachen,
and the body, speech, and mind of beings therein
are the perfect form, sublime speech, and
pure mind of mighty Chenrezig, the indivisible
union of appearance, sound, and vivid
intelligence with emptiness.

Next say a session of mantras, while counting them on a mala, which is a set of one hundred and eight prayer beads symbolizing the number of sutras. While doing this recitation, there are several visualizations you can use to discipline the mind's awareness of the union of wisdom and skillful means, the essential principle of tantrayana. You might, for instance, concentrate on seeing Chenrezig sitting on your head, while in your heart you pray for compassion and the realization of the emptiness of self and all phenomena. Sometimes you can concentrate on Chenrezig sending out light from his luminous body, which pervades the universe and transforms all sentient beings into forms of Chenrezig, following which you think of the whole universe as being his pure land. Or, while saying the mantra, you can rest the mind without any contrivance or effort in its natural state; or, you can begin to develop an intense compassion for all beings. Generally, start by thinking of one of these aspects and then try to remain with that thought or prayer for a while before trying another. At first, this will be tiring, but as you develop your capabilities, it will become relaxing and you will find your mind is calm and peaceful. After you have confidence in these beginning visualizations, please ask a lama to instruct you in more advanced visualization techniques.

When you have finished reciting the mantras, whether you said several hundred or thousands, visualize that all sentient beings are being transformed into Chenrezig, that they all melt into light and that this light is fully absorbed into the form of Chenrezig resting on top of your head. You should then visualize that you become inseparable from Chenrezig. When one pours milk and tea together, one loses the blackness of the tea as it becomes white like the milk; so too, you lose yourself in Chenrezig when you join your body, speech, and mind with his. Next, visualize that, in this inseparability, all form dissolves into the lotus and moon disk resting in Chenrezig's heart.

Concentrate and clearly see the letter *HRI* resting on the moon disk, surrounded by the six syllables of the mantra, each resting on one of the six petals of the white lotus. Visualizing this brilliantly white sacred letter *HRI*, you can see it is comprised of five parts that are known in Tibetan as the *tsedrak*, the *a-chung*, the *rata*, the *ha* consonant, and the *gigu*. Now, watch as these dissolve one into another. Starting on the left side of the *HRI* is what we Tibetans call the tsedrak, (namely, the Sanskrit aspirate comprised of two circles, one on top of the other) which dissolves into the lowest letter of the syllable *HRI*. This letter (a-chung) then dissolves upwards into the nearly horizontal stroke that is the rata. This, in turn, dissolves upwards into the main body of the syllable, the Tibetan letter *ha*. This main letter then dissolves upwards into the vowel sound that is known as gigu.

Visualization

My body, the bodies of others, and all appearances
are the perfect form of the sublime one;
all sound, the melody of the six syllables;
all thoughts, the vastness of the great *jnana*.

This last bit of dissolving vowel continues to dissipate until it is a tiny speck; this small speck or sphere of light gradually decreases in size, getting smaller and smaller, until it completely dissolves into emptiness. At that point, maintain your alert awareness, free of any conceptual discursiveness or thought. Be completely and extremely empty; feel for yourself this empty clarity. Meditate in this way. This is the stage of consummation that is the basis upon which you may realize the mahamudra in this lifetime if you have excellent capabilities, or with which you may gain liberation during the process of dying if you are of average capabilities and disciplines.

Then, to arise from this emptiness, again visualize yourself in a form of Chenrezig having one face and only two arms, and recognize that his body arises as the union of form and emptiness, his speech arises as the union of sound and emptiness, and his mind arises as the union of consciousness and emptiness. Having reappeared in the standing form of Chenrezig, you now dedicate the merit accumulated by doing this practice.

Dedication

Through this virtue, may I quickly achieve
the realization of mighty Chenrezig
and may I bring every single being
to that same state.

Traditionally, the practice of Chenrezig is followed by the prayer to Chenrezig's tsaway lama, Buddha Amitabha, in which you pray that you might be reborn in the state of the great bliss of the pure land called Dewachen.

You can always recite the mantra, anytime and anywhere, while you are driving, walking, talking, thinking, etc. I assure you that the compassion of the Three Jewels, in meeting with your faith and devotion, will definitely lead to your finding the path and in your having the ability to travel this path to enlightenment.

Another practice, encouraged by the Buddha Shakyamuni and open to one and all (with or without prior vajrayana initiation), is that of the deity known in Tibetan as Jetsün Drölma, commonly referred to as Green Tara. One can develop great faith by praying and meditating upon Green Tara and by very clearly visualizing her form before one in the sky. In praying to Green Tara for blessings and accomplishments, and by then visualizing them descending, one receives these blessings. It is said that through praying and developing faith in this way, whatever one requires or wants somehow arises because of the power of her blessings. It is also said that if one wants to have a child, the child will come;

if one wants to have wealth, then wealth will come; if one wants to have spiritual attainments, then these will arise, all from the power of having faith in her.

In such a short presentation, I am unable to give detailed descriptions of the visualization of Green Tara or of the other yidam practices taught by the Lord Buddha. Should your interest need satisfying, please contact the lama in a nearby center to direct your inquiry.

Now that you understand that perfection requires effort, you might well wonder, "Why bother?" If you had the existence of a cow, a dog, or a cat, you would not be able to practice the Dharma. You would not have even the degree of understanding required to enable you to recognize the need to practice the Dharma. Because you have obtained a precious human existence, replete with its many qualities and its many freedoms, you now have the opportunity to practice the Dharma in this very lifetime. You have no idea when this might happen again, and therefore you should bring this precious human existence to its full meaning right now, because it is through this existence that it is possible to realize full enlightenment.

Making no effort does not in any way offset your previously accumulated negative actions, and these will definitely ripen, if in not this lifetime, then in the ones to come. Therefore, even if one is carried away and constantly distracted by worldly activity for which one has a responsibility, then one can still practice the Dharma by considering the *four noble truths* [see glossary] and by reciting **Om Mani Padme Hung.** Even such a simple approach will allow you to attain some positive accumulation in this lifetime. In recognizing that this lifetime is very impermanent, it is important to consider future lifetimes and to take the steps toward rebirth in a higher state of existence, especially in the human realm. If only the present life were important, then one might just as well be concerned only with eating and drinking, like animals.

≈ 8 ≈

LINGERING SUNSET

Commentary on the Bodhisattva Vows

During the lifetime of the Lord Buddha, there lived a relative of his, a married man named Chungawa who had great faith and interest in the Dharma. However, he was prevented from developing this fascination by his very jealous wife, who forbade his curiosity and who continually connived and contrived to keep him from pursuing his interest. She guarded him so jealously that she accompanied him wherever he went.

Seeing Chungawa's predicament, the Buddha Shakyamuni decided to help him, and one day he came begging close to Chungawa's house. When Chungawa realized that indeed it was the Lord Buddha who was walking down the street outside his home that mid-morning, his whole instinct was to rush out to fill the begging bowl Lord Buddha held. This time his wife was neither able to stop him nor to go with him, as she was enjoying her bath. Deeply concerned at the news of Lord Buddha's presence and of her husband's eagerness to offer him food, she slung a pot of water at Chungawa, thoroughly wetting his shirt, and demanded that he return by the time his clothes had dried (which in the warm sun of India requires but a minute or two). Agreeing, Chungawa took his offerings to Lord Buddha and filled the waiting bowl.

"That is very fine," said Lord Buddha, "now follow me."

So overcome by the Lord Buddha's presence and aura of compassion, Chungawa agreed and proceeded to follow for quite some distance. They were far from the town before his mind began to remember his promise to his wife. Anxious about returning to her, yet feeling compelled to remain with the Buddha, he pondered his dilemma as they walked together. Eventually, they arrived at a monastery quite distant from all other habitation. Once there, the Lord Buddha led him directly to his chambers, and, before excusing himself, he requested that in his brief absence Chungawa should sweep the shrine room. Although Chungawa expressed his nervousness about his wife's concern as to his whereabouts, he agreed to perform this simple task. Each time he swept the room, however, more dust than ever before appeared and it seemed that he was getting nothing accomplished. Further, the Buddha, who had said he would be but a minute, still had not returned.

Eventually, Chungawa gave up and set off for home. Leaving the monastery by the lesser used road that ran through the jungle, he hoped he would soon be home and that he would avoid meeting with the returning Lord Buddha. But, while rounding a bend in the road, he saw to his dismay that the Lord Buddha was approaching by the same road. In his chagrin, Chungawa sought to hide himself beneath a tree whose branches touched the ground. This was to no avail, however, for as the Lord Buddha walked passed, the branches lifted by themselves to reveal Chungawa's hiding place.

"Chungawa, where are you going?" asked the Lord Buddha.

"Well ... er, ... I am going home, ... or, ... I was going home ...," replied Chungawa.

Lord Buddha said once again, "Well, come, follow me."

Once they had returned to the monastery, the Lord Buddha then pointed to his monastic robes and instructed Chungawa to take hold of them. When Chungawa questioned why, the Lord Buddha replied that he had some sightseeing in mind. Still puzzled, Chungawa complied and no sooner had he clasped the fine saffron drape than they were flying into the sky. At last, they came to rest upon a very high mountain. There they found an old, wrinkled, bent woman.

"Well Chungawa, what do you think? Who is more beautiful, this woman or your wife?"

Chungawa replied, "Lord Buddha, there can be no doubt about it. My wife is a hundred thousand times more beautiful."

Humored by Chungawa's answer, the Lord Buddha again requested that they continue on this journey. Again they flew, and through the Lord Buddha's miraculous powers, they arrived in the Heaven of the Thirty-Three in the gods' realm.

Encouraged by the Lord Buddha to explore this wonderful place, Chungawa was amazed in his wanderings by all the beauty he saw, not only of the gods and goddesses, but of the surroundings as well. Eventually, he arrived at a place of great activity where several gods and goddesses were preparing a magnificent throne. Their absorption into completing this task made Chungawa think that perhaps an important event was about to take place. Curiously, he approached the group and began his inquiry.

"Excuse me, can you tell me for whom this truly wonderful throne is being built? Will the enthroning ceremony take place today?"

The god turned to Chungawa, smiled a warm greeting, and replied, "Oh, this throne will not be occupied immediately. We are preparing it in expectation of the arrival of a human named Chungawa. He will keep his ordination as a monk so purely that he will be reborn here in the Heaven of the Thirty-Three. Such great virtuous activity and pure moral conduct are seldom attained, even though they are often attempted. So, in joyous acknowledgment of his eventual great success, we anticipate his arrival and are working here today."

Chungawa was speechless. The beauty of the throne and of this wondrous heaven were overwhelming. The fact that such a reward would await him was exhilarating. Chungawa reeled at the thought of eventually living in such a fortunate place and promptly dismissed from his mind his former life on earth. He lost all thought of his wife and of returning to her. Once the Lord Buddha had returned him to the earthly monastery, Chungawa requested and received monk's vows at the feet of the Lord Buddha.

One day, while addressing all the monks at the monastery, the Lord Buddha grew serious and voiced a concern. "Most of you have taken ordination because you wish to benefit all beings by attaining full enlightenment. You wish to transcend the misery of samsaric existence, a most wonderful and worthwhile endeavor. However, there is one among you who has taken ordination solely because he believes that, in keeping his vows purely, the reward of rebirth into the Heaven of the Thirty-Three awaits him. This monk's name is Chungawa. Henceforth, do not speak or associate with him in any way. All of you who have set your sights upon the goal of enlightenment are traveling a very different path than he is."

From that time onward, Chungawa was excluded by the monks in their daily activities. Yet, Chungawa persisted in his strict observance of his moral code, uncaring and unconcerned at his ostracism, as he was indeed intent upon being reborn in that wonderful heaven.

One day the Lord Buddha invited Chungawa on a tour of the hell realms. Chungawa again took hold of the Lord Buddha's robes, and through the Lord Buddha's miraculous powers, they were soon standing in hell. Overwhelmed by the intense and immense suffering the beings there were enduring, Chungawa became deeply disturbed and cast his eyes downward to avoid these gruesome sights. Clinging closely to the Lord Buddha as they walked through one hell after another, Chungawa eventually noticed a large mansion filled with several horrific beings and implements of torture. In the center of this large room was a huge cauldron full of molten copper, into which more and more copper was being thrown. Stoking the fire to heat it to an even higher temperature were several beings, all intently involved in this task. Yet, unlike the other cauldrons Chungawa had seen on this horrific tour, this cauldron was without an occupant. His curiosity overcame him and he approached a denizen who was standing nearby.

"Excuse me, could you tell me why such care is being given to a cauldron that has no occupant?"

The denizen turned and sneered his reply. "We are preparing it for a human who is at that moment living in the southern continent. He is currently busy with preserving his moral conduct with such exceptional devotion and observation to his vows that he will be reborn in the Heaven of the Thirty-Three."

This had a ring of familarity to Chungawa, but it made no sense. Therefore, he inquired, "Why are you preparing a cauldron here in hell if the person to whom you refer is going to be reborn in the Heaven of the Thirty-Three of the gods' realms?"

The denizen laughed deeply from his belly and replied, "I would have thought you would know. The natural consequence of a throne in that heaven is a throne in hell. No heaven lasts forever, and when the glamour and lights have faded, all the former gods get their chance to live here with us!"

The smoke from the fire that now blazed, the sweltering heat, and the impact of the denizen's reply made Chungawa feel weak and near to fainting. But, his curiosity persisted and he managed one more important question. "Who is this virtuous monk, this god-to-be who might, as you say, end up here in this cauldron one day?"

The denizen replied, "Chungawa." Mortified to hear that this was the fate that awaited him, Chungawa became panic stricken at the thought of having to swim in a cauldron of boiling copper. Fleeing to rejoin the Lord Buddha, who had gone on without him, he pleaded that the Lord Buddha quickly return him to the earthly monastery.

I am sharing this story with you to illustrate that the concerns and activities of a buddha or a bodhisattva are boundless and are not limited to any one individual. Their intentions continuously translate into actions to help all sentient beings come to an understanding of the limitations of suffering in samsara, limitations that can become transformed into the bliss of liberation in enlightenment. In the instance of Chungawa, once the Lord Buddha had made all these efforts to help him correctly establish a true path in the Dharma, Chungawa devoted himself not only to keeping his vows purely, but also to practicing the Dharma in order to benefit all beings by becoming fully enlightened. So strong and determined was his effort that Chungawa completely terminated all desire in each of the five senses. And, upon reaching enlightenment, his great accomplishment was duly acknowledged and he was then named "the one who terminated desire through the five senses."

Another incident that is also illustrative of bodhisattva activity is the story of a demoness who constantly harassed the country-side by taking the lives of many humans and animals. The Bodhisattva Chenrezig, concerned not only for the demoness' negative accumulations but also for the harm she brought others, emanated in the form of a demon. In this form, he courted the demoness, and soon they were cohabitating. In the course of his daily life as a demon, Chenrezig would recite *"Om Mani Padme Hung,"* and, eventually, the demoness inquired what he was saying.

"Oh, it is simply an excellent mantra that gives me everything I want, especially everything I want to eat," replied Chenrezig.

Finding this amusing, the demoness decided to see if there was anything to it and began reciting the mantra. Having confidence in her lover, she placed similar confidence in the mantra he favored to the extent that even though she often grew hungry for flesh and thirsty for blood, she said the mantra rather than indulge her appetite. Gradually her stomach began to shrink and she lost her craving for sentient beings. Additionally, from the blessing of the mantra, her mind began to change, so that, eventually, she no longer had any wish to eat or drink freshly killed corpses. Simply saying this mantra caused her whole mind to change; she even began to practice the Dharma, proceeding to become enlightened. All this transpired because Bodhisattva Chenrezig's activity planted the seed of bodhicitta.

The importance of the buddhas' activity becomes apparent when we again recall that we are all sentient beings and that we all wander in samsara. We are fortunate enough to have the precious human existence, but if we do not make good use of it, what result awaits us? We know for certain that those beings in the superior realms of the gods and demi-gods are experiencing the fruition of their virtuous karma. We, ourselves, can also experi-ence the gods' realms by performing virtuous deeds in this life-time and by failing to correct our attitudes of jealousy and pride. However, we can also go to the lower realms where suffering is even more intense. In the hot hells, there is the experience of intense pain while being constantly burned and consumed by fire, or while molten metals are being poured upon the body. In the cold hells, there is the experience of intense shivering cold that splits the body, cracking it open and giving a great sensation of pain. These hells are not a short excursion, as they were for Chungawa. Rather, the experience endures for a great length of time; so long, in fact, that it seems like an endless experience in which the beings therein are completely consumed by their own anguish and suffering.

We know that the hungry ghost realm is a slight improvement over the hell realm; yet, hungry ghosts experience intense craving and hunger that they can never satisfy. This insatiable appetite is due to the obscurations of miserliness and greed accumulated from former lifetimes that result in bodies with immense stomachs continuously demanding food, together with tiny mouths and throats that can never consume enough to satisfy them. Even worse, the food is often searing, making consumption a totally unpleasant task. This experience of constant craving, of being starved and thirsty, is also very long lasting; it is many aeons longer than it would take to cross and recross the great deserts of this world.

In the slightly higher state of the animal realm, we know that the majority of animals live in oceans and jungles, far from our observation, making our understanding of their suffering somewhat limited. It is obvious, however, that they are suffering intensely from stupidity and from fear of being eaten by larger predators; they are in a constant state of needing to run somewhere to gain refuge. Even in the realms of the *nagas*, those serpent-like animals who dwell beyond our perception, there is very intense suffering. Though there are many, many different varieties of animals with different lifespans and kinds of suffering, it is obvious that all have lives pervaded with suffering. Additionally, one can remain in this realm a very, very long time, taking rebirth in various forms of animal and insect.

In seeing that all sentient beings do not recognize that the cause of happiness is the practice of virtue, that they cause their own suffering by the practice of non-virtue, and that they wander endlessly through the six different realms experiencing the accumulated results of the combinations of virtue and non-virtue, how can we not give rise to compassion like the countless buddhas before us? How can we not give rise to love for all sentient beings? The understanding and recognition of the plight of our fellow wanderers is essential to the development of compassion, and the key motivation behind buddha activity.

It is said in the Buddhadharma that all sentient beings, without exception, have been our mother at least once or twice, if not many more times. We can acknowledge that our own mother kindly brought us into this world, gave us sustenance, taught us the ways of the world, and so forth. We must also recognize that our very own mother, and all our mothers throughout all our lifetimes, are also suffering as wanderers in samsara. Realizing this, compassion rises naturally.

Unfortunately, we do not recognize our own mother in all other sentient beings, nor does the mother recognize her child in all other sentient beings. The reason for this is our obscuration, the great veil of ignorance that keeps this truth of interrelatedness from being recognized. Once we recognize the truth that all sentient beings are our very own mothers, then it is inevitable that we give rise to great compassion. It is also inevitable that we come to the determination that we must, under any circumstances, establish all sentient beings, our mothers, in the supreme state of buddhahood. We must liberate them from the cycle of samsara. This is the nature of compassion and the ultimate goal of loving kindness.

An example of this perception of samsaric existence is contained in the story of the Arya Katayana, who was one of the great arhats living during the time of the Buddha. As Arya Katayana approached a village one day, he saw a woman sitting by the roadside. She was cuddling a small boy to her breast while eating a grilled fish. Throwing down the waste of bones and fins, she became annoyed by a dog that was trying to eat the scraps. The arhat watched as she shooed the dog away, using foul language, wild kicks, and large rocks. With his great super-knowledge, or clairvoyance, Arya Katayana could see that this angry woman's father (having recently died) had been reborn as the fish, and that the woman's mother (also deceased) had been reborn again as the dog.

He also saw that during this woman's lifetime she had an enemy who had made an oath to constantly cause harm, bring disturbance, arouse irritation, and actually injure this woman in any way possible. The enemy, having died with the power of this oath in mind, had been reborn as this woman's child and was now suckling at her breast. Thus, in seeing all this, Arya Katayana perceived that this woman's experience of samsara was in eating the body of her late father, offering abuses to her late mother, and snuggling up to her late enemy in her great ignorance. In realizing this, the Arya Katayana gave rise to unfathomable, immeasurable compassion for the whole of samsara and was able to proceed beyond the stage of an arhat to reach full enlightenment.

It is obvious that, within all the realms of existence, we have attained this special level of precious human existence because we have the intelligence to be able to perceive the state of samsara. Additionally, we understand the need to meditate and to give rise to compassion; we definitely have the abilities and powers to apply ourselves to that practice. These qualities of character are rarely found within samsara, so thick are the veils that obscure pure view. In the six realms of suffering, there are more sentient beings than can be calculated or conceived by our limited minds; they are absolutely numberless. Thus, if we can give rise to the desire to free all countless sentient beings from the ocean of suffering, with the intention of conveying them to the supreme state of buddhahood — if we have that wish to any degree whatsoever — then that wish itself vivifies the bodhisattva vow.

The adoption of the bodhisattva attitude is required in the path and practice of the bodhisattva vow. Through giving rise to great love and compassion for all sentient beings, and by wishing to establish them in the state of buddhahood, which is completely free from all suffering, one has the correct disposition for the bodhisattva approach. Both the relative and absolute aspects of bodhicitta are contained in this remarkable vow. The absolute (or ultimate) bodhisattva attitude holds to the absolute view that all phenomena and all sentient beings are devoid of any substantial reality. Within this bodhicitta attitude, there are two divisions or approaches: the first being the *bodhicitta of intention*, the second being the *bodhicitta of actualization*. Basically, the bodhicitta of intention is the desire to liberate all sentient beings from their delusions; with this developed attitude, one then must actually apply the intention. In abandoning all habitual non-virtuous activities, in taking up the habit of all virtuous actions, and in developing the practice of the six perfections (the six paramitas), one is able to apply oneself especially to the path of the bodhicitta of actualization. In fulfilling the bodhicitta of actualization, one can accomplish the fulfillment of the bodhisattva vows by becoming enlightened, an immense, immeasurable benefit to all deluded sentient beings.

To illustrate this point, let us now consider another story. Once there was a dakini who was married to a dull-witted and simple man. Yet, simple as he was, his faith in his wife was unshakable; with great devotion and conviction he would do whatever she asked, unquestioningly. Moved to compassion by his dull wit, his wife resolved to help him and, at last, devised a solution. She innocently requested him to recite the mantra of the Yidam Lord of Knowledge, tne noble victor known as Manjushri. So, every day the husband would pray to Manjushri, repeating *"Om Āh Ra Pa Tsa Ņa Dhī,"* time and time again.

Time passed. Then, one day the dakini instructed her husband to go to the shrine on the following morning. There he was to prostrate before Manjushri's statue and to pray on bended knee for initiation. She instructed him to hold out his hand following his prayer, and to eat whatever Manjushri gave him. She assured him that were he to do so, Manjushri would bestow the blessing of wisdom and knowledge, which would be of great benefit, not only to him, but to all beings as well. Because the husband had great devotion to her, he had no doubt whatsoever concerning her instructions, and the next morning he did exactly as she had requested.

The dakini hid herself behind the large statue of Manjushri; from this vantage she watched as her husband entered confidently, prostrated himself devotedly, and prayed his request with great fervor. Then, closing his eyes, he held out his hand. When she saw this, the dakini removed from her mouth a piece of fruit that she had been chewing and placed it in his outstretched hand. Devotedly he ate it, whereupon he immediately received all the blessings of Manjushri. Due to his faith and conviction plus the actual blessing of Manjushri, the husband was no longer a dull-witted man. Soon after this incident, he actualized his bodhicitta of intention and became a great scholar, a *mahapandita*, famed throughout all of India for his wisdom. His insights were to be of immediate and immense benefit to all beings, indicative of his bodhicitta of actualization.

By recognizing that the mind in essence is emptiness, one recognizes that this mind thinks, "I am suffering," if some unpleasant or painful experience arises, or will think, "I am happy," if some pleasant or satisfying experience arises. When one does not understand the true nature of the mind, then in essence what is not understood is *emptiness*. This mind that we think of as being real is actually devoid of any descriptive characteristics, such as size, shape, color, or location. Because all phenomena arise from mind, and mind itself is empty, it follows that all phenomena are empty. Our intention to develop awareness to benefit others means that we need to recognize the emptiness of all phenomena. This recognition matures relative bodhicitta into the ultimate liberation of enlightened awareness.

Our body of karmic fruition, which, from our previously accumulated karmic acts, allows us the experience of these corporeal phenomena, is a projection of the mind. Causal karmic acts were committed by the mind; the seed of such karmic acts were stored within the mind, and therefore this body is the karmic fruition of the mind. Furthermore, when we fall asleep, we dream of another body, our body of habitual tendencies; while in the dream state, we actually perceive this as being our own self. After we die, we have a mental body that again is just another mind projection that has no substantial reality. As we do not recall our last bardo of death and rebirth experience while simultaneously experiencing this moment, it is difficult to illustrate its delusion without first making an analysis of the dream state.

When we conjure up the dream environment, it will seem just as real as any waking experience. Any experiences of happiness or suffering that the habitual body believes to be real during the dream state are recognized to be totally empty by the fully ripened body upon awakening. Each new day begins with an awakening from this dream state; we wake up with an awareness that all the habitual body's sensations, all those dream visions and phenomena, are empty and have absolutely no self-existence. These experiences are not to be found anywhere in the sleeping room, nor can they be found anywhere else. Even the faint tracings these dreams leave behind serve only to remind the fully ripened (physical) body that there is another body, a habitual body. These dream memories soon vanish, like clouds dissipating into a clearing sky.

During the time of the Buddha Shakyamuni, there lived a great arhat named Shariputra. His mother, who did not like the Dharma at all, would not agree with anything he said to convince her of the truth of the Dharma, despite the fact that he was a realized saint. Undaunted by his mother's disbelief, Shariputra devised a discipline for her. He strung a bell over the door so that, as she went in and out of her room, the bell would ring. He requested that she pay heed to the bell's ringing by saying *"Om Mani Padme Hung"* every time she heard the bell's sound. As she could find no mental reasoning not to indulge her son's insistence, she reluctantly began to comply with his seemingly harmless request.

When she died, she was destined through her negative accumulation to be reborn in hell realms. There is one hell in which one experiences the vision and sensation of being dropped into a great cauldron of melting metal, similar to the cauldrons Chungawa saw when he had his brief visit to that region. As Shariputra's mother arrived and was approaching this destiny, the hell denizens, who were stirring the molten metal, banged the side of the cauldron with the stirring spoon, making a bell-like sound. Immediately, she responded with her habitual tendency and said, *"Om Mani Padme Hung,"* whereupon the whole hell experience completely vanished. Her son's compassion had thus helped her deluded mind and had liberated her from untold suffering. In every moment of our precious human existence, we too should recognize the need to liberate sentient beings compassionately from believing phenomena to be self-existent, when in *absolute truth* all phenomena are empty.

In death, the mind discards the empty fruition body and goes into a kind of oblivion with a complete loss of any memory or consciousness for a period of approximately three days. The mind remains in this state of oblivion until consciousness awakens and begins to project myriad illusory appearances, all believed to be just as real as we believe this current phenomenal appearance to be real. The appearances that manifest in the after-death state — landscapes, environments, whole cities, and so forth — and the intense sensory experiences — pleasure, pain, fear, and so forth — are all projections that the mental body of the bardo believes to be real. In the same way that the fully ripened body of wakeful life and the habitual body of the dream state experience reality through delusion, so too is the bardo experience but a mere mental projection having no self-nature, having no reality in and of itself. In recognizing the mind's nature as being void of any substantial existence, one must conclude that self-conceptualization is, as such, unproduced and uncreated. All appearance, being mere mental projection coming from the mind, which is essentially emptiness, is likewise unproduced and uncreated. This view, this recognition, is itself *absolute bodhicitta*.

In seeing that all sentient beings do not recognize their own illusory nature or the insubstantiality of all appearances, one recognizes that these beings falsely cling to appearances, believing their bodies to be real. It is apparent that clinging to the insubstantial reality of both body and phenomenal appearances gives the experience of intense suffering. In seeing that all sentient beings do not recognize ultimate bodhicitta and are locked into clinging to a false reality, then in no way can we not give rise to immeasurable compassion. Having compassion for all sentient beings from both the absolute and the relative viewpoints (described earlier), one joins compassion with the recognition of emptiness, just as two hands that work together help each other. It is by these means — recognition of emptiness and an immeasurable compassion — that bodhisattvas acquire the merit of skillful means and the wisdom necessary to attain buddhahood.

In the ten directions of space, there are innumerable buddhas and bodhisattvas. At some time or another, all of them have taken the bodhisattva vow. By employing this vow and the relative and absolute bodhicitta attitudes, they traverse the ten levels of bodhisattva development. There is absolutely no instance of any buddha or bodhisattva who has not taken the bodhisattva vow, or who has not given rise to relative and absolute bodhicitta. It is impossible to reach such attainment without fulfilling these commitments.

You who are reading this discourse have attained a precious human existence. You have all the freedoms and material possessions required for your needs in this lifetime. Because you are able to traverse the path of the Dharma, you have arrived at the door of the Dharma and are standing at the threshold. This arrival is very wonderful, is very remarkable, and is unfathomable in its greatness. Therefore, I will solve your quandary and hesitation at this threshold — a threshold that will eventually lead you to full liberation as a fully realized buddha — by telling you that to reach this goal you must accumulate a vastness of virtuous activity so as to develop a vast accumulation of meritorious karma. This is the most effective thing to be done in this lifetime. This is the easiest way to walk the path that lies before you. Taking and keeping the bodhisattva vow helps instill the habit of virtuous activity, and all of this has meritorious karmic accumulations.

In former times, when individuals requested the bodhisattva vow, they would perform great meritorious actions in making offerings to the buddhas and bodhisattvas as well as to the lama from whom they were to receive this great vow. For example, an aspirant might supply the community of monks and nuns with meals, construct temples where the Dharma could be practiced, make several hundred thousand circumambulations, and so forth. Making these vast offerings to the buddhas and the sangha developed great positive virtue, so much so that, eventually, an individual would arrive at the point where he or she could naturally and unhesitatingly receive the bodhisattva vow. In this age of jet travel and modern technology, where things happen a lot more quickly, we can use very simple and quick methods of amassing vast accumulations of merit. Examples of these are sponsoring persons doing a three-year retreat; going on pilgrimages to the shrines and temples in Tibet, Nepal, and India; sponsoring the construction of stupas, shrines, and temples; giving land that can be used and developed for Dharma activity; sponsoring *ganacakra* ceremonies or initiations; and so forth.

As you all have some connection with the Buddhadharma, it is probable you have taken the bodhisattva vow many times before, in this and in several different lifetimes. One maintains one's vow not only through one's virtuous actions for the benefit of all beings, but also by regularly reciting the bodhisattva vow, ideally on a daily basis. Therefore, if, in your own circumstances, you find yourself far distant from a Dharma center, or without a lama in your life who has the permission from his superiors to give this very important vow, this does not prevent you from reciting the vow daily, from meditating upon its meaning, and from applying its virtue in your life! However, I urge you to take this sacred vow formally with a qualified lama at your earliest opportunity.

When you recite this prayer (which is also your vow), your motivation is very important. Pausing a moment to think about the buddhas and bodhisattvas in the past who have taken and kept this vow, emulate their motivation. Make firm your resolve that you will attempt to put your vow into action, just as they have done. This not only connects you to their efforts, but at the same time it allows them to know that you have the determination to mature this commitment for the benefit of all beings.

Now that you have set your motivation properly, visualize very clearly that in the sky in front of you there is a lama surrounded by a vast array of innumerable buddhas, bodhisattvas, and arhats who are filling all space. Next, visualize yourself makings offerings to this entourage, offerings of everything in the universe that is good. Offer oceans, mountains, and wonderful things, such as beautiful palaces in which it is pleasant to reside. Conjure up a vast array so that the sky is completely filled with offerings of flowers, music, butter lamps, incense, candles — in short, all kinds of auspicious offerings. Visualize yourself offering these wonderful riches to the lama and his attendants with the inner prayer, "I pray that the lama, the buddhas, and the bodhisattvas of the ten directions accept this vast array of offerings, so that all beings may benefit from my intentions and motivation to take and keep this vow." Having given rise to the conviction that you are accepting the bodhisattva commitment, just as the lama, the buddhas, and the bodhisattvas have done, recite this vow, either in English (as follows) or Tibetan (see pp. 136-137).

Bodhisattva Vow

Until the heart of enlightenment is reached,
I go for refuge to the buddhas, and in the same way,
I also go for refuge to the teachings of the Dharma and
the assembly of bodhisattvas.

Just as the previous transcendent buddhas developed the
thought of enlightenment and practiced the ten
successive stages of bodhisattva training,

In order to benefit beings, I also will develop the
thought of enlightenment and follow these
successive stages.   *Recite three times*

Now, my life is fruitful. I have obtained the most
excellent human existence.

Today, I am born into the lineage of the buddhas and
have become a child of the buddhas.

From now on, in all possible ways, I will make my actions
conform to this family, so that this faultless,
noble lineage will not be defiled.

In the presence of all the refuges, I have invited all
beings to come to happiness until they have attained
the bliss of buddhahood.

Gods, jealous gods, and other beings, rejoice!

May the precious thought of enlightenment which has not
arisen, arise! Wherever it has arisen, may it
not be destroyed, but increase more and more!

Without being separated from the thought of enlightenment,
may we strive to practice the bodhisattva conduct!

Having been given complete protection by the buddhas, may
we abandon wrong actions!

May all that the bodhisattvas intend for the benefit of
beings be realized!

Through the intentions of the protectors, may all beings
attain happiness!

May all beings have happiness!

May all the unfortunate realms be emptied forever!

May all the prayers of the bodhisattvas at all levels
of enlightenment be realized!

Recite one time

May all beings have happiness and the causes of happiness!

May all beings not have suffering nor the causes of
suffering!

May all beings never be without the supreme bliss which is
free from all suffering!

May all beings live in great equanimity, which is free
from all attachment and aversion!

Recite three times

Bodhisattva Vow

JANG CHUP NYING POR CHI KYI BAR

SANG GYE NAM LA KYAP SU CHI

CHÖ DANG JANG CHUP SEM PA YI

TSOK LANG DE SHIN KYAP SU CHI

JI TAR NGÖN GYI DE SHEK KYI

JANG CHUP TUK NI KYE PA DANG

JANG CHUP SEM PAY LAP PA LA

DE DAK RIM SHIN NE PA TAR

DE SHIN DRO LA PEN DÖN DU

JANG CHUB SEM NI KYE GYI SHING

DE SHIN DU NI LAP PA LANG

RIM PA SHIN DU LAP PAR GYI

Recite three times

DENG DU DAK TSE DRE BU YÖ

MI YI SI PA LEK PAR TOP

DE RING SANG GYE RIK SU KYE

SANG GYE SAY SU DAK DENG GYUR

DA NI DAK GI CHI NAY KYANG

RIK DANG TUN PAY LAY TSAM TE

KYÖN ME TSÜN PAY RIK DI LA

NYOK PAR MI GYUR DE TAR JA

DAK GI DE RING KYOP PA TAM CHAY KYI

CHEN NGAR DRO WA DE SHEK NYI DANG NI

BAR DU DE LA DRON DU BÖ ZIN GYI

HLA DANG HLA MIN LA SOK GA WAR GYI

JANG CHUP SEM NI RIN PO CHE

MA KYE BA NAM KYE GYUR CHIK

KYE PA NYAM PA ME PA DANG

The Bodhisattva Vow written in phonetic Tibetan.

GONG NAY GONG DU PEL WAR SHOK
JANG CHUP SEM DANG MI DREL SHING
JANG CHUP CHÖ LA SHÖL WA DANG
SANG GYE NAM KYI YONG ZUNG SHING
DU KYI LAY NAM PONG WAR SHOK
JANG CHUP SEM PA NAM KYI NI
DRO DÖN TUK LA GONG DRUP SHOK
GOM PO YI NI GANG GONG PA
SEM CHEN NAM LA DE JOR SHOK
SEM CHEN TAM CHAY DE DANG DEN GYUR CHIK
NGEN DRO TAM CHAY TAK TU TONG PAR SHOK
JANG CHUP SEM PA GANG DAK SAR SHUK PA
DE DAK KUN GYI MÖN LAM DRUP PAR SHOK

Recite one time

SEM CHEN TAM CHE DE WA DANG DE WAY
   GYU DANG DEN PAR GYUR CHIK

DUK NGAL DANG DUK NGAL GYI GYU DANG
   DRAL WAR GYUR CHIK

DUK NGAL ME PAY DE WA DAM PA DANG MI
   DRAL WAR GYUR CHIK

NYE RING CHAK DANG DANG DRAL WAY DANG
   NYOM CHEN PO LA NAY PAR GYUR CHIK

Recite three times

What does this vow mean to one's life? Its basic meaning is that the attitude of caring only for oneself, of cherishing one's own requirements, and of acting only for one's own benefit while not being concerned about the benefit of others is completely gone, completely abandoned. One develops the attitude of altruism and considers that the benefit of others is far more important than the benefit of self. As a bodhisattva, one gives rise to this attitude.

When you have the opportunity to receive this vow formally from a qualified lama, you must think that you have received this vow not only from the lama but also from all the buddhas, the yidams, and all the accomplished bodhisattvas. You will then have formally become a bodhisattva. You may have occasion when receiving certain initiations to be asked to use your bodhisattva name. If no special name was given to you when you formally took the bodhisattva vow, use the word "Bodhisattva" at the beginning of your refuge name; however, one should not use this prefix, "Bodhisattva," in a bragging or light-hearted manner under any circumstances.

If you plant a seed of rice or barley in good soil which has warmth, moisture, and nutrients, you are able to watch it grow as it spreads its roots, sends up a stem, and produces the stalk and shaft of grain. In just the same way, I have planted in you the seed of bodhicitta that will definitely grow, continuing to mature until you blossom into full buddhahood. Not only myself, but all the buddhas and bodhisattvas are determined to protect and help you with their great compassion, to help you give rise to this bodhisattva attitude. Additionally, there are many different beings on this same great path that have great love for the Buddhadharma. These are your friends and associates who will help and protect you while encouraging you to develop this bodhicitta. When one has requested and received this vow, then one works for the benefit of all sentient beings until they all attain buddhahood. A bodhisattva strives as much as possible to develop this altruistic attitude.

Keeping and maintaining this commitment is accomplished by considering two perspectives and their resultant conclusion. First, it is possible to develop mental exhaustion that makes delivering all sentient beings to buddhahood seem impossible. Rather than becoming disheartened and fearful that one will not satisfy the vow (and thereby abandoning the good intention) one should understand that such abandonment would break one's vow. Second, if in this lifetime (or another) an enemy arises who spreads maliciousness, the bodhisattva commitment is broken if the practitioner excludes that person from his or her bodhisattva intention. In thinking of excluding this enemy and in not working to help bring this person to enlightenment, one reduces the bodhisattva intention. This would also break the vow.

We are beginners on the path and are bound to continue experiencing anger, hatred, dislike, and so forth; these feelings will arise from time to time. However, because we have taken the bodhisattva vow in this or other lifetimes, we must recognize that if these negative emotions arise, we should immediately (or as soon as possible) try to make amends by realizing the mistake. We should not allow these negative emotions to hold sway when practicing and keeping the bodhisattva vow. At the same time, we should also remind ourselves of the intention of commitment, resolving definitely to work for the benefit of those beings who cause us anger, hatred, and so forth.

Our enemies must be saved just as much as our friends. By making such a resolve and by making amends, even though the vow was damaged by negative emotions, the commitment is reinforced and the vow can become stronger. Failure to compensate by correct forgiveness constitutes breaking the bodhisattva vow. It is important to remember that whether a sentient being is known or unknown to you, is an enemy or a friend, is human or inhuman, that each is, in fact, your own mother from previous, present, and future lifetimes. Thus, by simply remembering that our mothers, as limitless as space, need our help to deliver them from confusion and suffering, we are keeping the bodhisattva vow intact.

Should we feel so inspired as to practice the foundations of mahamudra by undertaking the practices of prostrations, mandala offerings, etc., each of these practices includes prayers that allow us to retake the bodhisattva vow again and again. Repeatedly renewing this vow has the great quality of enhancing understanding. Additionally, when performing yidam practices, such as Chenrezig's sadhana, the aspirant renews both the bodhisattva vow and the refuge vow. Whether in longer or shorter form, these two very important concepts always begin such practices. Even though these are often with different wording, the concept and the action of their recitation always has the same effect.

It is said that if the benefits of keeping the bodhisattva vow were to have some kind of substantial form, the whole of space could not contain them. Specifically, even if a person commits an action so negative that the effect is rebirth in hell, by taking and keeping the bodhisattva vow, the resultant negative karmic accumulation can instead be immediately, completely eradicated. If many such negative actions have been committed, the keeping of this vow with pure motivation will eventually eradicate all negative karmic accumulations. The life story of Jetsün Milarepa illustrates this point.

To help maintain and expand your understanding and the power of the bodhisattva intention, you can do the meditation of giving and receiving, known in Tibetan as *tonglen*. Visualize that while breathing in, you take away all the sufferings from all sentient beings, removing confusion, lack of clarity, and so on. This suffering is transformed into a kind of smoky black light that is absorbed through your right nostril into your heart center. While absorbing this suffering, think, "I have completely absorbed all the pain and suffering of sentient beings into myself, freeing them so they can have all the happiness that they could desire." Then, while breathing out, imagine that a white light leaves from the pure intention of your heartfelt prayer and carries with it all your goodnesses and pleasures, carrying these to benefit all the other sentient beings. This simple practice of giving and receiving is very powerful; it is considered to be an important part of development along the path to liberation. It not only benefits all beings by its efforts at purifying their suffering, but it also helps to eradicate the massive amounts of negative accumulations of the practitioner. Its practice will definitely strengthen your bodhisattva intention.

In the future, when you attain the first level of an accomplished bodhisattva, you will then experience a clairvoyant wisdom. You will be able to remember that in the distant past you received a teaching on the bodhisattva vow from an old man in some ancient city; in remembering this, you will be very happy. With the realization of the first blooming of the first level of an accomplished bodhisattva, you can manifest remarkable qualities. For instance, in an instant, an accomplished bodhisattva can emanate one hundred emanations to teach, train, and deliver one hundred sentient beings to liberation in single moment. As the stages of an accomplished bodhisattva progress, these powers and qualities increase tenfold with each level, becoming even more immense and immeasurable.

It is auspicious that you have the desire to become a bodhisattva. You have begun your bodhisattva path and this is acknowledged by all buddhas and accomplished bodhisattvas. You have the ability to increase your understanding and to develop your bodhicitta. This is a time of great rejoicing! You should remember with kindness the lama who has bestowed upon you the bodhisattva vow (in this and in other lifetimes) and offer prostrations to him and all the buddhas and bodhisattvas. I will continue to make auspicious prayers for your rapid realization, your long life, all benefits, and happiness. Always be comfortable and at ease, and work to develop a pure bodhicitta attitude. I pray this teaching will quickly liberate you, for the sake of all sentient beings, our mothers.

Kalu Rinpoche in the late 1960s, meditating in his audience room at his monastery in Sonada, India (Photograph by J.G. Sherab Ebin)

≈ 9 ≈

BRILLIANT MOON

Elucidation of the Mahamudra

Presently we possess excellent bodies, bodies that are characteristic of the human realm, giving us the physical freedom to move about pretty much as we wish. We do not, however, have any mental freedom, meaning our minds are controlled by our karma, our emotionality, and our ignorance. Until we destroy this control and eradicate these obscurations, we can not say that our minds are truly free. To illustrate the manner in which we lack mental freedom, simply consider our basic human tendencies. If we have a single thought of desire or attraction for something that pleases us, this easily gives rise to aggression, pride, jealousy and so forth. A whole net of different thoughts arises based on our one simple thought, yet usually we are helpless to stop or control this process.

When one begins to practice the Dharma, one is typically and immediately confronted with this lack of freedom. For example, when one practices tranquility meditation, it is very difficult to get one's mind to sit still for more than a minute without having a thought. Then, too, when one tries to meditate upon a yidam, such as Chenrezig (who is white in color), one continually experiences thoughts of a black Chenrezig, a yellow Chenrezig, and so forth. Different colored Chenrezigs appear and one cannot maintain a stable visualization of the white yidam. Therefore, to develop freedom of mind, it is very important to first recognize the actual nature of the mind whereby one can gain control over its operation. In that way, undisturbed and unobscured by what arises and subsides naturally, the mind is free. Those humans who enjoy their precious human existence and are able to understand this perspective are also able to examine this teaching and determine the truth of the nature of the mind. Knowing that one has such an existence might, however, produce a kind of pride, causing one to think, "I have this superior existence and all this superior wisdom," or "I know the nature of mind." In actual fact, it is very difficult to know precisely the true nature of the mind; apart from thinking, "I am," or "I exist," it is difficult even to observe the nature of mind, let alone recognize it. There are several reasons why such obscurations occur, reasons worth reviewing before discussing the mahamudra.

First, in not recognizing the mind's nature, we all believe in ourselves and our ego. We naturally think we see a "self." Yet the mind, being completely formless and lacking the characteristics of shape, size, etc., is devoid of a "self." If one were to observe the nature of mind through meditation and were to see the nature of mind, then were there a "self," one would be able to place a descriptive characteristic upon the mind. One would be able to say, "It is this size," or "It is located here," or something equally descriptive. If you yourself could find something definitive about this mind, then you would be perfectly entitled to say that there is a "self" that is self-existent. But, if you cannot, then you must recognize the truth of the mind's emptiness.

Second, we cling to this "self" as being something real. Such clinging is merely a conceptual clinging that associates a "self" with some kind of form. If there were any kind of shape or place that could be said to be "mind," then this intellectual, conceptual supposition of there being a "self" would be valid. However, this is completely without basis in any reality. The mind is emptiness without a "self."

Third, despite this, we cherish and love that "self" and are very concerned with preventing any kind of harmful occurrence, wishing only for pleasant experiences. Failure to recognize clearly the nature of this "self" is called the cloudiness or ignorance of self, which we have discussed at length throughout this entire discourse. Simply stated, having these three states of ego clinging — seeing, believing in, and cherishing a "self" — yet being totally unaware of its true nature gives us what we think of as being "I."

The entire body of the teachings of the Buddha is concerned with alleviating this erroneous view. The existing methods and varied instructions for pointing out this mistaken idea are extremely extensive. Through applying these teachings and the commentaries by the great tantric masters, by developing an understanding, and by gaining a good habit through meditation, one is able to do wonderful things. For example, visualization can be used to calm the mind through meditation. This may be done in the following way. Begin the meditation by visualizing a clear sphere of light in the heart. Once stability has been gained in that visualization, meditate on the sphere of light expanding and moving far away in front of you. When stability has been gained again, meditate simultaneously on both the distant sphere of light and the sphere of light in the heart.

Having gained stability in meditating on both lights at the same time, next visualize another sphere of light as being very far behind you, and gain stability on this visualization. Then meditate with clarity and stability on the visualization of the spheres of light in front, way behind, and in your heart. Through the development of this meditation, you will find that not only have you calmed the mind, but such stability of focus will additionally prove to be beneficial when you attain the first level of an accomplished bodhisattva. Applying concentration at that moment will enable you to experience one hundred samadhis, or different types of meditative absorption, the very instant this level is achieved!

From the point of view of Buddhism and Buddhist practice, the discovery of the true nature of mind must be established for Buddhadharma to be fully practiced. However, this does not mean that any meditation practiced before such realization arises is bad or useless; rather, it is just not as effective as it could be. Understanding the true nature of mind brings with it a benefit, in that anything done with the mind in meditation is far more effective and beneficial. Indeed, while it is true that the mind of each and every one of us possesses all the qualities of a buddha, these are unapparent because of obscurations and our clinging to an inherently existing ego, or "I," which binds our obscurations together like a chain. Clinging to egoistic self-perception prevents recognition of the inherent qualities of buddhahood, qualities which we naturally possess. Until the obscurations of ego clinging are cut through, we will never realize these transcendent qualities inherent in the pure alaya.

Generally, our qualities are masked or completely covered, as though they were held bound in a solid vessel, as in a clay pot. In many of the tantras, the Buddha has said that there are only two methods or techniques by which coemergent wisdom can be realized or attained. The first is dispelling the four obscurations, in combination with the gathering of the accumulations of merit and wisdom. The second is attaining the blessing of the tsaway lama who has this realization. However, it is very difficult in these dark times to find a lama of such a caliber, one who has not only all the good qualities of a superior teacher but also has the perfection of the mahamudra. Therefore, such an option is rare — there are few who can give such a blessing. Furthermore, for the student to benefit from such a blessing, he or she must have accumulated a great amount of positive karmic accumulations and have an insatiable desire for the mastery of the mahamudra. Fortunately, however, there are many lamas who have the ability to help one on the path by answering questions and sharing experiential awareness accumulated in their own development towards this goal.

In finding someone to help, most importantly one needs to locate a lama that has an unbroken lineage (of blessing, empowerment, literary authority, experience, and so on) and is able to give the initiations of vajrayana. Secondly, the lama should have a demonstrable great compassion for all sentient beings. Instead of having an attitude of wishing to gain wealth and self-aggrandizement in order to build up his or her own dharma empire, the lama holds but one main thought in mind, namely, leading sentient beings away from the confusion of samsara.

It may happen that some students with exceptional qualities come seeking the lama's guidance. Interestingly, whenever the Dharma is explained to such students, they have the kind of intelligence that can understand it automatically and with very deep comprehension. Furthermore, they are able to put the teaching into immediate practice. Within this world, the occurrence of such excellent students has nothing to do with their gender. The real reason for being able to step beyond obscurations so easily is that they have gathered accumulations of merit and wisdom for many, many lifetimes. Additionally, they have worked on dispelling the four obscurations in their stream of experience. In the case of such students hearing a lama explain the meaning of the mahamudra, the solid vessel of their obscurations develops tremendous cracks and holes in it through which their innate buddha nature can shine forth. Thus, along with the realization they experience when hearing such an explanation, such students of excellent capacity will immediately give rise to tremendous, genuine compassion for sentient beings who do not have this same realization. Furthermore, a tremendous faith arises in them for the lama from whom the transmission of the mahamudra was received. There are few people like this, however, and their rarity might well be compared to the rarity of snow on a summer day.

In the past, when faced with such an individual of excellent capacity, it was the custom among the great gurus of India and Tibet to recognize the student as having such potential, and to give this special type of teaching. I, however, do not have the kind of super-knowledge that can recognize such exceptional people. Instead, I teach everyone what will benefit anyone. Some people will be benefitted by the explicit meaning, and some people will be benefitted by the implicit meaning; therefore, I teach both.

In our beginning attempts to gain liberation, we are all like young babes. We have to be protected, guided, and helped along the path of the Dharma. We need assistance in overcoming our illusory bewilderment, confusion, and so forth, and so we need the help and guidance of the lama. A lama having an authentic lineage, a great compassion for sentient beings, and the ability to explain the Dharma of the Buddha without error is the helper we all need. As babes in this path of the Dharma, it is the help of the lama and the Three Jewels that gives us what we need to enable us to find the correct, straight, and rapid path of vajrayana, the path that will lead us to the perfect realization of buddhahood.

However, all the help in the world will not take us any farther along the path to liberation if we do not apply the lama's good advice and sincere instruction. You must practice in order to proceed; such practice can be as simple as sitting quietly to examine the nature of the mind. I have spent a lot of time telling you many things about the true nature of the mind, something that indeed has no substantiality, but it is up to you to see for yourself if the words I have spoken are true. In itself, such examination has gradations of progress that are useful in uncovering, or discovering, the mahamudra. Therefore, let us take a moment to detail such procedures.

First, sit correctly in a meditation posture with relaxed breath and an open, uncontrived mental awareness. Remain in that state, and simply watch what happens. Before too long, you will begin to be aware of thoughts that arise out of nothing, which have no substantiality in and of themselves, and which will again lose themselves to either the next thought or the next dull moment of being. Does this thought arise from inside or outside the body? Does it come from north, south, east, or west? If it is internal, does it come from the heart, the stomach, the legs, the arms, or the head? It is important for you to take the time to examine this issue and to know whence thoughts arise. Also, where does the thought stay while your are occupied with it, and where does it go when it fades from your attention?

Continuing with this approach, are the thoughts separate from the mind, being distinct entities in and of themselves, or are they the same as the mind, having no distinction other than demonstrating the nature of the mind? Pause a moment and reflect on this point. If you have a thought of some place near to you, for instance your closest big city, is that thought the city itself or is it the product of the mind? Or, take a far, distant city, like Bodh-Gaya in India; is the thought of Bodh-Gaya something different than the mind itself? Is the thought of Bodh-Gaya and the mind the same, or are the two separate? Look again and see if, in giving rise to the thought of a place very near and a place very far, it is the same thought, or are these two different thoughts?

It is necessary to meditate on these concepts for some time until you come to a decision about whether the mind and thoughts are the same or different, and whether thoughts come from outside or inside. You have to decide on this issue, and then you should consult with the lama for verification of your findings. If you are correct, the lama will then give you further instruction to help you proceed, and if you are incorrect, the lama can address issues presented by your answer and can direct you toward correct understanding.

In order to proceed with this introspection, it is useful to know that in the extensive writings that comprise the whole of Tibetan Buddhism, many sources state that the mind and the thoughts are the same, that thoughts arise out of the mind like waves rise out of the ocean. Further, these texts state that the mind is empty, that it has no form or color, and that, therefore, thoughts are the same in that they are empty and without form or color. It is the mind's quality of clarity that allows thoughts to arise, and although thoughts are insubstantial, they continue to arise due to the unimpeded nature of mind.

The next phase of this examination involves looking at the natural state of the mind, at the change occurring in the mind, and at the awareness of the mind. By now, you should recognize that we constantly have this mind and that changes transpire in it, but you should also be able to rest the mind in its natural state and, when thoughts arise and the mind changes, you should be aware of that change. Awareness is very important. A mind resting in a place where there is no awareness is no different from gross ignorance, and a mind ignorant of change gives no benefit because it is held in the sway of delusion. If there is awareness, there is meditation; if there is no awareness, there is no meditation. When the level of mahamudra is finally reached, one's awareness allows meditation to happen effortlessly. This is referred to by the Tibetan and Indian masters of tantra as being one of the *five paths,* also known as a 'state of non-meditation' in that it occurs spontaneously and without contrivance.

Let us carry our consideration of the nature of mind a bit further by comparing the mind with the ocean. If the state of mind is the ocean, and if changes in the mind are waves on the ocean, are the waves and the ocean the same or different in essence? Alternatively, if the state of the mind is compared to the ground, and if changes in the mind are compared to trees, are the trees and the ground of the same quality of being, or are they different? Furthermore, are the state of the mind, the changes of the mind, and the awareness of the mind the same, or are they different? If they are the same, in what way are they the same? If they are different, where is the state of the mind, where is the change of the mind, and where is the awareness of the mind?

It is important that this examination be followed in sequence, with several weeks or months beings spent in its investigation. First of all, you must examine the arising of thoughts, the duration of thoughts, and the cessation of these thoughts. After having meditated on these considerations some time, you should go to a lama for further instruction. Later, you should take into consideration the state of the mind, the changes of the mind, and the awareness of the mind. After meditating on these topics for some time, again return to the lama to gain further instruction to help you mature the mahamudra experience.

In making this examination, I am sure you will recognize for yourself that the mind does have a state of naturalness without thoughts, and that this natural mind state has no color, shape, or form. You will fathom for yourself that the mind is empty and vast; in fact, it is so expansive that it can be compared to the sky or the sphere of space. But, the mind is also tiny because even insects as small as dots have minds. So, the mind does not have size; rather it accords itself to thoughts. Vast or tiny, the mind appears to be all-pervading like space. The nature of the mind is experienced when it is resting in its own state, without thought. When thoughts arise in the mind, the mind changes, but these changes are also the mind itself. For instance, when waves arise out of the ocean, waves are in one sense different from the ocean, but they are the same in that they are the same body of water.

Hence, in the Kagyu tradition, thought (Tibetan: *namdok*) is said to be the change of the mind. But in essence, thought is none other than the dharmakaya because the thought itself is essentially suchness. Thus, one who is aware of both the state and change of mind is said to be mind itself. If there is no awareness, then there is no meditation, and this is delusion. Without awareness, resting in the state of the mind is stupidity and the change of mind is simply thoughts. If, however, there is awareness, then the

state of mind is meditation and the change of mind is also meditation, all because the state of the mind, the change of the mind,
and the awareness of mind are one and the same.

When you meditate, do not try to have good thoughts, do not
try to keep away bad thoughts, do not try to stop thoughts, and
do not try to go after them. Rather, rest in a state of being aware
of the thoughts as they arise. This way, when bad thoughts arise,
they arise out of the emptiness of mind and fall back into the
emptiness of mind. The same is true for good thoughts. This same
process of examination can be applied to the many other traps of
personality and physiology. For instance, are your emotions of
desire and anger coming from the same mind, or from different
minds? And, as to the sounds, tastes, sights, smells, and sensory
experiences which can be so pleasing or displeasing to you, are
these coming from the same mind, or from different minds?

When you take the time to thoroughly examine such issues,
you will eventually come to conclusions that help formulate later
stages of realization. In realizing the inherent emptiness of all
reality, you will realize that the essence of the mind (which is also
empty) pervades all things; as such, it is the seat of dharmakaya.
When you recognize that the clarity of the mind is also its natural
state of being, you will realize that clarity as such is the seat of
sambhogakaya. For a buddha, who rests in natural liberation in
dharmakaya, the clarity of mind, the seat of sambhogakaya,
allows knowledge of the three times of past, present, and future.
In recognizing that the many thoughts that arise in the mind are
essentially unimpeded, you will realize that unimpededness as
such is the seat of nirmanakaya. It is wholly because of the
unimpededness of pure mind that buddhas manifest in forms of
ordinary and supreme incarnations in the nirmanakaya state in
order to benefit all sentient beings.

Our great teacher, Tilopa, the father of the Kagyu lineage,
condensed the teaching of mahamudra into these words, "No
distraction, no contrivance, and no meditation." What did he
mean? Well, "no distraction" refers to the total awareness of the
mind in the state of rest. Whatever it is, whether or not it is
changing and having thoughts, the mind is not distracted; it is
always aware. "No meditation" means there is no thought of

either good or bad, and nothing at all is being forced or structured. The awareness is totally spontaneous. "No contrivance" means there are no requirements and nothing to be done when letting the mind rest in its natural state.

If you can meditate in this manner, purifying your defilements and accumulating merit and wisdom, then when you receive the blessing of your tsaway lama, all your efforts soon will combine to bring your mahamudra practice to fruition. However, there are several pitfalls along the path of meditation. Meditation here means that you first begin your practice by taking refuge in the Three Jewels and the Three Roots; you then engender bodhicitta, and with sincere devotion perform the yidam practice of Chenrezig. Following the recitation and visualization practice of Chenrezig, focus upon the tsaway lama seated on the crown of your head; with intense devotion, pray for his or her blessing so that you might experience the spontaneous arising of non-causal awareness. Next, watch the tsaway lama dissolve into light and melt into you, and in this state of inseparability with the tsaway lama, you may begin your examination and observation concerning the true nature of the mind. And, finally, of course, conclude each meditation session with the dedication of merit and with prayers of good wishes for all sentient beings.

It can sometimes happen that, after having meditated by watching the mind for a period of time, you may find that thoughts and emotions follow each other so quickly that there seems to be no space in between them. When this occurs, cut through this confusing process with one motion of the mind, remaining in the state of non-distraction. Or, perhaps while performing this meditation, you may find yourself in a state where no strong thought process happens, where no awareness is present, making the mind dark and cloudy. This is the arising of stupor, and you should deal with it by instantly cutting through it. You should then strengthen or tighten awareness and remain undistracted in a state of inseparable emptiness and clarity.

Sometimes while doing this sort of practice, a state will arise that is almost like sleep, in which the mind becomes completely dark. This kind of state, or meditation, is of no benefit, either for the practice of zhinay (shamatha) as tranquility, or for the practice of lhatong (vipashyana) as insight. If you can arise from that state and let the mind rest without distraction in a state of clear emptiness, with a very precise yet elusive clarity, then this is a useful form of tranquility meditation. This progressive stage will bring about the attainment of many qualities.

If, while meditating, the aspirant has gained a certain understanding indicative of knowing something of the mind's true nature, fathoming a glimpse of true wisdom, then this is the practice of lhatong. And, if while meditating in such a manner, the student becomes aware and recognizes that the mind's essence is empty, that it is vast like empty space, and that the quality of this emptiness is clarity or lucidity, then in seeing this, he or she can take a great step forward. In such understanding, recognition dawns showing that both clarity and emptiness are inseparable and that their essential nature is unimpeded awareness. If, while recognizing this, the aspirant does not remain in conceptualization, but rather, in a state that is completely apart from any kind of manipulation or contrivance within the mind, then this is the beginning of the practice and realization of the mahamudra. Maturing this view culminates in the full blossoming of buddhahood. This can have a number of implications. Considering the different aspects of the nature of mind that become full blown at the moment enlightenment is achieved, then to say that the mind is essentially empty and intangible like space is to say that, when experienced directly, mind is everywhere, and so too is the consciousness of a buddha. The awareness of an enlightened being extends everywhere; there is no limit to it. It has no center or circumference, as it does not obey such rules. Hence, it connotes an all-pervading, omnipresent awareness. This has been termed *dharmakaya*.

As well, there is a luminous potential of mind that gives the ability to know. This, again, has an all-pervading quality in the sense that wherever there is space, that space is illuminated. Wherever there is mind, there is clarity. Wherever there is intangible awareness, there is luminosity. The unimpeded or dynamic manifestation of the mind's awareness becomes full blown as a kind of transcendent (or panoramic) awareness experienced by the being who attains the full level of buddhahood. This has two aspects. One is a qualitative experience that is aware of the essential nature of all experience and all phenomena. The other is a quantitative awareness that is aware of all the little details. Omniscience is not only knowing definitively the distinctions of samsara, it is also the understanding of the underlying essence.

All our definitions are just mental constructs, simply ideas we have concerning the nature of enlightenment. There is no way we can really talk about what it is like, because enlightenment is beyond any kind of mental concept. Not to come to some conclusions about what constitutes or contributes to liberation, however, is to avoid the issue and to keep endlessly turning the wheel of samsara. Therefore, it is useful that we try to describe enlightenment. In so doing, we are naturally forced to say that it is both a universal and an individual experience, yet it appears to be neither one nor the other, partaking of both. Each and every being that attains enlightenment experiences essentially the same thing. Buddhas are involved in the same state of being; their awareness has the same omniscient, all-pervading, luminous, unimpeded experience of both the essence and details of everything. Otherwise, enlightenment could not be said to be omniscient, and therefore one would have to conclude that enlightenment was not full and complete; this is simply not the case.

With regard to mahamudra, there are said to be three stages, namely, *ground mahamudra, path mahamudra,* and *fruition mahamudra;* and the three together incorporate or accomplish the entire array of the eighty-four thousand collections of the Buddhadharma. By recognizing the ground mahamudra, the practitioner proceeds in the practice and, after a while, this practice becomes the path mahamudra. Then, when the aspirant realizes the path mahamudra totally and fully, he or she attains the fruition mahamudra. Ground mahamudra is the basis of all mahamudra. It points out the nature of mind. Let me remind you that the word *mahamudra* has four syllables in the Tibetan language. When analyzed individually, the first syllable, *chak,* means hand, which refers to the seal of voidness and indicates that all phenomena are insubstantial. The second syllable, *ja,* refers to the fact that all phenomena and all experience are not beyond voidness but are none other than voidness. Because this realization is extremely

south, receive unequal lighting. A given situation can have differing aspects, and in that sense, there is an individual quality to enlightenment. But, this is not individuality as we normally understand it. Our ordinary definition of individuality says that the something that is me is separate from the something that is you, and, consequently, I am different from you, because I am not you. We think, "If I were you, I would not be me, but because I am me and not you, then I have an individuality." This sort of framework is wholly unnecessary for an expression of enlightened energy to take place. On the one hand, buddhahood is a universal experience and all buddhas experience the same thing, but, on the other hand, in certain instances there are particular manifestations of buddhahood. Neither of these statements is false, nor are they mutually contradictory.

A traditional verse begins by stating that the dharmakaya, the absolute direct experience of the emptiness of mind, is all-embracing and pervades everywhere like space or the sky. The verse continues by saying that the sambhogakaya, the direct experience of the clarity and luminosity of mind, is like the sun shining in that sky. The verse concludes by describing the physical form manifestation of an enlightened being (termed the *nirmanakaya*, or the direct experience of the unimpeded and dynamic quality of mind) as being like rainbows appearing everywhere for the benefit of all beings. However, it is not as though space, sun, or rainbows were thinking to themselves, "I will make myself appear over there, because you are separate from me." Not at all: for quite simply, there is a space in which the sun shines and in which rainbows appear. In the same way, there is a universal experience that all enlightened beings attain, which, nevertheless, can manifest in unique ways. Manifestation does not require our normal perspective of "self and other" in order to appear.

Here it is necessary to distinguish between absolute reality, the label for something that really cannot be conceptualized, and relative reality, which can be. Anything that can be conceptualized with the intellect is, by definition, relative reality. Whatever cannot be conceptualized is absolute reality. The dharmakaya of buddhahood is absolute reality and its experience is the absolute truth or ultimate reality, whereas relative or conventional truth is anything that can be limited by any conceptual framework. It should not surprise us that we can only approximate what enlightenment may be, because as sentient beings still bound by our delusions, we do not have the capacity to do otherwise.

We are working with a limited and confused state of awareness. If we had the panoramic awareness to describe enlightenment, we would be enlightened! But because we lack that quality, we also lack the awareness necessary to describe the experience accurately. However, we can begin to talk about it, and that is what we try to do when we use the words buddha or buddhahood. These terms give the idea of elimination of all that is limiting, hindering, negative, or obscuring in the mind, so that the potential of mind can fully blossom. This is, perhaps, the single most concise and accurate statement we could make about enlightenment.

In the Buddhist tradition, one finds reference to the state called buddhahood as being an awakening from the sleep of ignorance and an elimination of any imposed limitations. This awakening allows consciousness to extend itself infinitely, to embrace everything that is possible to be known. Something inherent becomes actualized, similar to the quality of a lotus flower opening. Beyond these explanations and descriptive phrases, the state of liberated being called buddhahood cannot really be described accurately because we are not yet in its frame of reference.

For the process of spiritual development to take place at all, certain qualities and elements are not only necessary but are extremely crucial. One of these is having faith and confidence in the spiritual principles and goals to which one is aspiring, and in the teachers who show one the way to that goal. It is the quality of compassion that allows one to hold all beings as close and as dear as one's own parents. The more energy you put into developing these qualities of faith, confidence, and compassion, the more effective your spiritual practice will become. The moral choices you make in life, those practical day-to-day decisions made between virtuous and non-virtuous actions, are also an important factor in your spiritual development and should never be underrated.

It is additionally important to inquire into the mind's true nature with either a process of analytical or investigative meditation or with an intuitive approach in meditation. The aspirant can either examine experience and analyze it so that he or she comes to a deeper understanding of the nature of mind and the nature of experience, or the student can simply allow a fundamental experience of the empty, clear, and unimpeded nature of mind itself to arise. Either way, the practitioner is developing qualities that are extremely important; a great deal of attention and effort should be focused toward these issues.

When the beginnings of the recognition of mind's true nature arise, then you should instantly think of the Buddha Shakyamuni, of all the bodhisattvas, and especially of the tsaway lama, with the recognition that they all have attained full realization of the true nature of the mind. You can then advance rapidly by simply thinking how wonderful this is. Additionally, if you then can cultivate a naturally arising great faith filled with continuous prayers and can continually supplicate the buddhas and bodhisattvas, you can have an easy path to true fulfillment of the goal.

The whole point of this sort of discussion is to make use of these concepts, so that they become the basis for a whole, on-going process of spiritual development. Thus, the aspirant can attain the true benefit of this kind of teaching, the benefit being the attainment of enlightenment itself. When that transpires, you will have a sense that the tsaway lama from whom one has received the transmission of mahamudra is more kind than all the buddhas of the three times and the ten directions. Even though this feeling arises mostly because the aspirant has not met the buddhas and has not received the mahamudra teaching from them, nevertheless, the tsaway lama is now seen as being extremely wonderful and benevolent. It is through the loving kindness and compassion of the tsaway lama that you are actually given the keys to liberation; once you have received the mahamudra instructions, it is as though you hold the key in the palm of your hand.

If one has realization of the nature of the mind coupled with complete, impartial compassion and inconceivable devotion and gratefulness to the source of the teaching, then in one instant the aspirant will be able to obtain full buddhahood. Thus, even though one might not be able to fully understand the meaning of mahamudra at the time of hearing it explained, the receiving of the teachings serves as a great blessing because it creates a connection between the student and the teaching that will eventually ripen to fruition in some future circumstance. The fact that you have the faith to read these teachings, and that you have read them, is extremely wonderful, being a source of great merit. Therefore, please join me in dedicating this merit to all sentient beings with the aspiration that all beings, without any exception whatsoever, will obtain full liberation and complete buddhahood.

≈ 10 ≈

CLOUD MOUNTAINS

Challenges of Samaya and Dharma

You will live, perhaps, one hundred years. Human life is transitory and impermanent; it is completely uncertain when the moment of death will arise. The main reason for practicing diligently right now, especially with the type of mantra recitation I have explained, is that you have the opportunity to progress along the spiritual path. You have no idea when this opportunity will vanish, or when there will be another. Therefore, at every moment it is to our advantage to recognize this and to apply ourselves diligently. In daily life, the fulfillment of mundane activities, laziness, and the cloudiness of bad meditation often serve to distract us. Let us now examine each in turn.

Laziness predisposes a person to overlook the importance of carrying out a given activity, either out of naiveté or out of a lack of normal comprehension. Even if a person understands the importance of certain activities, laziness leaches away any interest in undertaking them, and so no effort is made. Laziness does not limit itself to worldly affairs but applies itself as well to spiritual affairs. One may not understand the content of spiritual practice, or one may understand it and still not really care enough to want to do anything about it. In the first case, laziness comes either from not understanding the continuity of mind from one state of rebirth to the other, or from refusing to accept or to believe this to be true. If one does not have a comprehension of the continuity of mind from one relative state of rebirth to another, then one cannot have an appreciation for how one influences what the mind experiences through what one does. Without such an understanding, one does not have the necessary motivation to practice, because such motivation is something that arises by itself if and when one understands the situation. Without an understanding of the different possibilities of higher or lower rebirth, or of the particular karmic process that leads to these states giving happiness and unhappiness, pleasure and pain, etc., then one does not have a framework in which that motivation can grow.

Motivation is found through understanding, and on the spiritual level it is through understanding that we can work most directly against laziness. The sense of being ineffectual or unable to practice can lessen because, as understanding about the limitation of sentient beings' experience (and how it can be influenced or changed through practice) increases, so does the desire to benefit others. The more one is motivated, and the more one actually goes about using the karmic process in a positive way, the better are the chances that the results of that causality will bring the benefit of progressive development on the spiritual path.

Dullness of mind during meditation inhibits progress. When a person is asleep, the alert factor dissipates as the mind sinks into a dulled state; there is no way one can meditate in that situation. Now, even though a person might be awake in the ordinary sense of the word while in meditation, there can be a lack of alertness to the meditation. The traditional vocabulary of meditation teaching gives several different levels of alertness. The first is called thinking, which indicates that the spark of awareness that is inherent to mind has become dulled. The second is termed fog and refers to the mental condition that results when the dullness begins to thicken, causing things to get thicker and duller in the process. The third translates into the idea of nearly blanking out, which means a real obscurity exists. Thus, when meditation is obscured with dullness, the practitioner can still be awake in the physiological sense of the word but the mind appears to be asleep. There is no alertness at all. Now, if any one of these three levels is the case, then, of course, real meditation is not taking place. In fact, if there is any meditation with such mental qualities present, then it is a meditation of stupidity, because such meditation only reinforces stupidity and the dullness of mind.

In real meditation, a bare state of awareness is necessary, so that the meditation has a spacious quality, a clarity and transparency to the experience. This is the experience sought. There is no need to think, "This is emptiness; this is luminous; this is transparent." Instead, it is easily recognizable; it is just there to be experienced. This is not to say that thought will not arise, because thoughts do arise in the mind. In fact, during meditation one is aware of thoughts arising, but one is aware without being distracted by the thought process. For it is not as though the thought arises, the mind becomes distracted, and, only afterwards, does one realize that a thought has arisen. Rather, as the thought arises, one is aware of its arising and remains undistracted by either the arising or the content.

In Tibet, there is a proverb that states that the best introduction to sleep is bad meditation, meaning that if one has a dull approach in meditation, it leads straight into a state that is not significantly different from sleep. In fact, this dullness is the bridge between sleep and waking. It is considered to be a twilight zone, an interim level of dull stupidity to which one goes while in bad meditation. Sleep is distinguished from waking consciousness by more than simple awareness, because being awake also implies physical activity. Likewise, waking consciousness differs from meditative consciousness in the quality of alertness present; implicit to the state of meditation is bare awareness.

It is remarkable and indeed very wonderful that there are many people having a strong aspiration to practice the Dharma, who wish to practice in order to realize the fruit of Dharma. Yet, the most common complaint is, "I do not have enough time!" This is perfectly true! You need money, so you have to go to work, which takes a good portion of your day. Additionally, more time is taken up by personal needs, for you have to eat and to sleep, you have to watch TV and go to the movies, plus you have to do a great many other things. And, because you definitely have to do these things, you do not have time to practice the Dharma. However, if you were to meditate on the preciousness of this human existence, the rarity of its being obtained, and the certainty of its being impermanent, then in contemplating and recognizing these truths, you would find you have a lot of time. Why? Because you would realize the real requirements for life in our 'Southern Continent' world (Sanskrit: Jambudvipa, in the Mt. Sumeru cosmology) can be easily and simply satisfied. On a rudimentary level, one definitely needs to eat, and one definitely needs clothing and shelter. With these three basic necessities, plus a strong desire to practice the Dharma, one can become an extremely good practitioner, *if* one takes the time.

You might well ask yourself, at some point or another, whether you are meant to abandon the world and go off into a cave and meditate. Well, it would not be a bad idea, and it certainly would not hurt, but be practical. How many of us are ready to give up everything and go off alone to practice like Milarepa did? As a teacher of Western students, I do not consider this to be a particularly sensible approach. Such strict and continual seclusion is not necessary. It is possible that one can practice while still actively involved in the world. Such a combination of spiritual practice and worldly activity allows the aspirant to use his or her faculties in a very skillful way.

Ideally, if we were embarking on something as important as discovering the nature of mind in order to attain some kind of significant experience, then obviously this is going to take some time and effort. There should be at least a month for a student and a teacher to work together in the slow process of familiarizing the student with the experience, bringing the student through an on-going process to that experience. This amount of time would be ideal, but even a week would do. We begin by developing an approach to meditation that is of total relaxation and of an uncontrived state of awareness. This is our basis for meditation. One is inculcating the appreciation of the intangible emptiness of mind, of its luminous clarity, and of its unimpeded and dynamic manifestation as awareness as being the fundamental, inherent nature of mind itself.

At this point, we can simply touch on the experience of the fundamental nature of mind itself. Remember that physical posture is important, especially when first developing meditation, because an erect posture facilitates the arising of this experience. Now, use a process of meditation to analyze the mind; try to discover something that is the mind, try to define mind as being shaped, colored, or experienced in such-and-such a way. You could look for a year, and still you would be wasting your time. Why? Because you are not going to find any of these. You are not going to find any color or shape, or any size or location, or any limitation that you can ascribe to mind at all; so stop trying.

Rather, let the mind rest in its own nature, a state of spacious awareness. By spacious, I am referring to the way that space pervades everything, solid or otherwise. We cannot say that space begins here and ends over there. Neither can it be said that mind behaves according to such limitations. Fundamentally speaking, mind is all-pervading, in that it pervades every aspect of awareness. Thus, there is an open, spacious, intangible quality inherent in the experience of the nature of mind itself. All that is necessary for the experience to arise is for the mind to be in a state of totally uncontrived relaxation. So, without any effort, without any attempt to force the mind at all, without doing anything with the mind, allow the mind to experience its own inherent, intangible emptiness.

The quality of this experience has a recognizable spaciousness in which there is no lack of illumination. In any given space, if there is no sun, no moon, no source of illumination, it is obscured space, and we cannot see anything in it. On the other hand, if there is a source of illumination — the sun, the moon, or some artificial source (like a light bulb) — the space is illuminated. Without being able to separate the two, we can say that there is space and illumination. Mind has an illuminated space in which one can see in perfect clarity. The point of this approach in meditation is to realize that not only is there a spacious, empty quality to the experience as indicative of its intangibility, but that the experience is also characterized by a luminosity. Such clarity is the perfectly unimpeded ability (or potential) of the mind to know, without there being anything obscured or not known. This clarity and transparency are thus part of the experience as well, and we have labeled this the luminosity of mind. It is something we also need to make note of in using this kind of meditative approach.

The nature of mind is characterized not only by its spacious quality, but also by its transparency and clarity. Despite the fact that there is this clear, intangible, and spacious quality, it is still possible to be in a kind of trance in which there is no thought or dynamism taking place. This I have referred to earlier as bad meditation, because it is such a dull experience. The dynamic, unimpeded manifestation of mind is missing, so nothing can arise. It is important that this dynamic manifestation be a part of the experience of mind's true nature, something additional to the spaciousness and the transparent clarity. Such alertness, or such awareness, can (and, in fact, does) manifest as conscious, conceptual thinking. When one is meditating properly, it is entirely possible to think, and the point is, that for the thought to arise at all, there must be an alert and aware quality of mind. Thus, when one is using this approach in meditation, given that there is a spacious and transparently clear quality to the experience, there is also the dynamic spark of awareness. To be aware of the thoughts that arise in the mind, be they nominally good or bad, is itself an expression of that spark. The specific nature or content of the thought is not the issue; it is the awareness which is important.

You will recall from our earlier discussions that, since beginningless time, it is the mind that has been experiencing rebirths, and it is mind that will continue to experience an infinite cycle of rebirth without end, given that the person does not attain enlightenment. Should, however, a being attain enlightenment and arrive at that direct experience of the mind, it does not mean that the mind disappears. Rather, all the obscuration and all the ignorance have been eliminated, and the full manifestation or unfolding of the incredible, inherent potential of mind is now possible. By no means should enlightenment be misunderstood as being an elimination of the mind. The mind does not evaporate, is not severed, nor does it disintegrate when enlightenment is attained. Whether enlightened or unenlightened in the experience of the practitioner, the mind endlessly continues to be empty, clear, and unimpeded. For sentient beings, it is only a case of whether this will be a continued experience of samsara, or one of nirvana.

Many times during the two past decades I have been asked to visit North America and Europe. After I had been there several times and was beginning to think that perhaps I was getting too old to be traveling around the world, and wondering about the wisdom of going again, I had occasion to speak with His Holiness the XVIth Gyalwa Karmapa. He had just returned from what proved to be his last teaching tour to the West, and naturally he spoke to me about his travels. He remarked in passing on the spread of the Buddhadharma outside of Asia, saying that each time he went abroad, he saw more and more activity spreading from the teachers of all the vajrayana orders of Tibet. He noted that associated with the Karma Kagyu tradition alone, there were then more than 325 centers worldwide. He felt that these centers required an on-going source of instruction and advice, especially since interested people would need to be able to continue their practice. As his own health was already on the decline, he told me he had encouraged many important and well-known teachers to return to the West to further the teachings they had already given.

He encouraged me to return to the West with the following words. "I want you, Kalu Rinpoche, to go back to the West. I want you to undertake this, even though you are old, because there are many centers in need of instruction and guidance. It would be extremely beneficial if you could visit as many centers as possible."

There are many activities in the West that could use assistance. Thus, when these needs were coupled with His Holiness' request, it helped me make my decision to return to the West each successive time. You might well wonder what activities require my close supervision, and in answer, one of my major concerns is the establishment of *three-year retreat* centers. Already several exist in central Europe and along the West and East Coasts of North America. Several more are planned for Hawaii, New Zealand, and South America. There also have been requests and plans to increase the number of retreat facilities in both North America and continental Europe. In most retreat centers, ten men and ten women, plus two cook-attendants and the resident teacher for the retreat, have successfully started their three-year retreat, and they are currently involved with practices that form the content of this long and intensive program.

A three-year retreat is something that is very new to the West. It might seem strange, or at least a bit overdone. But, to the many people of Asia, it is not a strange idea at all. Among the Tibetans, retreats were a well-established part of the culture, and many Tibetans chose to devote at least some part of their lives to intense retreat and practice. Eventually, the rather formal institution of the three-year, three-month, three-day retreat developed. During such a retreat, one does not leave the retreat facility, nor do other people come to visit. The practitioner is isolated for that brief period of time, in order to devote all of his or her time and energy, without distraction, to the study and practice of the Dharma. Such application is very useful and important in the successful development of vajrayana practice.

You might well wonder what is done in such an isolated retreat for such a long time. When one is following the curriculum that is established for the three-year retreat in the Karma Kagyu and the Shangpa Kagyu traditions, the retreatant begins with the foundation practices and then proceeds through various tantric ritual practices involving yidams. This culminates in practice of the advanced tantric techniques of the six yogas of Naropa, the mahamudra approach, and so forth. During this whole three-year, three-month, three-day period, there is a carefully graded program of study and practice that enables one to be exposed to the spectrum of techniques available to the practitioner of vajrayana.

During this length of time, the retreatant does his or her best to assimilate what is given in these practices, following which the practitioner is free to decide the particular course his or her life is going to take. Some people may go on and take full monastic ordination. Some go back for another retreat. Some people choose to go on to become lamas: teachers who are qualified to guide others in meditation, to give advice concerning the practice of the Dharma, and to teach the Buddhadharma. Other people go back to the life that they were leading before the retreat. It is strictly an individual decision what one does after the retreat is finished. The point is that during such a retreat, one is devoting one's life, with intense concentration, solely to the study and practice of the Buddhadharma.

The fact that these retreat centers exist at all, and that more and more are being built, reflects well upon the growth of Buddhism in the West. When I first came to Europe and North America in 1971, Buddhism was still very, very new to most Westerners. There were very few centers and little activity, but in the past fifteen years this has changed quite a bit. In Tibet, there is another saying, "Things are as different as heaven and earth." I would say that the situation of my first visit and the way I now find the West are as different as heaven and earth. I find that many people, despite the obstacles they encounter on a cultural and a material level, have developed an interest in the Buddhist teachings. The men and women who are working to establish this tradition throughout the Western world are not necessarily wealthy or influential people in society. Nevertheless, they have sufficient commitment to gather as groups, found and maintain centers, and involve themselves in trying to provide access to the teachings. Hence, the teachings are growing and spreading. In seeing these efforts, I am reminded of Milarepa and of the trials and tribulations he went through in his spiritual development, and I am encouraged that many Westerners are demonstrating a similar level of commitment.

In noting this spread of Buddhism in the West, there are some factors that can perhaps explain why it is taking place. The first of these is the influence exerted by the monotheistic traditions that has imbued Western cultures with concepts that are as fundamental to Buddhism as they are to these approaches. In both, there exists the same emphasis on having faith and confidence in a spiritual (or exalted) ideal. There is also a similar emphasis on compassion and loving kindness towards other beings. And, there is emphasis on the fundamental qualities of generosity and morality. Although the context may differ slightly, these concepts and ideas have resulted in a tradition in Europe and the Americas that reflects, at least to some degree, the same intent as the practices within Buddhadharma.

Another factor is the general level of education and intelligence in Western countries. As a whole, people in these countries tend to be far more educated and intelligent than people in less developed countries. There is more opportunity to develop intellectual potential, and this is something very important in appreciating the profundity of Buddhism. The Buddhadharma possesses a logical and internal structure that is impressive, especially when one understands all of the different aspects of this tradition. And, Tibetan Buddhism especially presents a complete and profound path of spiritual development, in all its aspects of gradations and attainment that represent the development of the *nine yanas* or vehicles.

Westerners are very well prepared, perhaps more so than people of other cultures, to be able to understand what really is being said in Buddhist teachings and what the implications are. Therefore, it is my feeling that the influence of the values of human kindness characteristic of many monotheisist traditions, plus the general intelligence and education of Westerners, which will play really key roles in allowing the teachings to make this current transition.

During my travels in Asia, I have noticed that, in countries where Buddhism has been part of the culture for centuries, there is a sympathetic and wide-spread popular response to the Dharma. When a teacher there gives a teaching, sometimes thousands of people show up. When a teacher gives the vows of refuge, hundreds of people take refuge. There is an incredible show of popular faith and devotion to the teachings of Buddhism. There is, as well, a strong tradition of patronage by wealthy and influential individuals. Usually Asian centers are either sponsored by such wealthy patrons or come under their care, and thus the general spiritual community has very little trouble meeting the center's expenses. In the West, the centers have managed to gather necessary funds a bit differently, and although the Western centers do not maintain themselves in a manner similar to their Asian counterparts, they do function, they do offer activities, and they are growing in membership.

As I have already explained, the basis of practice is, first, the abandoning of non-virtuous actions and the practicing of virtuous actions, upon which, secondarily, rests the practice of developing compassion and recognizing emptiness, and, third, one has the swift and powerful practice of the two phases of arising and consummation yogas of the vajrayana practice. With the teachings I have given you upon these three points, you have the essence of the Buddhadharma. To further your understanding of these points, you have available centers where there is usually a lama in residence who can add to your knowledge concerning various aspects of these three paths.

No matter what your level of knowledge or insightful understanding, it is important to study continually so as to enhance your practice. A serious student will take classes and study at a university or college until he or she finally receives a degree. The student then applies this knowledge in his or her work. In just the same way, in finding out about the basic principles of the Buddhadharma practice, you can increase your understanding by referring to the lama's teachings and, in this manner, you will develop your understanding until you have realized enough to be able to practice very easily, in a perfect manner.

The Tibetans refer to the teachings of Buddhadharma as the inner teachings, because these teachings relate to the inner level of experience, focusing most expressly and clearly there. This is not to suggest that the other outer level of experience is ignored; rather, these teachings concentrate on the understanding of mind, on working with mind.

When the inner teachings were absorbed from India into the Tibetan culture not so many centuries ago, a number of different traditions developed. Through the activities of several kings, translators, and teachers, many generations passed before the whole tradition of Buddhadharma could be successfully transplanted to a new culture in a new land, Tibet. Although all of the traditions that arose from the successive generations of absorbtion have authentic roots from the Lord Buddha himself, they differ slightly in approach and they are known by different names, e.g., Nyingmapa, Kagyupa, and so forth. The orders developed due to the particular circumstances in which the teachings were brought to Tibet. The names of the teachers who introduced them (or the names of the particular places in which they were introduced) produced superficial differences leading to identity labels, but the fundamental approach among all the major orders remains the same. The sutras and tantras, the exoteric and esoteric teachings of Buddhism, are revered and taught by all of these orders.

In the West, a similar process has begun; and, in the beginning, it may appear confusing. It might be difficult for you to figure out where to begin, what to study, and so forth. Even more so, it might be very difficult to know what to do when, or even what to do at all, given the immensity and variety of approaches. It is my feeling that to take the best advantage of one's current and impermanent precious human existence, one must develop faith in the tsaway lama. One must have faith by recognizing that the Three Jewels are part and parcel of the tsaway lama: the tsaway lama's body is the Sangha, his or her speech is the Dharma, and his or her mind is the Buddha. Further, to recognize the Three Roots of vajrayana, one develops the view that the tsaway lama's body is the essential Buddha Vairocana, his or her speech is that of the Dakinis and Dharmapalas, and his or her mind is the Yidam. Thinking in this way, one has faith in the tsaway lama as being the combined essence of the Three Jewels and the Three Roots.

An electric wire, however long, carries current from the generator to the light fixture, thereby allowing it to provide light. If the wire is broken or cut any place, the light will be immediately extinguished, as obviously the power from the generator cannot be transmitted along a broken wire. In the same way, the power or the current of flow of spiritual realization comes through enlightened masters in a completely unbroken way, and it is able at any moment to demonstrate its full power, or its complete enlightenment.

Tsaway lama is a vajrayana idea. In the hinayana and mahayana, one relies upon the preceptor and the spiritual friend, respectively, and in these two traditions, the preceptor and the spiritual friend bring wonderful benefit as they perform a very great service for those practicing these paths. In the vajrayana, this role is fulfilled by the tsaway lama and the lineage lamas. And, what exactly is the benefit of having a tsaway lama? This is similar to putting a piece of paper in the sunlight; even though the sun is very hot, it cannot set the paper on fire. But, putting a magnifying glass in the sun's beams creates a hot spot on the paper, causing the paper to catch fire and burn within only a few moments. By connecting one with the power of the lineage, the tsaway lama, like a magnifying glass, concentrates the spiritual energy of the lineage right into the student — right then, right there, at that very moment. It is the tsaway lama who transmits the spiritual energy of the lineage and gives the blessings, initiations, teachings, and so on. Lineage refers to the lineages of blessing, the lineages of initiation, the lineages of instruction, the lineages of literary authority, and the lineages of experience of realization, and so on. If all the lamas of a lineage stem from Buddha Vajradhara, and the lineage is completely intact, then you may receive those blessings, initiations, and experiences directly through the lineage as though you were personally receiving these directly from Buddha Vajradhara himself!

The tsaway lama is that being who connects the aspirant to all these necessary lineages of transmitted knowledge, awareness, and clarity. For instance, the Karma Kagyu lineage stems from the Dharmakaya Dorje Chang (Sanskrit: Vajradhara), and the teaching of the mahamudra transmission came directly from Dorje Chang to Lodrö Rinchen, then to Saraha, then to Nagarjuna, Shawari, Maitripa, Tilopa, and Naropa. These were the lineage founders whose lives were spent in India. Then, in the eleventh century A.D., the lineage came to Tibet, due to the efforts of Marpa, the translator, who was a student of Naropa. From there, the lineage was transferred from Marpa to Milarepa, then to Gampopa, from whom it was transmitted as follows:

The founding fathers of the Kagyu lineage, in order of transmission of the lineage:
top center, *Saraha, student of Lodrö Rinchen;* top right *Nagarjuna* and top left,
Shawari, both students of Saraha; middle center, *Maitripa;* middle left, *Tilopa;*
middle right, *Naropa;* bottom center, *Marpa Lotsawa;* bottom left, *Milarepa;*
and bottom right, *Gampopa* (Woodblock prints from Tibet, early 20th century)

Dusum Khyenpa	*The First Gyalwa Karmapa*
Drogon Rechen	*Disciple of Dusum Khyenpa*
	(Became Tai Situpa Rinpoche
	by title given by Yung Lo)
Pomdrakpa	*Disciple of Drogon Rechen*
Karma Pakshi	*The Second Gyalwa Karmapa*
Urgyenpa	*Disciple of Karma Pakshi*
Rangjung Dorje	*The IIIrd Gyalwa Karmapa*
Yung Tonpa	*Disciple of Rangjung Dorje*
Rolpay Dorje	*The IVth Gyalwa Karmapa*
Kachö Wangpo	*The Second Sharmarpa Rinpoche*
Dezhin Shekpa	*The Vth Gyalwa Karmapa*
Ratnabhadra	*Disciple of Dezhin Shekpa*
Tongwa Dönden	*The VIth Gyalwa Karmapa*
Jampal Zangpo	*Disciple of Tongwa Dönden*
Paljor Döndrup	*The First Gyaltshap Rinpoche,*
	(Main Disciple of Jampal Zangpo)
Chödrak Gyatso	*The VIIth Gyalwa Karmapa*
Tashi Paljor	*The First Sangye Nyimpa Rinpoche*
Mikyo Dorje	*The VIIIth Gyalwa Karmapa*
Konchok Yenlak	*The Vth Sharmarpa Rinpoche*
Wangchuk Dorje	*The IXth Gyalwa Karmapa*
Chökyi Wangchuk	*The VIth Sharmarpa Rinpoche*
Chöying Dorje	*The Xth Gyalwa Karmapa*
Yeshe Nyingpo	*The VIIth Sharmarpa Rinpoche*
Yeshe Dorje	*The XIth Gyalwa Karmapa*
Chökyi Döndrup	*The VIIIth Sharmarpa Rinpoche*
Jangchup Dorje	*The XIIth Gyalwa Karmapa*
Chökyi Jungnay	*The VIIIth Tai Situpa Rinpoche*
Dudul Dorje	*The XIIIth Gyalwa Karmapa*
Chödrup Gyamtso	*The Xth Sharmarpa Rinpoche*
Pema Nyingche	*The IXth Tai Situpa Rinpoche*
Thekchok Dorje	*The XIVth Gyalwa Karmapa*
Lodrö Taye	*The First Jamgon Kongtrul Rinpoche*
Khachab Dorje	*The XVth Gyalwa Karmapa*
Pema Wangchuk	*The XIth Tai Situpa Rinpoche*
Khyentse Özer	*The Second Jamgon Kongtrul Rinpoche*
Rigpay Dorje	*The XVIth Gyalwa Karmapa*
Norbu Döndrup	*The Disciple of Rigpay Dorje*

This comprises the whole of the Karma Kagyu mahamudra lineage to date. It is said that by merely hearing the names of these great enlightened masters, a great blessing is given in that defilements and obscurations of one's being are purified. This lineage is but one example of the varying lines of transmission that weave into Tibetan Buddhist traditions. Each order has its own progression of transmission; additionally, of all the varying aspects of sutra and tantra commentary and the vast complexity of vajrayana initiations, each has its own unique path of transmission.

The tsaway lama should have certain qualities, the first among them being an unbroken lineage. Secondly, he or she must know the meaning of the Dharma. Finally, he or she must have great compassion for sentient beings. These are the main basic qualities of the tsaway lama. The student must also have qualities: there must be unwavering faith and devotion for the tsaway lama. With the steadfast devotion of the student, and the advice of a qualified tsaway lama, the practitioner can experience the arising of great siddhis or accomplishments.

If, however, the practitioner doubts the tsaway lama and only sometimes joins hands together in reverence to the lama, and later the same practitioner speaks disparagingly about the same lama, this actually defiles that relationship, making the task of obtaining buddhahood difficult for that student. Disparaging the tsaway lama is very serious in that it damages the *samaya* or bonds of commitment with the tsaway lama and also makes the practice of visualization difficult; it causes pure vajra pride to be unstable. You will remember that the authorization to practice in this vajrayana manner was originally given by the tsaway lama during the initiatory process. Disparaging one's tsaway lama is comparable to living on extensive credit without having the means to satisfy the obligations. If, however, a student maintains respect and devotion to the tsaway lama, the bond of samaya remains strong, making it is easier to stabilize vajra pride. The result of having a stable vajra pride is that it enables one to see oneself clearly as the deity, allowing for quick advancement along the path to full enlightenment.

Additionally, comprehension of the symbolism inherent in the form assumed by the deity occurs spontaneously and with apparent clarity, rather than being contrived through intellectual fostering. For example, consider the symbolism inherent in the items that the Yidam Chenrezig holds: a white lotus and a crystal mala held aloft, and a wish-fulfilling gem cupped to his chest in prayerful hands. His holding of the white lotus flower is the symbol of the absolute purity indicative of the deity's freedom from any impurity, and his ability to completely purify any sentient being. The crystal mala that he is turning is demonstrating (or symbolic of) his compassion acting as the hook that draws sentient beings out of the ocean of samsara. The wish-fulfilling jewel that Chenrezig holds is symbolic of his being able to fulfill the wishes of all sentient beings, and of his giving total fulfillment to whatever wishes sentient beings might have. His hands being joined in prayer are symbolic of his constant supplication to the buddhas and bodhisattvas to rain down benefits to help sentient beings along their path. When your samaya is pure, your vajra pride stabilized, and your visualization complete to the last detail, and if your consciousness of the symbolic meaning and your recitation of the yidam's mantra are done with the awareness of the emptiness of all phenomena, the nature of mind will become absolutely apparent! And, in this recognition of mind's true nature, you will quickly and easily become enlightened through the path of perfection of vajrayana.

As you can see from this lengthy discourse, when one involves oneself in the practice of Tibetan Buddhism, the student encounters all of the techniques and methods that are used as part of this approach. One will find many references to certain qualities that are to be developed as part of the practice. These include faith and confidence in the Three Jewels and in the spiritual teachers and gurus, the development of compassion and loving kindness towards all beings, and spiritual exercises such as prostrations, circumambulation, various prayers and mantras, and meditative techniques. All of these have a single common function — to slowly eliminate or cleanse the levels of confusion in the mind and thus permit the direct perception of the nature of mind to take place.

In the beginning, when one is first entering into the practice, there is a level of exerting oneself using physical, verbal, and mental capabilities. Using these to develop the virtuous and meritorious tendencies in oneself is a cumulative process. At the beginning of the five paths, termed the *path of accumulation,* the process first brings together all of the things in the student's practice that reinforce positive qualities, merit, and deepening awareness. Eventually, at a certain point, this sort of activity becomes a spontaneous and natural part of the aspirant's nature. Even in cases where efforts still must be made, aspirants are able to bring a great deal of patience and forbearance to the practice.

When the practice begins to take over and to carry itself along without much effort, one has reached a second stage, known as the *path of application.* When this purificatory process of cleansing the veils of confusion comes to the point where the student has a direct glimpse of the nature of mind, this first stable on-going experience is termed the *path of vision.* In illustration of this term, when we perceive the first sliver of the new moon, we recognize that the moon is fully there but that only a faint trace of it is being perceived. In the same way, on this path of vision, the student has had a direct experience of the nature of mind that does not vanish but remains a stable part of one's experience. However, this first direct perception has not yet grown to the fullest extent, and just as the moon will continue to grow, this experience will continue to grow. It is simply not possible to forget that experience, nor to slide back into a lower stage of development. Once one has had that significant direct experience of the nature of mind, one is at a level that is termed irreversible. At that point, the aspirant cannot lose the experience, forget it, or somehow end up as a confused, unenlightened being again, even though this realization is not yet the full experience of enlightenment.

The stage of irreversibility is recognized as the first level of an accomplished bodhisattva realization; there are ten of these levels (or bhumis) of incomplete but also irrefutable enlightenment. With this partial yet extremely important development, an accomplished bodhisattva continues toward the complete attainment of enlightenment, developing through the various bhumis, just as the moon continues to grow throughout the first phases of the lunar month. The ultimate result of that kind of process is the actual elimination of all ignorance, confusion, faults, and obscurations of the mind, so that the inherent potential of mind can express itself completely, without any hindrance or limitation. This is enlightenment; this is buddhahood! The common comparison made to the full state of enlightened liberation is of the full moon. Realization of the potential as an enlightened being has expanded to its fullest extent, so that an accomplished bodhisattva is now fully enlightened, a buddha liberated from samsaric suffering.

With the experience of complete enlightenment, there is no limitation, no hindering factors, no obscurations, just the direct experience of the full manifestation of the inherent potential of mind. Now, what this implies is that there is a state of omniscience (or of total awareness) because, as mind is essentially empty, there is no thing that can be described in any tangible or limited way. Because there is no limit to the mind, there is an all-pervading quality in the mind that includes every aspect of experience: samsaric and nirvanic, unenlightened and enlightened. The inherent, natural luminosity of mind, which is its ability to experience, becomes full blown at the level of buddhahood in that there is no limit to the experience of a fully enlightened being. This luminosity, combined with the mind's all-pervasiveness, means that enlightenment is a state of omniscience that is not limited by time, space, or distance. Past, present, and future pose no barriers to that kind of awareness. Additionally, there is the dynamic and unimpeded awareness that is also the manifestation of mind. It is this quality that gives rise to the compassion and loving kindness that is inherent in this enlightened experience and that gives the ability for a buddha to effectively demonstrate the *four activities of buddhahood.*

Right now, when we think of loving kindness or compassion, we think in a very dualistic way. If we see another being suffering, we think, "Oh, what a pity, what a shame; I should really try to help." That is not the compassion of buddhahood, which is a completely non-referential compassion, having nothing to do with any particular sentient being feeling any certain way, or with one's sympathetic or empathetic response to that being. There is absolutely no need for a completely liberated enlightened being to even think about being compassionate; he or she just comes from that state. When the sun is shining in the sky, it simply shines. It does not think, "OK, I am going to send light down there because it needs some light." No, the sun just shines and the light radiates in all directions. In the same way, direct experience of the nature of mind implies compassion simply radiating in all directions, without any necessary framework of reference. Thus, all of these qualities of buddhahood — the all-pervading luminous or clear omniscience, the compassion, the effective manifestation of the four activities — all arise from the fact that the potential of pure alaya is naturally inherent in the mind and is simply expressing itself freely, without any limitations of impure alaya.

It is my prayer that all of you who have read this will apply yourselves wholeheartedly in that one direction, and that you may all easily and with great certainty attain this liberation. I thank you, and bid you a safe journey! And, I ask you to remember that all beings, as numberless and as vast as space, are our mothers; I urge you to dedicate the merit from reading this discourse towards their enlightenment.

Old formal portrait of right *His Holiness the XVIth Karmapa and* left *theVery Venerable Kalu Rinpoche, flanking His HolinessDilgo Khyentse* (Photographer unknown, courtesy of J.G. Sherab Ebin)

Kalu Rinpoche seated before a shrine in Bhutan, taken shortly after his arrival from Tibet in 1956 (Photographer unknown, courtesy of J.G. Sherab Ebin)

Kalu Rinpoche in Tibet in the early 1940s (Photographer unknown, courtesy of J.G. Sherab Ebin)

During a visit to Rumtek Monastery in the late 1960s, center *Kalu Rinpoche,* right *Lama Gyaltsen, and Rinpoche's translator* left *Sherab Ebin pause to talk on the monastery's upper balcony, while* upper left *unidentified monk observes them.* (Photograph by J.G. Sherab Ebin)

During the visit by Kalu Rinpoche, Lama Gyaltsen, and Sherab Ebin to Rumtek in the late 1960s, the XVIth Gyalwa Karmapa held an informal audience with their party. (Photograph by J.G. Sherab Ebin)

Kalu Rinpoche and Lama Gyaltsen, with unidentified monk, standing on the upper balcony overlooking the Rumtek Monastery courtyard (Photograph by J.G. Sherab Ebin)

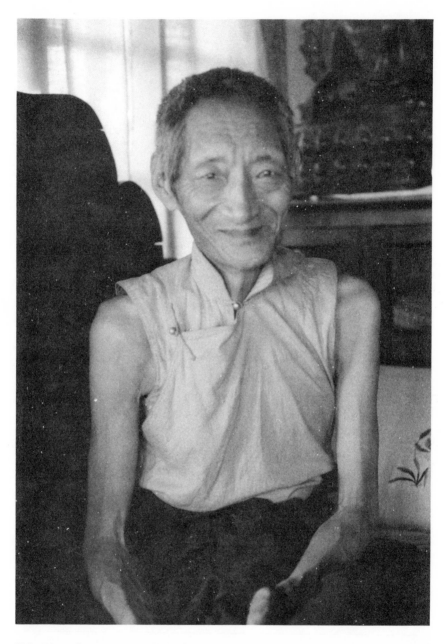

Kalu Rinpoche pauses to smile for the camera in his audience room at the monastery at Sonada, India. (Photograph by J.G. Sherab Ebin)

Appendix A

Open Letters to Disciples and Friends of The Lord of Refuge, Khyab Je Kalu Rinpoche

From Bokar Tulku Rinpoche, Lama Gyaltsen, and Khenpo Lodrö Dönyo, 15 May 1989

Concerning the last moments of Kalu Rinpoche and the religious activities following

From His Eminence the XIIth Tai Situpa

Concerning the passing of Kalu Rinpoche

Khyungpo Naljor, founder of the Shangpa Kagyu lineage, and, floating above him, are two of his main tsaway lamas: the yoginis left, Niguma *and* right, Sukhasiddi. (Pen and ink drawing, courtesy of Gega Lama of Darjeeling, 20th century)

Open Letter to Disciples and Friends of
The Lord of Refuge, Khyab Je Kalu Rinpoche

What follows is an open letter addressed to all disciples of the lord of refuge, Khyab Je Kalu Rinpoche, from Bokar Tulku Rinpoche (Kalu Rinpoche's principal disciple and Dharma heir), Lama Gyaltsen (Kalu Rinpoche's nephew and lifelong personal attendant), and Khenpo Lodrö Dönyo, the abbot of Sonada Monastery. Written by Bokar Tulku Rinpoche, the letter expresses their shared experience.

Sonada Monastery
15 May 1989

At 3:00 P.M., Wednesday, the 10th of May 1989, our precious lama, Khyab Je Kalu Rinpoche, passed from this world into the pure realms. In the interest of bringing Rinpoche's presence closer to each of his disciples at this time of our shared loss and grief, we would like to present an account of the events of the last few months, as well as the events that will now unfold in the next several weeks.

In late November, Rinpoche traveled with the lamas and monks of his monastery, as well as with the members of his translation committee, a total of about a hundred persons, to Beru Khyentse Rinpoche's monastery in Bodh-Gaya. Rinpoche made it clear that he wanted everyone to travel together with him, and so the monastery sangha joined Rinpoche to drive in a caravan (of two busses and two cars) from Sonada to Bodh-Gaya. Having established the activities of the lamas, monks, and the translators, Rinpoche traveled to Los Angeles for a visit of a few weeks, during which he gave a number of empowerments and teachings. While there, Rinpoche was invited to stay in America to build up his strength, but he was determined to return to India to support the translation committee's work, a work that has been his principal concern for the past two years.

Upon returning to India, Rinpoche visited Bodh-Gaya briefly, encouraging his monks and translators in their activities and meeting with Dilgo Khyentse Rinpoche, who was completing a drupchen at the Kagyu Monastery. Then Kalu Rinpoche traveled to Sherab Ling, the monastery of Tai Situ Rinpoche. Kalu Rinpoche had been invited on many occasions to visit Sherab Ling and had been unable to go there previously. He felt this journey would allow him to both participate in the Losar (Tibetan New Year) festivities with Tai Situ Rinpoche at Sherab Ling, and also to visit His Holiness the Dalai Lama, who was in residence in Dharamsala at that time. He stayed about one week at Sherab Ling.

In fact, while there Rinpoche was able to visit His Holiness the Dalai Lama in Dharamsala. They had a long visit, took a meal together, and discussed a number of subjects. His Holiness expressed his pleasure with Rinpoche's activities, promised to do whatever he could to further the work of Rinpoche's translation project, and showed his concern for Rinpoche's health by having his own personal physician give Rinpoche a check-up. His Holiness commented that, of all the lamas working to spread the Dharma throughout the world, there was *no one* whose activity and kindness was greater than those of Rinpoche.

Rinpoche returned to Bodh-Gaya and stayed there another two weeks before moving all his lamas, monks, and translators back to the Darjeeling District on the 22nd of February. Since Rinpoche had embarked on the construction of a major stupa in Saluguri (near Siliguri), he remained there for a period of three weeks with all of his monastery sangha. During this time, the lamas and monks worked on painting relief sculpture adorning the enclosing wall, and on the making of one hundred thousand *tsatsa* for the stupa's eventual consecration. Also, the translators continued their work on the translation of Jamgon Kongtrul Lodrö Thaye's *Treasury of Knowledge*. Throughout this time, Rinpoche spent several hours each day at the stupa site personally supervising the various projects, and his health remained good, his activity undiminished.

On the 21st of March, Rinpoche moved his monastery sangha back up to Sonada. Over the next several weeks Rinpoche seemed to become weaker, although medical opinion was that he had no specific illness. Lama Gyaltsen, myself, and others in Rinpoche's entourage encouraged Rinpoche to travel to Singapore or France in order to take advantage of the better conditions there, but Rinpoche steadfastly refused to travel at that time. It was difficult for Rinpoche to eat, and the weakening of his body continued. On the 15th of April, Dr. Wangdi of Darjeeling insisted that Rinpoche enter a hospital in Siliguri. Rinpoche was visited in the hospital by many Rinpoches, including Chadral Rinpoche (a great Nyingma lama and a close friend), Jamgon Kongtrul Rinpoche, Gyaltshab Rinpoche, and others. Rinpoche's health improved slightly while he was in the hospital, but he continued to refuse suggestions that he seek medical help elsewhere. After two weeks, Rinpoche was determined to return to his monastery in Sonada. The doctor there felt strongly that Rinpoche should remain in the hospital another three weeks. Finally, at the encouragement of myself and Khenpo Dönyo, he agreed to remain one more week before returning to Sonada.

Rinpoche arrived home late afternoon on Friday the 5th of May. As he was carried up to his house, seated in a sedan-chair that was carried on the shoulders of several of his lamas, he was smiling and waving to different individuals, and it was obvious that he was happy to be home. There, Rinpoche remained in strict retreat, except for a short period during the morning following his arrival, when he received the traditional welcoming scarves from all the members of the monastery. He remained alert and engaged throughout, occasionally addressing individuals, and showing concern for their well-being.

During these few days, Rinpoche was in good spirits and his health seemed stable. Lama Gyaltsen always found that when asking after Rinpoche's health, Rinpoche would respond that he was well. Even when there would seem to be some external sign of physical difficulty, Rinpoche would apparently be feeling no suffering. So it was during those days. When asked how he was, Rinpoche responded:

Daytime is the cultivation of the experience of illusion.
Nighttime is the cultivation of the experience of dream.

Lama Gyaltsen and I both felt that this was a statement of Rinpoche's own state of mind at that time.

On one occasion, Rinpoche expressed the sentiment to me that, having lived eighty-five years, he felt his life had been full and complete. While an ordinary person is never satisfied with his or her life, or craves to live on indefinitely, Rinpoche had no regrets. However, the one concern he did express was the fact that the translation of Jamgon Lodrö Thaye's *Treasury of Knowledge* had not been completed and that perhaps his efforts to establish the translation committee had begun too late. Khenpo Dönyo and I assured him that the committee was well established and the work was well underway. We both promised to see the project through to completion; even if Rinpoche were not able to see its realization, the work would be finished and would bear Rinpoche's name.

At 2:00 A.M. on the 10th of May, Rinpoche's condition deteriorated dramatically. (Only later did we discover he had suffered a heart attack; the doctor in Siliguri had said that Rinpoche's lungs were then working at 40% capacity, which, no doubt, had placed an additional strain on his heart.) Khenpo Dönyo was sent immediately to Siliguri (three hours away) to call the doctor from the hospital to come to the monastery. Another car was sent to Darjeeling to call Dr. Wangdi. Also called to come were Chadral Rinpoche (from his nearby monastery) and Jamgon Kongtrul Rinpoche (from Rumtek). Chadral Rinpoche and the doctor from Darjeeling were able to arrive quickly. Rinpoche was encouraged to return to the hospital in Siliguri, but he refused. He indicated that the doctors could be called, but that he was not leaving the monastery. Later in the morning, after all of us had insisted that he return to the hospital, Rinpoche finally said we could do what we liked. All was prepared for the move and the luggage was in the cars when Rinpoche indicated he wanted to rest a few moments in his inner room. As he moved into the inner room he still had full mastery of his body.

In the inner room he was put on oxygen and given glucose intravenously. His bed was pulled out from the wall, and to Rinpoche's right were Lama Gyaltsen and Khenpo Dönyo; to

Rinpoche's left were myself and Chadral Rinpoche. At one point Rinpoche asked to sit upright. The doctor and nurse forbade him to do so. A short time later he again indicated he wanted to sit up, and again the doctor and nurse adamantly refused to allow this, no doubt fearing the action might worsen his condition. Lama Gyaltsen felt terrible, but powerless to contradict the doctor.

Then Rinpoche himself tried to sit up and had difficulty in doing this. Lama Gyaltsen, feeling that perhaps this was the time for Rinpoche to sit for the beginning of the lama's final meditation and that for Rinpoche not to sit up at that moment could create an obstacle for this, supported Rinpoche's back as he sat up. Rinpoche extended his hand to me, and I also helped him aright himself. Rinpoche indicated that he wanted to sit absolutely straight, both by saying this and by gesturing with his hand. The doctor and nurse were upset by this, and so Rinpoche relaxed his posture slightly. Nevertheless, he assumed the meditation posture.

Tears were flowing down our faces uncontrollably and our hearts were filled with anguish. Rinpoche placed his hands in the meditational posture, his open eyes gazed outward in the meditational gaze, and his lips moved softly. A profound feeling of peace and happiness settled on us all and spread through our minds. All of us present felt that the indescribable happiness that was filling us was the faintest reflection of what was pervading Rinpoche's mind. Lama Gyaltsen also felt a passing experience of the profound sorrow characteristic of the compassionate awareness of the suffering pervading the cyclic existence of samsara. It was also felt to be a gift of Rinpoche's awareness.

Slowly Rinpoche's gaze lowered, his eyelids closed, and his breath stopped.

I have been witness to a number of people passing from this world. On such occasions their dying is accompanied with a short rasping of breath, a long exhalation, or a long inhalation. With Rinpoche, there was none of these. Rather, his was a most extraordinary passing into profound meditation.

The doctor and nurse wanted to try some extraordinary means to revive the breath, but Chadral Rinpoche indicated that Rinpoche should be left alone, resting peacefully as he was. Then the doctor performed his examination.

Chadral Rinpoche and I arranged his clothing and left Rinpoche in his *tuk-dam,* the lama's final meditation. The environment had to be kept quiet, and Rinpoche was to be left undisturbed so long as the tuk-dam lasted. An hour or two later, Jamgon Kongtrul Rinpoche arrived and spent a short time with Rinpoche. Later in the evening, Sharmar Rinpoche arrived and also sat with Rinpoche. Both remarked how vital Rinpoche's form was, as though at any moment he might begin to speak.

The morning of the third day, Saturday, the 13th of May, all the signs which indicate that the tuk-dam is completed had appeared. As we washed Rinpoche's body and changed his clothes, there were none of the usual traces of body waste or impurity. Also, the body had remained soft and flexible, without any stiffness whatsoever. Rinpoche's body, now called *ku-dung,* was then placed in a prepared case which was covered in brocade, and this now resides in Rinpoche's audience room.

In consultation with Jamgon Kongtrul Rinpoche and Chadral Rinpoche, the decision has been made to prepare the ku-dung as a *mar-dung,* rather than cremate it, thus assuring that it will always be with us. This is a practice that was a tradition in Tibet. In this way, the physical aspect of the lama's form remains as a relic, a basis for religious inspiration. The lama's activity thus continues, because, as visitors come in contact with the mar-dung through seeing, hearing, contemplating, touching, and/or praising the relic, they increase their opportunity for liberation. It is said that any connection whatsoever becomes beneficial, whether the mind of the being who has formed any degree of contact with the mar-dung is positively inclined or not. In this way, the mar-dung becomes the basis for both the spreading and longevity of the doctrine and, thereby, it becomes a basis for both temporal and ultimate benefit of beings.

For a period of forty-nine days, disciples and students of Rinpoche will express their devotion and gratitude through the performance of a continually ongoing series of ceremonies. In the presence of the ku-dung (which still remains in Rinpoche's audience room), the schedule will be as follows: during the first week,

Jamgon Kongtrul Rinpoche and Chadral Rinpoche will preside over the Shangpa offering to the lama; during the second week, Tai Situ Rinpoche will preside over the five tantric deities practice; during the third, Gyaltshab Rinpoche will preside over Hevajra practice; during the fourth, Sharmar Rinpoche will preside over Gyalwa Gamtso practice; during the fifth, Beru Khyentse Rinpoche will preside over Vajra Yogini practice; during the sixth, Nyengpa Rinpoche, Ponlop Rinpoche, Garwang Rinpoche, Drugram Gyaltrul Rinpoche, and Derya Druppon Rinpoche will preside over Cakrasamvara practice; and, during the final week, all the regents and rinpoches will preside over Kalacakra practice. The final culmination of this period of offerings and ceremonies will occur on the 28th of June, 1989.

In addition to these ceremonies, the higher retreat center will perform the five tantric deities during the third week, the Shangpa Cakrasamvara during the fourth, and Vajrasattva during the seventh. The lower retreat center will perform Shangpa Cakrasamvara during the third week; Vajrasattva during the fourth; and the five tantric deities during the seventh. The retreat centers are also performing the Shangpa ceremony of aspiration prayers every evening.

The monks of the monastery will be performing the Shangpa ceremony of aspiration prayers in the main temple, accomplishing ten bhumi repetitions of Samantabhadra's prayer of noble conduct during these forty-nine days. This prayer was considered very important by Rinpoche. At one point in his life, Rinpoche had sponsored ten bhumi repetitions of the prayer in Lhasa. Also, beginning the 4th of June, the annual group recitation of a thousand bhumi mantras of Chenrezig, the Mani Dung Drup, will take place in the lower temple.

As well, on the Wednesday concluding each of the seven weeks, ceremonies of offering to Rinpoche will be performed in the major monasteries of the different schools. On Wednesday, the 17th of May, the Rumtek Monastery will perform the Kagyu Gurtso. Namgyal Tratsang, the Dalai Lama's college in Dharamsala, will perform an offering to the lama on the 24th of May. Sakya Trizin's monastery will perform an offering ceremony on the 31st of May. A ceremony will be performed at Sherab Ling, the monastery of

Tai Situ Rinpoche, on the 7th of June. A ceremony will be performed on the 14th of June at the monastery of Dilgo Khyentse Rinpoche. On the 21st of June, all the Kagyu monasteries in Kathmandu (those of Chökyi Nyima Rinpoche, Pawo Rinpoche, Daptsang Rinpoche, Trangu Rinpoche, Tenga Rinpoche, and the Swayambunath Monastery) will perform offering ceremonies. Wednesday, the 28th of June, will be the culmination of this period of offerings and the many practices when the Kagyu regents and many other rinpoches will be in attendance here in Sonada at Kalu Rinpoche's own monastery.

During this time, disciples of Rinpoche are welcome to come and pay their respects to the ku-dung. Each day there will be two periods — 8:00 to 9:00 A.M., and 2:00 to 3:00 P.M. — during which one can visit and make aspiration prayers before the ku-dung. This is a particularly auspicious time to do so. If, however, you are not able to travel to Sonada at this time, the ku-dung will remain here as a mar-dung, and it will be possible to pay your respects at a later time.

The departure of Khyab Je Kalu Rinpoche from this world is a moment of extraordinary sadness for all sentient beings. The world has become a darker and a poorer place in his absence. The gentleness of his being, the pervasiveness of his kindness, the brilliance of his wisdom, and the irresistiblity of his sense of humour has touched hearts in every part of the world. The subtlety of his insight and his total mastery of mind and phenomena is beyond the grasp of our ordinary understanding. It is difficult to fathom our extraordinary good fortune to have met and established a Dharma connection with such an enlightened being. Yet, there is no avoiding a feeling of a profound personal sorrow at our loss.

Through Rinpoche's teaching and our understanding of the Dharma, however, we know that all composite phenomena are impermanent and that where we truly meet our lama is in the ultimate openness of mind. The lama has never been separate from us and never will be separate from us. *What remains for us to do is to be true to Rinpoche's vision, his example, his teachings, and his advice.* This we can do through shedding our sorrow and celebrating the gifts of immeasurable kindness he has given us, through maintaining the purity of our commitments and our vajra (samaya) bonds, and through cultivating the qualities of enlightened being that Rinpoche so clearly demonstrated to us. And, we should do all this with the deepest prayers to Rinpoche that he quickly take human form and return again to be with us.

With sincere best wishes to you all,

Bokar Tulku Rinpoche
Gyaltsen Lama
Khenpo Lodrö Dönyo

Situ Padma Wangchuk, the XIth Tai Situpa Rinpoche, who installed Kalu Rinpoche both as the retreat leader at Kunzang Dechen Ösal Ling (founded by Jamgon Kongtrul the Great) and that at the Palpung monastery retreat center, positions Kalu Rinpoche held for many years before traveling in 1956 to Jang Chub Ling monastery in eastern Bhutan. (Photographer unknown, courtesy of J.G. Sherab Ebin)

The Twelfth Tai Situpa

To all followers of the incomparable Shakyamuni, the ordained and the laity, who bear the magnificent qualities of faith and diligence, I address these words:

At this time, the sublime Lord of Refuge, Khyab Je Kalu Rinpoche, supreme upholder of both the Buddha's doctrine as a whole, and of specific transmissions, has accomplished a great wave of activity meaningful to beings throughout both the eastern and western hemispheres of this world. As the magnificent protector of the teachings of all traditions and of beings, he has brought his enlightened activity to fulfillment.

On the fifth day of the third month of the female earth snake year of the seventeenth sixty-year cycle of the Tibetan calendar, at his principal seat of Sonada, his mind entered the expanse of totality amid a display of many wondrous signs.

In consideration of all those connected to this supreme being, and as an enhancement to his fulfilled vision, there will now be a gathering to recite the mantra of six syllables -- the mantra that is the very essence of Chenrezi -- 100,000,000 times. There is no doubt that this will be a great wave of virtue, beneficial both in this life and the future, for anyone who forms a connection to this practice. This opportunity should not be wasted. Participation in this gathering in any way possible is extremely important.

With my prayers to the Three Jewels, and with my completely pure aspiration, I, Tai Situpa, strongly encourage you to engage in this virtue.

Wearing the formal hat characteristic of the lineage of Gampopa, Kalu Rinpoche is seen here in the late 1960s seated in the original temple located on his land in Sonada, India. (Photograph by J.G. Sherab Ebin)

Appendix B

Chenrezig Sadhana

Prayers and Practice of Yidam Chenrezig

With Commentary adapted from Kalu Rinpoche's teachings

&

A Vajra Melody Imploring the Swift Return
of the Lord of Refuge, Khyab Je Kalu Rinpoche

As translated from the illustrated letter
of H.E. Jamgon Kongtrul Rinpoche

Tang Tong Gyalpo, a Tibetan yogi, one of the lineage holders of the Shangpa lineage.
(Woodblock print from Nepal, 20th century)

Prayers and Practice of Yidam Chenrezig

On the following pages are the sadhana of Chenrezig together with a commentary on the stage by stage meaning of the prayers and explanations concerning the visualizations.

The commentary was derived from a lecture given by the Very Venerable Kalu Rinpoche in Vancouver, British Columbia, Canada, during his second visit to North America in 1974. The teaching has been condensed to allow usage of the important directions for meditation in a pertinent manner.

The translation used for the English rendition of this Tibetan liturgy is the work of J. G. Sherab Ebin.

Sections marked with a ⬤▬⬤ are considered essential if performing the shortened version of the practice. Generally, all sections are said if no time restrictions are present.

Traditionally the recitation of any sadhana(s) is followed by either a prayer for the teacher's long life or a prayer the swift return of the emanation, depending upon the circumstances. Presented here is a translated version of the prayer written by H.E. Jamgon Kongtrul Rinpoche for the swift return of Kalu Rinpoche, included as per his personal request. The phrase "may you swiftly return" has been replaced with the phrase "may you live long" since the reincarnation of Kalu Rinpoche has been recently recognized by His Eminence the XIIth Tai Situpa. Of joyful news to his followers, this newest, young reincarnation is once again living at his monastery at Sonada!

E.S.

Commentary on the Sadhana

1 Begin by visualizing that the refuge tree is in front of you, and that on either side of you are sentient beings. Visualize this while simultaneously engendering devotion to the objects of refuge, the Three Jewels and the Three Roots.

2 Not only your tsaway lama, but all the lamas of the lineage transmission look upon all sentient beings with the same deep, passionate concern of a mother for her only child.

3 Cakrasamvara and other high tantric deities have many attendants who gather around the central yidam. These are joined to the devoted practitioner by the lama's initiations and teachings until eventually there is no distinction between yidam and practitioner.

4 The conquerors of the enemy defilements, who have all the perfect physical and verbal qualities as well as the fully awakened enlightened mind, are the buddhas.

5 *Dharmas* refers to teachings given by enlightened masters (most particularly Buddha Sakyamuni) to enable all sentient beings to find a path to reach full and complete enlightenment.

6 The sanghas comprise all the bodhisattvas, arhats, conquerors, etc., as well as the circle of disciples of the Lord Buddha, and those who have continued to observe the obligations of monastic ordination as either a monk or a nun.

7 These are your helpers in clearing away non-conducive circumstances and impediments to Dharma practice, thus enabling the creation of conducive circumstances to help you continue your efforts on the path to full enlightenment.

Chenrezig Sadhana

1   ❦❦❦ REFUGE ❦❦❦

From this moment onward,
until the heart of enlightenment
is reached, I, and all sentient beings,
as limitless as the sky,

2   Go for refuge to all the glorious and holy lamas;

3   Go for refuge to all the yidams
gathered in the mandalas;

4   Go for refuge to all the buddhas,
conquerors gone beyond;

5   Go for refuge to all the supreme dharmas;

6   Go for refuge to all the noble sanghas;

7   Go for refuge to all the dakas, dakinis, protectors and
defenders of the Dharma, who possess the
eye of transcending awareness.

Commentary on the Sadhana

8 Praying to awaken from the sleep-like ignorance through the development of all forms of knowledge (the Dharma), you go for refuge in the Buddha and the assembly of bodhisattvas and arhats.

9 By the practice of the six paramitas (generosity, morality, forbearance, diligence, meditative stability, and wisdom), virtuous actions are accumulated and offered to benefit all beings so that you and all others may attain nirvana.

10 The mahasiddha Tang Tong Gyalpo was a lineage holder of the glorious Shangpa Kagyu [of which the Very Venerable Kalu Rinpoche was also a holder]. Usually, Tang Tong Gyalpo is pictured as a large, rotund, white haired man, with a long, pointed beard, wearing the loose robes of a yogi.

Chenrezig Sadhana

BODHICITTA

8   To the buddhas, Dharma, and noble sangha,
I go for refuge until enlightenment.

9   May I, meritorious from making offerings,
Accomplish buddhahood, not forsaking any
being suffering in the six realms.

10   *The Chenrezig sadhana begins at this point. Called*
The Recitation for the Meditation of the Great
Compassionate One for the Benefit of Beings as Vast
as the Sky, *this text was composed by the great saint,
the mahasiddha Tang Tong Gyalpo and bears the blessing
of his speech.*

Commentary on the Sadhana

11 Thinking of yourself and all sentient beings as reflecting the infinity of space, you visualize that on the crown of everybody's head is an eight-petaled white lotus, above which rests a flat disk of the moon. The lotus symbolizes one's rising above the mud of samsara in a stainless manner, while the moon symbolizes the totality of enlightened awareness.

12 When Chenrezig was formed as the embodiment of all the buddhas' compassion, the first appearance was that of the white letter *HRI*, which turned into a recognizable deity now known as the Noble All-Seeing One. *HRI*, therefore, is considered to be his seed syllable. More advanced meditators may visualize the following: once you see the **HRI** on the moon disk and lotus, visualize that brilliant light shines outward from the **HRI** as an offering to all the buddhas in every direction. This light reminds them of their vows to help all beings who suffer and they rain down blessings upon all sentient beings. This brilliant light from all the buddhas, bodhisattvas, and sentient beings returns and is reabsorbed into the **HRI**, which instantly changes into Chenrezig. Either method is satisfactory, for **HRI** definitely changes into Chenrezig. Being of the purest brilliant white possible, Chenrezig is so splendorous that light of the five colors (symbolizing the attainment of the five transcending awarenesses of which he is an embodiment) radiate now from his form in all directions.

Chenrezig Sadhana

❧ VISUALIZATION ❧

11   On the crown of my head
and that of all sentient beings
pervading space, there rests a white lotus
and a moon seat.

12   From *HRI* appears the Noble All-Seeing One.
He is white,
bright, and radiating five-colored light rays.

Four-armed Chenrezig. (Woodblock print from Tibet, early 20th century)

Commentary on the Sadhana

13 He smiles with inner understanding and love as he gazes with compassion upon all sentient beings, just as a mother smiles upon her child.

14 His four hands signify the four immeasurables: love, compassion, joy, and impartiality. The first pair are joined at his heart and hold a wish-fulfilling jewel signifying his prayer to all Buddhas to remain to help all beings. The second right hand holds a mala made out of clear crystal quartz. This symbolizes his drawing sentient beings upward out of samsara. In his left hand, he holds a white lotus, which symbolizes his absolute purity and freedom from samsara.

15 He is adorned with a crown, a necklace, and several bracelets, all of which are wrought of the finest gold and studded with beautiful gems which signify his having perfected the six paramitas and his having the thirty-seven requisites for full enlightenment. His silken robes, covering his lower torso and legs, are white, gold, and red in color. Resting on his left shoulder is a soft pelt of an antelope called the krishnasara, which is found only in the gods' realm. The antelope's wholly peaceful nature symbolizes Chenrezig's total non-violence.

16 His tsaway lama, Buddha Amitabha, the Buddha of Boundless Light, rests on a lotus and moon disk above Chenrezig's head. Seated in the vajra posture of Vairocana while wearing the robes of a monk and holding a begging bowl, Buddha Amitabha's color is red. The wheel of the Dharma marks both his palms and soles, and he has as well the 111 other marks of perfection of a buddha.

Chenrezig Sadhana

13   He smiles charmingly
and gazes with eyes of compassion.

14   He has four arms, the upper two joined at his
heart and the lower two holding a white lotus
and a crystal mala.

15   He is adorned by precious jewels and silks;
an antelope skin covers his shoulder.

16   The Buddha of Boundless Light
adorns his head.

Commentary on the Sadhana

17 Completely still and calm, Chenrezig is seated in full lotus posture (the seven postures of Vairocana), signifying that he does not rest in either samsaric bewilderment or nirvana, but acts for the benefit of beings by being both a bodhisattva and a yidam. The moon at his back, being stainless, reflects Chenrezig's total purity.

18 You should think of Chenrezig as being the union of all the sources of refuge, the Three Jewels and the Three Roots. Now, clearly see Chenrezig resting on the crown of your head and upon the heads of all sentient beings; while fostering a tremendously deep faith and devotion, pray to him with the following prayer of confidence in his purity of being and his intentions.

19 Chenrezig's first and most outstanding quality is his complete freedom from any kind of fault and defilement. He has no vestige of dualistic clinging to objective reality or subjective existence. He is completely free from any karmic accumulation.

20 His tsaway lama, Buddha Amitabha, lord of the western paradise, the pure land known as Dewachen, crowns Chenrezig's head as a seal of his own perfection.

21 Chenrezig's compassionate concern for all sentient beings' welfare is reflected in his unceasing gaze as he looks continually upon all sentient beings.

22 One pays homage with body, speech, and mind to Chenrezig. Joining your hands together is the physical devotion, reciting his sadhana is the verbal devotion, and the performance of the visualization given in the sadhana is the act of mental devotion.

Chenrezig Sadhana

17   He sits in vajra posture, his back supported
by a stainless moon.

18   He is the essence of all the sources of refuge.

19   ❧ PRAYER ❧

Lord, whose white body is not clothed by
fault,

20   And whose head is adorned by a perfect Buddha,

21   You look upon all beings
with the eyes of compassion.

22   To you, Chenrezig, I offer homage.

Commentary on the Sadhana

23 This prayer is beneficial whether one is engaged in the practices of the path of sutras or the path of tantras. This prayer
can be incorporated into all acts of devotion, such as offering
prostrations, mandalas, and all forms of devotion and meditation.

24 In this branch, you offer homage principally to Chenrezig
and also to all the buddhas and their children, the bodhisattvas,
who dwell in the totality of space in the eternity of time: past,
present, and future.

25 In the second branch, both real and imagined flowers,
incense, etc., are offered, both by placing them on your shrine
and by also imagining vast amounts of these objects filling
space and being offered principally to Chenrezig as well as
the other buddhas and bodhisattvas who surround him. You
pray that these are accepted so that all sentient beings might
derive direct and indirect benefits.

26 In this third branch, you offer confession by remembering
the unwholesome actions committed since beginningless time.
By fostering regret and remorse, you openly admit these,
while you pray that the blessings of the buddhas, bodhisattvas,
and compassionate Chenrezig will purify these karmic
accumulations. You should think, "I vow not to repeat these
unwholesome acts," and then you should consider that all
this unwholesomeness has now been cleared away and
removed.

27 In this fourth branch, you develop an attitude of rejoicing in
the good works of others. The shravakas and pratyekabuddhas,
the arhats, the bodhisattvas, and ordinary beings are all
oriented to achieving liberation from samsara, and all this
virtue, accumulated in the past, present, and future, makes
one extremely happy and joyous.

Chenrezig Sadhana

23   ❧ SEVEN BRANCH OFFERING PRAYER ❧

24   To the sublime one, the mighty Chenrezig,
to the buddhas and their children,
who reside in the ten directions
and in the three times, I pay homage
with complete sincerity.

25   I offer flowers, incense, butter-lamps, perfume,
food, music, and other real and imaginary
offerings, and beseech the noble assembly to
accept them.

26   I confess all the unskillful actions done from
beginningless time until now,
that were caused by the power of
conflicting emotions — the ten unvirtuous deeds
and the five sins of limitless consequence.

27   I rejoice in the spiritual merit of whatever virtue
has been gathered by the shravakas,
pratyekabuddhas, bodhisattvas,
and ordinary beings,
throughout the three times.

Commentary on the Sadhana

28   In this fifth branch, you pray that the teachings be given (as symbolized by the turning of the wheel of the Dharma) so that the particular attitudes and motivations of sentient beings might find immeasurable benefit when these are employed and put into practice.

29   In this sixth branch, you beseech the buddhas not to pass into parinirvana, but to stay and to help, until the cycle of sentient existence is completely emptied of all sentient beings. One pleads for their compassion and assistance in eliminating the tremendous suffering of all beings.

30   In this seventh branch, you pray to dedicate all the merit you have accumulated throughout your Dharma practice to becoming the primary cause for the enlightenment of all sentient beings. You also pray to become a buddha or bodhisattva, an excellent leader who can really bring sentient beings to full enlightenment in a direct and immediate way.

31   This portion of the prayer was composed by a nun named Palmo, who had great devotion to Lord Chenrezig. She was accustomed to spending the summer months fasting totally every other day and eating but one meal on the interim days. It is said that she prayed throughout her whole life to Chenrezig and had many visions of him. In the prayer, she expresses her understanding of his totality of representation, his embodiment of love and compassion, and his universality as a source of refuge.

Chenrezig Sadhana

28   I pray that, in accordance with the wishes and
aptitude of beings, the Dharma wheel of teachings
common to both mahayana and hinayana
be turned.

29   I beseech the buddhas not to pass into nirvana as
long as samsara is not emptied, but to look with
compassion upon sentient beings who wallow in
the ocean of suffering.

30   May whatever merit I have accumulated be the
cause for the enlightenment of beings; may I
quickly become a splendid leader of beings.

31   ❧ PRAYER ❧

I pray to you, Lama Chenrezig;
I pray to you, Yidam Chenrezig;
I pray to you, perfect noble Chenrezig;
I pray to you, Lord Protector Chenrezig;
I pray to you, Lord of Love Chenrezig.
Great compassionate victor, please hold us with
your compassion! For the numberless beings who
wander endlessly in samsara, experiencing unbear-
able suffering, there is no other refuge than you!
Protector, please bestow the blessings to obtain
omniscient buddhahood!

Commentary on the Sadhana

32 Here, one begins to consider the six realms of samsara that sentient beings have endured since beginningless time. The lowest realm is that of hell, where one undergoes karmic retribution of anger by experiencing extreme heat or cold. In thinking about this suffering, you pray to end the suffering of hell beings, that they might be born in Chenrezig's presence. Then, after the consideration of each of the six realms in turn, you say his mantra.

33 In the next lowest realm of samsaric suffering, hungry ghosts suffer greatly from their prior actions of greed. You pray they be liberated to be reborn in Chenrezig's pure land and again recite Chenrezig's mantra.

34 The realm highest in the three lower realms (and that which is closest to the human realm) is that of the animals who suffer domestication, dullness, and stupidity as a result of past gross ignorance. You pray they might all be liberated and come in contact with the presence of protector Chenrezig.

35 The human realm is the lowest of the three higher realms, and, while it enables one to develop a precious human existence, few humans have the interest to do so. As a result, they lead lives of constant and continual struggle and frustration, all because of their desires. Here, you pray that all human beings be fortunate and that they might be reborn in Buddha Amitabha's pure land of Dewachen.

Chenrezig Sadhana

32   In accumulating negative karma from
beginningless time, sentient beings, through the
force of anger, are born as hell beings and experience the suffering of heat and cold. May they all
be born in your presence, perfect deity.
OM MANI PADME HUNG!

33   In accumulating negative karma from
beginningless time, sentient beings, through the
force of greed, are born in the realms of pretas
and experience the suffering of hunger and thirst.
May they all be born in your
perfect realm, Potala.
OM MANI PADME HUNG!

34   In accumulating negative karma from
beginningless time, sentient beings, through the
force of stupidity, are born as animals and experience the suffering of dullness and stupidity. May
they all be born in your presence, protector.
OM MANI PADME HUNG!

35   In accumulating negative karma from
beginningless time, sentient beings, through the
force of desire, are born in the human realm and
experience the suffering of excessive activity and
constant frustration. May they all be born in the
pure land of Dewachen.
OM MANI PADME HUNG!

Commentary on the Sadhana

36 The beings of the demi-gods' realm suffer disputation due to the past karmic accumulations of jealousy, and they are born into a realm where they continually bicker, quarrel, and fight. You pray that they might be reborn in Chenrezig's pure land.

37 The gods' realm derives its population from those beings who have performed many countless good deeds but who have failed to reach enlightenment because of their pride. While in the heavenly gods' realm they experience great pleasures, but these are of no lasting value as eventually they must leave (change) and fall into the lower realms again. You pray their impermanent environment be ended and that they, too, will be reborn in Chenrezig's pure land.

38 Considering the whole of samsara, you regard your karmic accumulations, both positive and negative, and pray to maintain a bodhisattva commitment equal to that of Chenrezig's in order to liberate beings from samsara's impure realms. The sound of the six syllable mantra is perfect and beneficial, causing untold cessation of suffering and producing the causes of liberation in all directions.

39 You pray that your bodhisattva skills improve through devotion to Chenrezig so that the beings that you are trying to help will take the vehicles of hinayana and mahayana into consideration in all of their actions. You pray that all those that you help will be virtuous and that they will help spread the Dharma for the benefit of all sentient beings.

Chenrezig Sadhana

36   In accumulating negative karma from beginningless time, sentient beings, through the force of jealousy, are born in the realm of the demi-gods and experience the suffering of fighting and quarrelling. May they all be born in your realm, Potala. OM MANI PADME HUNG!

37   In accumulating negative karma from beginningless time, sentient beings, through the force of pride, are born in the realm of the gods and experience the suffering of change and falling. May they all be born in your realm, Potala. OM MANI PADME HUNG!

38   Wherever I am born, may my deeds, by equalling Chenrezig's, liberate beings from impure realms, and spread the perfect sound of the six syllables in the ten directions.

39   Through the power of praying to you, perfect noble one, may the beings who I am to discipline pay the greatest attention to action and result, and may they diligently practice virtue and the Dharma for the benefit of beings.

Commentary on the Sadhana

40 In response to your prayers, light radiates forth from Chenrezig's body and reaches all sentient beings without exception. Thus, the four buddha activities of (1) enriching and (2) magnetizing all their positive karmic accumulations while (3) destroying and/or (4) pacifying all negative karmic accumulations are performed.

41 With all defilements thus transformed by this light, all the general appearances of our outer delusion in which we live become the pure land of Dewachen. You see this land and all sentient beings born into it as having the perfect form of Chenrezig, complete with his sublime speech and pure mind. In this pure realm, which is inseparable and indistinguishable from Chenrezig, all appearances become simultaneously appearing and empty. All sound becomes mantra: the indivisibility of sound and emptiness. All mental activity becomes the indivisibility of awareness and emptiness.

42 The mantra does have a literal translation, namely, Hail Jewel of the Lotus. But its power is not bound by any meaning, whether literal or non-literal. Rather each of the six syllables is said to close one of the doors to the six realms of samsara. Thus, OM closes the door to the gods' realm; MA, the demi-gods' realm; NI, the human realm; PE (PAD), the animal realm; ME, the hungry ghost realm; and HUNG closes the door to the hell realms. Reciting this mantra can effectively help all sentient beings by either implanting the seed of liberation, or by helping those who have this seed to mature their development along the path to liberation.

Chenrezig Sadhana

🐚 VISUALIZATION 🐚

40 Through this one-pointed prayer, light radiates
from the body of the sublime one, purifying
impure karma, impure appearances,
and the deluded mind.

41 The outer realm is the pure land of Dewachen,
and the body, speech and mind of beings therein
are the perfect form, sublime speech, and pure
mind of mighty Chenrezig, the indivisible union
of appearance, sound, and vivid
intelligence with emptiness.

42 *In this meditative state, say the mantra **Om Mani Padme
Hung** as many times as you are able. Finally, let the mind
remain absorbed in its own essence without making distinction between subject, object, and/or action.*

The mantra Om Mani Padme Hung in Tibetan sacred script. (Courtesy
of Tinley Drupa)

Commentary on the Sadhana

43 Light goes out from the heart of yourself (as Chenrezig), and the whole of Dewachen and all sentient beings (also in the envisioned purified form of the Yidam Chenrezig) dissolve into light and are absorbed into your own form (still visualized as being Chenrezig). Then, this form also dissolves into light and is absorbed into your heart where there rests a six-petaled lotus. Atop the moon disk resting on the lotus is the letter *HRI* surrounded by the six syllables of the mantra, each on a petal of the lotus. Next, the lotus and mantra dissolve upwards [as described in Chapter Seven]. In this way, you let the mind come to rest completely, without contrivance or discursiveness, in its own natural state of luminosity, clarity, and unimpededness. You rest as long as possible in this state of natural mind. You conclude this meditation by seeing yourself as Chenrezig and the world of form as that of Dewachen, and then you dedicate the merit.

44 There are four important parts to the Tibetan Buddhist tradition: taking refuge, the visualization of the yidam, the experience of the true nature of the mind, and the dedication of merit. Through the accumulation of merit, you can develop both wisdom and skillful means with which to experience the mahamudra. Therefore, all practices and teachings end with this important aspect of practice.

45 No commentary.

Chenrezig Sadhana

43   ❧ VISUALIZATION ❧

My body, the bodies of others, and all
appearances are the perfect form of the sublime
one; all sound, the melody of the six syllables; all
thoughts, the vastness of the great *jnana*.

*(Visualize the dissolution and rest as long
as possible in this state of natural mind.)*

❧ DEDICATION ❧

44   Through this virtue, may I quickly achieve
the realization of mighty Chenrezig and may I
bring every single being to that same state.

45   *One traditionally concludes with the prayers for quick
rebirth in Dewachen, not only because Buddha Amitabha
was Chenrezig's tsaway lama, but especially because it
is in Dewachen that one can easily perfect the final
accomplishments of the various levels of bodhisattvas.*

Commentary on the Sadhana

46   The western paradise of Buddha Amitabha, the pure land of Dewachen, is said to be the easiest pure land rebirth to attain because rebirth in other pure lands requires strict adherence in all aspects to the observance of one's vows. Here, you pray that your actions of meditation and dedication will allow you this privilege.

47   In Dewachen, one perfects the hinayana and mahayana vehicles by performing meritorious actions and by crossing the ten levels of bodhisattva development while emanating countless forms in the ten directions to benefit all beings.

48   Here, again, the merit is dedicated for the recitation of the pure land prayer. The two bodies considered to be supreme are the sambhogakaya and the wholly purified dharmakaya, which naturally arise from efforts made along the path. Bodhicitta is both the beginning and end of the bodhisattva commitment and is a necessary and important inclusion in all vajrayana practices.

Chenrezig Sadhana

⬥⬥ PRAYER FOR QUICK REBIRTH ⬥⬥
IN THE PURE LAND

46

Through the merit of reciting and meditating,
May I, and every being to whom I am connected,
be miraculously born in Dewachen when these
imperfect forms are left behind.

47

May I then immediately cross the ten levels
and, for the benefit of others, may I
emanate in the ten directions.

⬥⬥ PRAYER ⬥⬥

48

Through this virtue, may all beings perfect
the accumulations of spiritual merit
and awareness.

May they attain the two supreme bodies which
arise from merit and awareness.

Bodhicitta is precious! May it arise in those who
have not cultivated it. In those who have
cultivated it, may it not diminish.
May it ever grow and flourish!

Dharma Chakra Center
P.O. Rumtek via Ranipul
Sikkim, India

Telephone: 363

Seat-Holder of
His Holiness the
Gyalwa Karmapa

HIS EMINENCE
JAMGON KONTRUL RINPOCHE

༣། །སྨྱུར་ཐོན་གསལ་འདེབས་རྡོ་རྗེའི་སྒྲ་དབྱངས་ཞེས་བྱ་བ་བཀུགས་སོ།།

ཨོཾ་སྭ་སྟི། །མི་ཤིག་སྟོང་ཉིད་སྙིག་ཡེ་དི་གཱ་ལ་དུ། །བཅུ་གཉིས་ཡོ་འི་དྲངས་མ་བསྟོམ་
པ་འི་ང་མཚར་ལས། །ཡིག་ལ་འོང་སྐྱེ་ལ་གགས་ཡོལ་ལུལ་རྡོ་རྗེ་རིག །ཡེན་
མ་ནས་རྩ་ག་སུ་ས་ལུ་ཚོགས་ རྒྱལ་རྒྱར་ཅིག །དཀ་པ་འི་ཚུལ་དབྱུལ་ལེ་ས་
སྲུས་ཕྲེན་ལ་སྔེ །འོལ་པས་འགྲོ་ཚོགས་ཡེད་དགར་བ་བྱོད་པ་ལ། །འཇམ་
མགོ་མཚོ་མ་འི་རྣམ་པར་ཡོ་ལས་འཁར་པ་འི། །མ་ཆུ་ལས་མེད་སླ་མ་འི་མ་ཆོག་སྒྱུལ་
སྒྱུར་འཕྲེན་གསོལ། །རྒྱལ་བ་བསྟ་ནབ་ཐིམས་ཀྱི་འཇི་ནོ་མར་རེས་འགྱུང་གི་།ལྷོ་རྨོ་
རུ་བཅུ་ནུ་བསྐྱབ་གསུས་འཕྱས་བུ་འི་དུ། །འཁོར་ལོ་གསུ་མ་ཀྱི་མ་ཇོད་པ་འགྲ་
ཚོགས་ཡེད། །དགོ་པར་འལ་འཚོ་བགྱོད་ཕྱེ་ར་སྒྱུར་འཕྲེན་གསོལ། །འཆེ་ཆེ་ནན་སྤྲོང་
རྗེ་རིག་འི་འཇོན་འཁྲུགས་པ་འི་དུ་དུས། །ཆེབ་གསང་སྤྲགས་ཀྱི་འཕྲུལ་སྣུལ་རྫས། །
བསྐྱལ་བས། །གང་འདུལ་མེ་ས་འཁམས་མ་འདུས་ཉིང་ལ་སུ། །རྣུ་དུ་སྦུང་ཆེས་
ཆར་འབེནས་པ་ར་སྒྱུར་འཕྲེན་གསོལ། །སྐྱེ་གས་མ་འི་དུས་འདེ་སྟེ་སྟོངས་
ཤུམ་མེད་པས། །རྒྱལ་བ་འི་ནབ་སྟུན་རྒྱུན་སྒོལ་ལ་མཐུ་ཕིན་པ། །འདང་སྦུར་གུན་
ཕུན་ཞེས་བྱགས་རྫ་མ་རྗེ་འི། །མ་ཆོག་སྤྲུལ་དེན་ཕྱེ་རྟེ་སྒྱུར་དུ་འཕྲེན་གྱུར་ཅིག །

དེ་ལྱུར་གསོལ་འབང་བསྐུ་མེད་མ་ཆོག་གསུ་མ་དང་། །བྱང་ཕྱོང་
སྨྱོན་ཚོག་བདག་གི་ལྷུག་ནས་མ་གྱི། །མཐུ་ཡེས་དེ་བཞིན་ན་འགྱུ་
སྟེ་བགང་བ་རྒྱུད་ཀྱི། །བསྟུ་ནུ་པ་འཇོ་མ་སྒྱིང་གྲོགས་མམར་རྒྱུ་ལ་ གྱུར་
ཅིག །ཞེས་པ་འི་བྱུ་ས་རྗེ་ན་མ་ཀུ་རེ་ས་ཆེ་བ་ར་ཕི་སྒྱུར་འགྲེ་ན་གསོལ་འདེ་བས་འ་དེ་ཀི།
བཆོག་གི་སྤྲུ་ཆོ་རྒྱལ་མཆོ་དགས་རེ་བ་སྒྱུལ་སྒྱུ། །དཔལ་རྒྱལ་དང་ཀྲཱ་བ་ཆུ་ཕུག་པ་འི་གདུང་
དགས་འདུན་བྱོན་ཆོ་ལ་སྒྱུར་འཕྲོན་གསོལ་འདེ་སར་སུ་འཁམ་མགོན་སྒྱུལ་སྒྱུས་ལ་བཀུར་བ་
དགེ་ལེགས་འཕེལ།།

A VAJRA MELODY IMPLORING THE SWIFT RETURN OF THE LORD OF REFUGE, KHYAB JE KALU RINPOCHE

May all be auspicious!
Within the very sphere
 of indestructible great emptiness,
From the wonder that is the convergence
 of the very essence of all that
 is animate and inanimate,
Arise vajra songs, completely free
 of origination or cessation;
Masters of such songs, assembly of
 deities embodying the Three Roots,
 may you be victorious!
Through the display of activity,
 enhanced by the nine modes
 of proficiency of an exalted one,
You bring delight to the minds
 of a multitude of beings;
You embody the continuation
 of the perfect qualities of
 Jamgon Kongtrul,
Incomparable lama, may your
 sublime emanation live long!

In the ground of the discipline
 of the victorious one's teaching,
You plant firmly the roots
 of the tree of your renunciation,
 a tree heavily laden with
 the fruit of the three trainings.

Through the three cycles of activity
  you restore the minds of a
  multitude of beings in virtue.
May you live long!

When space is churned by
  the gathering clouds of your great
  love and compassion,
And is shaken by the resounding
  thunder of the profound
  vajrayana,
The rain of your marvelous Dharma falls
  on the fields of those to be
  influenced, without error as to their
  inclination or potential.
May you live long!

At this time of degeneration,
  through your indomitable courage,

You have the mastery that causes the
  transmission of the victorious one's
  teaching to flourish.
Noble lama, Rangjung Kunkhyab by name,
  may your illuminating sublime
  emanation live long!

As I pray in this way,
  by the power of the infallible
  Three Jewels,
By the power of the words of
  aspiration of the sages, and by
  the power of my own noble intentions,
May these very prayers be realized,
And may the Kagyu teachings
  spread throughout the world.

This prayer for the prompt rebirth of the lord of refuge, Khyab Je Kalu Rinpoche, is given in response to the request of Lama Gyaltsen, the sublime one's own nephew. To this end, the words of aspiration for longevity of the lord of refuge that were spoken by the glorious XVIth Gyalwa Karmapa himself, have been changed into this prayer for the swift return of Kalu Rinpoche by H.E. Jamgon Kongtrul Rinpoche in the third month of the female earth snake year in the seventeenth sixty-year cycle of the Tibetan calendar.

This prayer has been translated from the Tibetan by Drajur Dzamling Kunkhyab, on 20 May 1989, at Samdrub Darjay Chöling Monastery, in Sonada, Darjeeling District, West Bengal, India.

May virtue and excellence increase!

Kalu Rinpoche pauses to smile for the camera in his audience room at the monastery at Sonada, India. (Photograph by J.G. Sherab Ebin)

APPENDIX C

*Glossary
of
Vajrayana Terminology*

Pen and ink drawing by Kalu Rinpoche depicts his translator Sherab Ebin as he saw him. (Courtesy of J.G. Sherab Ebin)

The glossary is compiled from teachings given by Kalu Rinpoche and other highly respected Kagyu teachers, and from references already available. It should be understood that Buddhism recognizes many approaches, and the same terms explained here might well be explained somewhat differently in other vajrayana orders. Moreover, some terms have significantly different meanings in different contexts.

I would like to thank J. G. Sherab Ebin and Richard Barron, and Steven Goodman of Yeshe Nyingpo for taking the time to correct the spelling of the Tibetan and Sanskrit transliterations and to indicate the associated Tibetan or Sanskrit words for several of the terms defined herein.

Terms that traditionally are grouped by number should be looked for by the numerical reference. Tibetan spelling is italicized throughout, with approximate pronunciation given in square brackets for the main listing only. Sanskrit terms have been supplied in addition to the Tibetan in several instances but not throughout. Those listings in Sanskrit that begin with Ś should be looked for under **Sh**.

Buddhist terminology, especially that which is related to the vajrayana, is seldom simple or concise. The translators and my editorial assistants both have been very helpful in seeing that the glossary did not mushroom into an encyclopedia. To facilitate further study, I have provided a bibliography and draw your attention to the books that contain the translated teachings of Milarepa as being an invaluable source of illustration and reference.

E.S.

Absolute Reality (Tib. *don.dam.* [don dam]) A term used to describe the enlightened awareness that is beyond duality and the confusion of the four veils of obscuration. *See* RELATIVE REALITY, OBSCURATION

Ālaya-Vijñāna (Skt., Tib. *kun.gzhi.rnam.par.shes.pa.* [kun zhi nam par she pa]) Often abbreviated as ālaya. It is also used in the *Yogācāra Abhidharma*, as attributed to Asaṅga (fifth century, A.D.), to describe the fundamental nature of mind, and is considered to be the eighth consciousness, having two qualities. One is considered to be pure and undefiled in that the buddha nature is incorruptible, and, in this sense, it is often translated as *primordial consciousness.* The other is considered to be impure, in that the reaping of either positive or negative karmic actions is indicative of the delusion concerning the true nature of being, and, in this sense, the term is often translated as *storehouse consciousness. See* EIGHT CONSCIOUSNESSES

Amitābha Buddha (Skt., Tib. *'od.dpag.med.* [Ö pag me]) Literally "boundless light;" the buddha of the western direction, whose elemental association is fire, whose wisdom is discrimination, and whose practice is said to be an antidote of greed. Also, the saṃbhogakāya buddha of the lotus family. *See* BUDDHA FAMILIES, DEWACHEN

Anuttarayogatantra (Skt., Tib. *rnal.'byor.bla.na.med.pa'i.rgyud.* [nal jor la na mey pay gyü]) The highest of the four levels of tantric yoga. *See* FOUR LEVELS OF TANTRIC YOGA, FIVE PATHS, MĀHAMUDRĀ, DZOGRIM

Arhat (Skt., Tib. *dgra.bcom.pa.* [dra com pa]) Literally "one who has slain the foe," referring to the hīnayāna ideal of overcoming emotional complexities and intellectual discursiveness. An arhat is said to have reached a state in which there is a cessation of suffering.

Auspicious Coincidence (Tib. *rten.'brel.* [ten drel], Skt. *pratitya samutpāda*) Refers to a coming together of factors to give the characteristics of any given occurrence or situation. In the viewpoint of the vajrayāna, each moment has the potential for transcendence, no matter what the circumstances, and is therefore considered auspicious.

Āyatana (Skt., Tib. *skye.mched.* [kyem che]) The field of sense perception for each of the six sense faculties and their sensory objects, totalling twelve in all.

Bardo (Tib. *bar.do.* [bar do]) Literally "between two," referring to the characteristics of the illusory appearance of change experienced by sentient beings within the six realms of saṃsāra. Traditionally, it is thought that six bardos sustain the processes of birth, death, and rebirth. First, our current life of ordinary waking consciousness is termed the *bardo between birth and death* (Tib. *skye.shi.bar.do.*). Second, the interval in our daily lives that contains our pursuit of equanimity, with its moments of meditative stability, is called the *bardo of meditative concentration* (Tib. *bsam.gtan.bar.do.*). Third, the interval between sleep and waking, in which the mind experiences the dream state, is known as the *dream bardo* (Tib. *rmi.lam.bar.do.*). These are the three bardos associated with life; the next two bardos deal with the process of death and after-death. The fourth bardo begins from the moment an individual starts to die, lasting until the moment of the separation of body and mind, and is called the *bardo of the death process* (Tib. *'chi.kha'.bar.do.*). Fifth, the interval immediately following death is considered to be one of several experiences and qualities, the most immediate of which is the mind being plunged into dharmatā where it experiences a state of unconsciousness. This experience is termed *chönye bardo* (Tib. *chos.nyid.bar.do.*), which may be translated as *bardo of the ultimate nature of phenomenal reality*. Finally, the interval between the realization of death and the karmic fruition that influences the choices directly affecting the coming rebirth, together with the process of being reborn, is called the *bardo of becoming* (Tib. *srid.pa'i.bar.do.*).

Bhūmi (Skt., Tib. *sa.* [sa]) Literally "ground," referring to any of the ten stages (Tib. *sa.bcu.*, Skt. *daśabhūmi*) of accomplishment and realization through which a bodhisattva progresses towards enlightenment.

Bindu (Skt., Tib. *thig.le.* [tig le]) Literally "drop" or "circle." In this text, the term is used in a meditation employing the visualization of circles of light. It is also used when referring to the essential energies received from both the father and the mother in the bardo of becoming, ingredients which will dissolve during the process of dying. As the essence received from the father is considered to be white and those received from the mother to be red, these are also often referred to as the red and white elements.

Bodhi (Skt., Tib. *byang.chub.* [jang chup]) The state of realization of buddhahood. See ENLIGHTENMENT

Bodhicitta (Skt., Tib. *byang.chub.kyi.sems.* [jang chup kyi sem]) The enlightened attitude which is one both of altruism (in that it evokes the motivation to practice with the intention of benefiting all sentient beings) and of direct expression of the liberated awareness itself (in which case it is frequently referred to as absolute bodhicitta); it is considered to have four aspects: mundane (Tib. *kun.rdsob.*), transcendental (Tib. *don.dam.*), aspiration (Tib. *smon.pa.*), and practice (Tib.

'*jug.pa.*). A prayer engendering bodhicitta is considered a prerequisite beginning to all practice within the vajrayāna.

Bodhisattva (Skt., Tib. *byang.chub.sems.dpa'.* [jang chup sem pa]) The aspirant who takes and keeps a set of vows that focus upon the implementation of the six pāramitās to liberate all sentient beings from saṃsāra. The term may be used to refer to two qualitative levels. On the level of the mundane bodhisattva, the aspirant engenders bodhicitta and observes the bodhisattva vows. The transcendent bodhisattva level is that of a developed meditator who has reached the concluding stages (the ten bhūmis). An aspirant on these levels is referred to as an accomplished (or realized) bodhisattva. *See* BHŪMI, BODHISATTVA VOWS

Bodhisattva Vows (Tib. *byang.sdom.* [jang dom]) The formal set of vows which motivates the dedication of one's actions for the benefit of others. *See* BODHISATTVA

Body of Fully Ripened Karma (Tib. *rnam.smin.gyi.lus.* [nam min gyi lü]) The physical body from birth to death as sentient beings experience it, as well as the environment in which the individual finds him- or herself.

Body of Habitual Tendency (Tib. *rgyu.lus.* [gyu lü]) The experience of the dream, including the body perceived in the dream and the dream environment.

Body of Karmic Fruition *see* BODY OF FULLY RIPENED KARMA

Body of the Bardo Experience (Tib. *yid.lus.* [ye lü]) The attachment of the mind to a "self" during the interval between dying and rebirth. Also called the *mental body*.

Body of the Dreamer *see* BODY OF HABITUAL TENDENCY

Buddhadharma (Skt., Tib. *sang.rgyas.kyi.chos.* [sang gye kyi chö]) The collected teachings (Dharma) of Buddha Śākyamuni as well as the path to enlightenment that is described therein. In this text, it can also mean the combination of the understanding of the path, the degree of maturity in that path, and the development of aspiration (bodhicitta) peculiar to each member of the saṅgha.

Buddha Families (Tib. *sang.rgyas.kyi.rigs.* [sang gye kyi rik], Skt. *buddhakula*) Refers to the maṇḍala of the five saṃbhogakāya buddhas who embody the transcendent wisdom that arises when the obscurations of emotional complexities are resolved. The designation "family" comes from the saṃbhogakāya view that all phenomena are in essence none other than the dharmakāya manifesting as the five wisdoms and the five saṃbhogakāya buddhas' bodies and their environment. The names of the five saṃbhogakāya buddhas (and their respective families) are Vairocana (Buddha family), Akṣobhya — sometimes represented as Vajrasattva — (Vajra family), Ratnasaṃbhava (Jewel family), Amitābha (Lotus family), and Amoghasiddhi (Karma family). *See* FIVE WISDOMS

Buddha Nature *see* TATHĀGATAGARBHA

Buddha, Saṃbhogakāya (Skt., Tib. *longs.sku.* [long ku]) A manifestation of enlightened mind in the saṃbhogakāya that is said to have five qualities, known as the *five certainties* (Tib. *nges.pa.lnga.*). The qualities are: *(1)* that the form of the Buddha as teacher is unending; *(2)* that the environment of the Dharma discourses is always one of a pure land; *(3)* that the Dharma transmitted is always in the mahāyāna or vajrayāna traditions; *(4)* that the saṅgha receiving the teachings is always composed of those accomplished bodhisattvas on the eighth, ninth or tenth bhūmis; and *(5)* that such manifestation is unchanging and is not subject to time.

Buddha Śākyamuni, Prince Siddhārtha (sixth century ? B.C.) (Tib. *thub.pa.sangs.rgyas.* [thub pa sang gye]) The most recent historical Buddha, who is said to be the fourth in a lineage of one thousand historical Buddhas that will appear in this kalpa. His title *Lord* comes from various sources. One is his having been born a prince of the Śākya family. Several Tibetan lamas consider the term to be a poor English translation of the epithet tathāgata (Tib. *de.bzhin.gshegs.pa.*) meaning "thus gone" or "thus come," which usually precedes his name in Sanskrit writings. Siddhārtha means literally "he who has accomplished the siddhās."

Cakras (or Chakras) (Skt., Tib. *'khor.lo.* [khor lo]) "Wheels" or "circles," referring to the subtle energy centers of the physical body. In the Tibetan vajrayāna tradition, there are five main cakras: at the crown of the head, at the throat, at the heart, below the navel, and in the area referred to as secret, or the genitalia.

Cakrasaṃvara (or Chakrasaṃvara) (Skt., Tib. *'khor.lo.bde.mchog.* [khor lo dem chok]) One of the five main practices of the Kagyu lineage, this yidam is a heruka belonging to the Lotus (or Amitābha Buddha) family, who plays an important part in the six yogas of Nāropa. (The four other yidam practices are those of Mahāmāyā, Vajrabhairava, Guhyasamāja, and Hevajra.)

Chenrezig (Tib. *spyan.ras.gzigs.* [chen re zig], Skt. *Avalokiteśvara*) The buddha of compassion who is the patron buddha of Tibet. Kalu Rinpoche taught that the daily performance of the sādhana of Chenrezig fulfills all the samaya for all the initiations one has ever received.

Circumambulation (Tib. *'khor.ba.* [khor wa], Skt. *parikrama*) The reverent act of walking clockwise around a holy person or a holy place. There are two places here on earth where performing circumambulation is said to bring the highest rewards: Mt. Kailas in western Tibet, and the great stūpa at Bodhnath, Kathmandu, Nepal. Sometimes, the circumambulation is also done prostration-by-prostration. It is said that just to circumambulate once around Mt. Kailas erases the negative karmic accumulations of one lifetime.

Clarity (Tib. *gsal.ba.* [sal wa]) Corresponding to the saṃbhogakāya aspect of enlightenment, this is considered to be one of the three basic qualities of the nature of the mind, giving the mind its inherent ability to experience. *See* COEMERGENT MIND

Coemergent Appearance (Tib. *snang.ba.lhan.skyes.* [nang wa lhen kyi], Skt. *āloka sahaja*) Refers to the appearances characteristic of sambhogakāya, which are said to be insubstantial yet apparent, thus demonstrating the luminous nature of mind.

Coemergent Mind (Tib. *sems.nyid.lhan.skyes.* [sem nye lhen kyi], Skt. *sahajamānas*) Refers to the true nature of mind, which is said to have the three qualities of clarity, luminosity, and unimpededness.

Coemergent Wisdom (Tib. *lhan.gcig.skyes.pa'i.ye.shes.* [lhen cik kyi pay ye she] or *lhan.skyes.ye.shes.* [lhen kyi ye she], Skt. *sahajajñāna*) Alternatively translated coemergent awareness, it refers to the simultaneous arising of nirvāṇa and saṃsāra; this essential thought in vajrayāna implies that, in the natural arising of phenomenal existence, wisdom is inherently present.

Compassion (Tib. *snying.rje.* [nying je], Skt. *karuṇa*) "Noble heart and mind," referring to the empathy for the suffering of all sentient beings and to the desire to personally end that suffering. Considered the basis for practice throughout the triyāna, each yāna stresses various methods to develop and practice compassion. In the vajrayāna, it is developed primarily through yidam practice, in which the practitioner skillfully develops loving kindness and matures the bodhicitta into the union of skillful means and wisdom; thus, in vajrayāna, the term can apply to either the practice or the principle. *See* NIRMĀṆAKĀYA

Cutting Through Instruction (Tib. *gzhi.rtsa.chod.pa'i.gdams.nag.* [zhi tsa chö pay dam nak]) Literally "the clear-cut precept that clarifies the basis or core of the issue;" when followed, the instructions from the tsaway lama are said to give the student dramatic progress.

Dakini (Skt., Tib. *mkha'.'gro.ma.* [khan dro ma]) Literally "one who goes to the sky," referring to the wisdom manifestation of enlightened awareness, which is usually pictured in a semi-wrathful feminine form.

Dark Age (Tib. *snyigs.ma'.dus.* [nyek may dü], Skt. *kaliyuga*) Characterization of epochs of time in which no historical Buddha has or will appear and in which no Buddhadharma is available. Also used to refer to the degeneration of morality, discipline, and spiritual wisdom within various eras and societies, including that of our present world and age.

Dependent Origination *see* TWELVE LINKS OF DEPENDENT ORIGINATION

Dewachen (Tib. *bde.ba.can.* [de wa chen], Skt. *sukhāvatī*) The pure land of Buddha Amitābha. *See* AMITĀBHA, PURE LANDS

Dhāraṇī (Skt., Tib. *gzhungs.* [zhung]) Invocation; an unusually long mantra.

Dharma (Skt., Tib. *chos.* [chö]) In Buddhism there are three essential meanings: the teachings given by Lord Buddha Śākyamuni, collectively termed the *Dharma;* all phenomena, including ideas and emotions, called *dharmas;* and the essential truth or ultimate nature of the mind, which is termed *dharmakāya.*

Dharmakāya (Skt., Tib. *chos.kyi.sku.* [chö kyi ku]) A term denoting the aspect of essential truth in the nature of all existence, a perspective recognized by those attaining enlightenment. Said to be wholly without form, distinct and yet inseparable from any sentient expression or experience, it is the mind quality of the buddhas. *See* TRIKĀYA

Dharmapālas (Skt., Tib. *chos.skyong.* [chö kyong]) Literally "protector of the Dharma," referring to the quality of immediacy and power of the buddhas' enlightened awareness that demonstrates itself through the four buddha activities to eliminate the obstacles encountered along the path to liberation though the display of compassion that is embodied in a terrifying or wrathful appearance.

Dharmatā (Skt., Tib. *chos.nyid.* [chö nye]) The nature or truth of being; experience in its totality, just as it is; the fundamental nature of all phenomena.

Dorje Chang *see* VAJRADHĀRA

Dorje Sempa *see* VAJRASATTVA

Dzogrim (Tib. *rdzogs.rim.* [dzog rim], Skt. *sampannakrama*) Often translated as completion stage or perfecting yoga of the anuttarayogatantra. In this stage of meditation, the practice focuses upon identifying one's mind with that of the yidam, thereby perfecting the accomplishment of the first level of mahāmudrā *See* KYIRIM

Eight Consciousnesses (Tib. *rnam.shes.tshogs.brgyad.* [nam shi thsok gye], Skt. *aṣṭa vijñāna*) According to the Yogācāra school of Buddhism, when one has attained the level of full realization one's awareness (or consciousness) becomes transmutated. Thus, the yogi's five sense awarenesses (that are contingent upon the organs of eye, ear, nose, tongue, and skin) become the wisdom of performance (or activity) (Tib. *bya.grub.ye.shes.*); his sixth awareness, that of dharmas and ideas, becomes the wisdom of observation (Tib. *sor.rtog.ye.shes.*); his seventh awareness of ego consciousness becomes the wisdom of equality (Tib. *mnyam.nyid.ye.shes.*); and his eighth awareness of ālaya-vijñāna becomes the wisdom of the great mirror (Tib. *me.long.ye.shes.*).

Eightfold Noble Path (Tib. *'phags.pa'i.lam.yan.lag.brgyad.* [phak pay lam yen lak gyü]) The path leading to the cessation of suffering, consisting of right understanding, thoughts, speech, action, livelihood, endeavor, mindfulness, and concentration.

Eight Non-Freedoms (Tib. *mi.khom.brgyad.* [mi khom gye]) Refers to the eight conditions that prevail when sentient beings are predisposed by their karma not to have the inclination to seek the Dharma, or to obtain it only after great difficulties. Also, although an attraction and a connection might exist, the Dharma practice is difficult to implement into life. The non-freedoms are to be found in the eight unrestful states of rebirth. A sentient being who is *not* bound by the eight non-freedoms is said to be free and well-favored (Tib. *dal.'byor.*, Skt. *kṣana sampad*). *See* EIGHT UNRESTFUL STATES, SIX REALMS OF SAMSĀRA

Eight Unrestful States (Tib. *mi.khom.pa'i.gnas.brgyad.* [mi khom pay ne gye]) The unrestful states are those births: *(1)* as a hell-being, *(2)* in a pretā realm (Tib. *yi.dwags.*), *(3)* as an animal, *(4)* as a god, *(5)* in a social situation where the Dharma is unknown, *(6)* in an age when no historical Buddha has appeared, *(7)* birth either as a holder of extreme views (Skt. *tirthika*), or as a person suffering from mental or sensory impairments that inhibit the understanding of Dharma, and *(8)* in a life that hinges upon the wrong views that neither the Dharma nor karma are of any meaning. *See* PRECIOUS HUMAN EXISTENCE

Eight Worldly Winds (or Dharmas) (Tib. *chos.brgyad.* [chö gye]) Denotes those influences that fan the flames of passion, i.e., sorrow and joy; ridicule and praise; loss and gain; and, defamation and fame. This term is alternatively translated as eight worldly desires.

Emotional Affliction *see* KLEŚA

Emptiness *see* ŚŪNYATĀ

Enlightenment (Tib. *byang.chub.* [jang chup], Skt. *bodhi*) This term is used to convey an awareness that, in and of itself, is beyond definition. However, after having studied extensive Kagyu tantra and sūtra teachings, one might logically consider that enlightenment could include any and all of the following qualities: the end of delusion; the clear realization of the true nature of mind's luminous unimpededness; the transcendent experience of primordial buddha nature; the freedom from karmic causality; the union of wisdom and skillful means; the wisdom of allowing loving kindness be the instrumental means of compassion; the effortlessness of meditative absorption; the freedom from restriction of the five elements; freedom from hindrances of the six consciousnesses; freedom from frustrations of the six sense objects; freedom of the limitations of the six sense organs; the liberation from the delusion of the duality of self and other; the fulfillment of ground, path, and fruition; the completion of mahāmudrā practice; the fullness of the trikāya; the realization of absolute reality in relative reality; the recognition of relative reality in absolute reality; and the true enjoyment of the simplicity of vajrayāna approach as engendered by the cutting through instructions of the founders of the Kagyu lineage, namely, Tilopa, Nāropa, Marpa Lotsawa, and Milarepa.

Five Certanties *see* SAMBHOGAKĀYA BUDDHA

Five Paths (Tib. *lam.lnga.* [lam nga], Skt. *pañca mārga*) The way to enlightenment is traditionally arranged into five paths. The first, the *path of accumulation* (Tib. *tshogs.lam.*, Skt. *sambhāra mārga*), is one of purification and accumulation of merit in which the meditator learns what to cultivate and what to weed out in his or her daily life. The second, the *path of application (or unification)* (Tib. *sbyor.lam.*, Skt. *prayoga mārga*), is one of integrating the profundity of the four noble truths with the meditative investigations of vipaśyanā, thus enabling the meditator to cut desire at its root. The third, the *path of vision (or seeing)* (Tib. *mthong.lam.*, Skt. *darśana mārga*), is one of stepping beyond saṃsāra, thus attaining the first stage of an accomplished bodhisattva. The fourth, the *path of meditation* (Tib. *sgom.lam.*, Skt. *bhāvana mārga*), is one of passing from the first stage of an accomplished bodhisattva to complete the tenth bhūmi. And, the fifth, the *path of no more learning (or fulfillment)* (Tib. *mi.slob.pa'i.lam.*, Skt. *aśaikṣa mārga*), is one beyond the tenth bhūmi, in the stage of absolute liberation realized by an enlightened being.

Five Sciences *see* PANDITA

Five Skandhas (Tib. *phung.po.lnga.* [phung po nga], Skt. *pañca skandha*) In several sūtras, notably the *Śūrangama Sūtra*, Buddha Śākyamuni taught that the constitution of the sentient being is comprised of five aggregates, which describe both the physical and mental aspects of existence of all sentient beings. These are form (Tib. *gzugs.*, Skt. *rūpa*), sensation (Tib. *tshor.ba.*, Skt. *vedanā*), recognition (Tib. *'du.shes.*, Skt. *saṃjñā*), formation (Tib. *'du.byed.*, Skt. *saṃskāra*), and consciousness (Tib. *rnam.shes.*, Skt. *vijñāna*).

Five Virtues (Tib. *rtsa.ba.lnga.* [tsa wa nga]) Also known as the five basic vows, refers to the vows taken by lay people in which the abjuring of killing, stealing, lying, adultery, and intoxication are adapted as a moral lifestyle. Alternatively entitled lay-person's vows. *See* GENYEN

Five Wisdoms (Tib. *ye.shes.lnga.* [ye she nga], Skt. *pañca jñāna*) The aspects of awareness that are associated with the wisdoms of the five buddha families are: *(1)* Vajrasattva's mirror-like awareness (Tib. *me.long.ye.shes.*, Skt. *ādarśā jnāna*), *(2)* Ratnasaṃbhava's even awareness (Tib. *mnyam.nyid.ye.shes.*, Skt. *samata jñāna*), *(3)* Amitābha's discerning awareness (Tib. *sor.rtogs.ye.shes.*, Skt. *pratyaveksanā jñāna*), *(4)* Amogasiddhi's spontaneously fulfilling awareness (Tib. *bya.grub.ye.shes.*, Skt. *kṛtyānuṣthāna jñāna*), and *(5)* Vairocana's all-encompassing expanse of awareness (Tib. *chos.dbyings.ye.shes.*, Skt. *dharmadhātu jñāna*). *See* BUDDHA FAMILIES

Formless Stage of Meditation *see* DZOGRIM

Form Stage of Meditation *see* KYIRIM

Foundation Practices (Tib. *sngon.'gro.* [ngön dro]) Also known as the four extraordinary preliminaries, referring to the four practices in the major orders of Tibet that are undertaken to eliminate obscurations and to develop the accumulations of merit and wisdom. These generally include one hundred thousand each of prostrations, refuge recitations, Vajrasattva visualizations, maṇḍala offerings, and guru yoga supplications.

Four Activities of Buddhahood (Tib. *'phrin.las.bzhi.* [trin ley zhi]) The activities that are said to embody the energetic compassion of enlightenment, which are those of pacifying, enriching, integrating, and destroying.

Four Demonstrations (or Seals) of Mahāmudrā (Tib. *phyag.rgya.bzhi.* [chak gya zhi]) The development stage known as the mahāmudrā is said to have four demonstrable parts (which are called *seals*): *(1)* the seal of mystical performance (Tib. *las.kyi.phyag.rgya.*); *(2)* the seal of spiritual commitment (Tib. *dam.tshig.gi.phyag.rgya.*); *(3)* the seal of awareness (Tib. *ye.shes.kyi.phyag.rgya.*); and *(4)* the seal of the true nature of mind (Tib. *chos.kyi.phyag.rgya.*). The same stages in Sanskrit are, respectively, *karmamudrā, samayamudrā, jñānamudrā,* and *dharmamudrā.*

Four Eminences (Equivalent title in Tibetan is the name of the lineage in which the tulku is recognized, e.g. XIIth Tai Situpa) Generally known as the spiritual sons of the Kagyu lineage, the current holders of the seat of the Gyalwa Karmapa chosen by him to be his successor: the Tai Situpa, the Sharmarpa, the Gyaltshap, and the Jamgon Kongtrul Rinpoches. Western students have adapted the Catholic tradition of using the title *Eminence* to distinguish the responsibility entailed in the position. Each Eminence is an acknowledged teacher in his own right, and each has hundreds of thousands of students.

Four Infinite Wishes (Tib. *tshad.med.bzhi.* [tshe mey zhi]) The four wishes are: that all sentient beings might always sow and reap the seeds of happiness; that all sentient beings never sow or reap the seeds of sorrow; that all sentient beings will enjoy the pure ālaya which is free from suffering and never separate from happiness; and that all sentient beings will remain in equanimity, free from attachment and aversion. *See* BODHISATTVA

Four Levels of Tantric Yoga (Tib. *gyu.sde.bzhi.* [gyu de zhi]) Tantric yoga is considered to have four levels of development, beginning with the lower tantras, those of kriyātantra, caryātantra, and yogatantra, plus the highest tantra, known as the anuttarayogatantra.

Four Major Doctrines *see* MAJOR ORDERS

Four Noble Truths (Tib. *'phag.pa'i.bden.pa.bzhi.* [phak pay den pa zhi]) During his first public teaching following his enlightenment (an event referred to as the first turning of the wheel of Dharma), Lord Buddha Śākyamuni formulated the teachings of the truth of suffering (Tib. *sdug.bsngal.pa.*), the truth of the cause or origin of suffering (Tib. *kun.'byung.ba.*), the truth of the cessation or annihilation of suffering (Tib. *'gog.pa.*), and the truth of the path leading to the cessation of suffering (Tib. *sdug.bsngal.'gog.par.'gro.ba'.lam.*).

Four Powers (Tib. *stob.bzhi.* [top zhi], Skt. *catvāri bala*) The method of purifying negative actions through (1) sincere repentance while (2) expressing the determination not to commit the negative action again with (3) the use of a conceptual framework to purify oneself and (4) the willing acts to generate positive karmic consequences in compensation. This method rectifies all levels of commitment, including the bodhisattva vows.

Four Stages of Mahāamudrā (Tib. *phyag.chen.bzhi.* [chak chen zhi]) Mahāmudrā is considered to have four levels of experience. The first is *one pointedness* (Tib. *rtse.gcig.*), in which the tranquility of the zhinay practice eventually eradicates dualistic thought. The second stage is termed *away from playwords* (Tib. *spros.bral.*), in which the primordial awareness is now recognized, and the yogi finds no further need for comparative descriptions. The third stage is called *one taste* (Tib. *ro.gcig.*), in which the meditator is freed completely from the hindrances of delusion concerning the nature of nirvāṇa and saṃsāra. The fourth and final stage is that of *non-practice* (Tib. *sgom.med.*), in which the non-effort (Tib. *rtsol.med.*) or non-doing technique of meditation becomes natural in the fully liberated awareness experience of enlightenment. *See* MAHĀMUDRĀ

Four Thoughts that Turn the Mind (to the Dharma) (Tib. *blo.ldog.rnam.bzhi.* [lo dok nam zhi]) Traditionally, one begins the foundation practices by considering: *(1)* the rarity of having obtained a precious human existence and the foolishness at wasting the opportunity; *(2)* the inevitability of death and the impermanence of all phenomena; *(3)* the all-pervasiveness of samsaric suffering and the foolishness of clinging attachment; and *(4)* the inerrant law of karma and the unending fruition of impure ālaya awaiting the sentient being trapped in saṃsāra.

Four Veils of Obscuration *see* OBSCURATION

Freedom From Obstacles *see* ZANGTAL

Gampopa (1079-1153) (Tib. *sgam.po.pa.* [gam po pa]) The successor to Milarepa, Lord Gampopa was persuaded by his wife on her deathbed to follow seriously the path of the Dharma. He became a monk in midlife and eventually found his way to Milarepa, who was his tutor in the final stages of accomplishment. A scholar of the Kadampa tradition of Atīśa, he united the Kadampa teachings with the teachings of the mahāmudrā, which resulted in his founding of the Dakpo Kagyu tradition. He had several brilliant students, among them Dusum Khyenpa, who was to become the first Gyalwa Karmapa and the first holder of the Karma Kagyu lineage, one of the four major subdivisions of the Kagyu tradition. *See* KAGYU LINEAGE, KARMAPA

Gaṇacakra (Skt., Tib. *tshogs.kyi.'khor.lo.* [tshok kyi khor lo]) A ritualistic offering to the tsaway lama and all the buddhas and bodhisattvas, thought to be extraordinarily meritorious. Usually all present partake in a feast of "white" food, which consists of sweet and delicious foods arranged in beautiful maṇḍalas. As this is a tantric ritual, meat and wine are essential ritual offerings. In addition to food offerings, there are other traditional offerings, including flowers, incense, butter lamps, tormas, having extra prayers said for long life, and so forth.

Gelong (Tib. *dge.slong.* [ge long], Skt. *bhikṣu*), **Gelongma** (Tib. *dge.slong.ma.* [ge long ma], Skt. *bhikṣuṇī*) A term denoting full ordination for a monk or nun, which involves over two hundred vows. Currently, the Tibetan tradition does not offer this level of ordination for women, and those desiring it receive vows preserved in the Chinese or Korean traditions. *See* GENYEN, GETSUL

Gelug Lineage (Tib. *dge.lugs.pa.* [ge lug pa]) The most recent of the divisions of Tibetan Buddhism, established in the late fourteenth century by Je Tsong Khapa as a synthesis of the teachings then current in Tibet. *See* MAJOR ORDERS

Genyen (Tib. *dge.bsnyen.* [gen yen], Skt. *upāsaka*), **Genyenma** (Tib. *dge.bsnyen.ma.* [gen yen ma], Skt. *upāsikā*) Refers to a layman or lay woman who has taken the beginning vows of the five virtues; although it is the stage of commitment prior to that of novice monk or nun, the majority of holders of these vows remain at this level of commitment for life. *See* FIVE VIRTUES, GETSUL

Getsul (Tib. *dge.tshul.* [ge tsul], Skt. *śramaṇera*), **Getsulma** (Tib. *dge.tshul.ma.* [ge tsul ma], Skt. *śramaṇerikā*) Refers to a novice monk or nun who has taken thirty-six vows, the stage of vows prior to full ordination. Novice nuns receive ten vows which are subdivided into thirty-six; at present most Tibetan nuns are getsulma. *See* GELONG, GENYEN

Golden Ground of the Universe *see* MT. SUMERU

Ground, Path, and Fruition (Tib. *gzhi.lam.'bras.gsum.* [zhi lam dre sum]) *Ground* refers to the realization of the basic view of the trikāya from the vajrayāna perspective. *Path* is the implementation of meditative absorption to remain true to that view. *Fruition* refers to the actual realization of the unity of ground and path. Here duality transcends into the tathāgatagarbha's spontaneously arising wisdom as the meditator now fully realizes the true nature of the mind and skillfully transmutes time and space into unending liberation.

Guru *see* LAMA, TSAWAY LAMA

Hīnayāna (Skt., Tib. *theg.pa.dman.pa.* [tek pa man pa]) Literally "the lesser vehicle," which refers to its being the first of the three yānas. Its focus is upon pure moral conduct and upon resting the mind in equanimity. *See* MAHĀYĀNA, NINE VEHICLES, VAJRAYĀNA

Historical Buddhas (Tib. *sangs.rgyas.stong.* [sang gye tong]) The central figures, who are born with all the one-hundred and twelve marks of body and speech characteristic only to this level of incarnation, from whom the spread of their teachings of the Dharma flows and flourishes, due to the efforts of the saṅgha. Kalu Rinpoche has explained that one thousand historical Buddhas will appear within this present kalpa, known as the smaller kalpa (Tib. *skal.pa.chung.ngu.*). Following this round of buddhas, a very long period is expected; it is characterized as being an age of darkness because no historical Buddha will appear and no Buddhadharma will be found. Once completed, another ten thousand historical Buddhas will incarnate into this world, in the time referred to as the great kalpa (Tib. *skal.chen.*). Mathematically, the length of these kalpas is astronomical; the rarity of the appearance of even one historical Buddha is thus truly marvelous, and the auspicious coincidence of coming in contact with either the historical Buddhas themselves or their teachings is considered to be extremely fortunate. *See* BUDDHA ŚĀKYAMUNI

Hundred Peaceful and Wrathful Deities *see* MAṆḌALA OF THE HUNDRED PEACEFUL AND WRATHFUL DEITIES

Initiation *see* WANG

Interdependence of Phenomena *see* TWELVE LINKS OF DEPENDENT ORIGINATION

Interdependent Arising of Phenomena (Tib. *sgyu.'phrul.dra.ba.* [gyu drul dra wa]) Literally "web of myriad forms," referring to the spontaneous interdependent arising of all phenomena that demonstrates a delusory and unsubstantial quality in its manifestation (giving it a dream-like quality), which allows manifestations to arise in the same place without either hinderance to one another or any obstacle to this interpenetration, a quality often compared to a magic web, also known as the manifestation web.

Jamgon Kongtrul the Great (1813-1899) (Tib.*'jam.mgon.kong.sprul blo.gros.mtha'.yas.* [jam gon kong trul lo dro thay ye]) One of the famous founders of the Rime Movement, this teacher was considered to be an emanation of Ananda, Lord Buddha's cousin and attendant. He is responsible for several hundred commentaries and for gathering many practices into a body of teachings and initiations known as the five great treasuries. Following a custom among Tibetan authors, he used the Sanskrit equivalent for his monastic name of Yonten Gyatso (Tib. *yon.tan.rgya.mtsho.*), Guna Sagara, meaning "ocean of good qualities." *See* RIME MOVEMENT

Jetsün (Tib. *rje.btsun.* [je tsün]) Respectful term allotted to religious leaders, saints, and great teachers.

Jñāna (Skt., Tib. *ye.shes.* [ye she]) The wisdom awareness that is pure ālaya; primordial awareness.

Kadampa Tradition (Tib. *bka'.gdams.pa.* [ka dam pa]) A style of teaching popular throughout Tibet (especially visible in the some of the branches of the Kagyu lineage) that emphasizes study, the development of compassion through training disciplines, and the observation of monastic precepts. Introduced into Tibet in the eleventh century by the Indian teacher Atīśa, it influenced many teachers, including some of those from whom Gampopa received teachings. It was incorporated into the Kagyu lineage by Gampopa following his succession of Milarepa.

Kagyu Lineage (Tib. *bka'.brgyud.pa.* [ka gyu pa]) The name of the lineage descendent from several great Indian paṇḍitas and from early Tibetan translators that traces its unbroken path of transmission through numerous great yogis, most notably Milarepa. Its name is an abbreviation of the lineages of the four authorized ones (Tib. *bka.bzhi.brgyud.pa.*), referring to its early founders. It is known as the whispered lineage, or the lineage of oral transmission, because Marpa restricted the number of recipients for thirteen successive transmissions. Today, we find four major and eight minor branches. The major branches are *(1)* Karma Kagyu (or the Karma Kamtsang), *(2)* Tsalpa Kagyu, *(3)* Baram Kagyu, and *(4)* Phagdru Kagyu. The disciples of Phagmo Trupa, the founder of the fourth branch, were to develop eight of the lesser branches. The branches are known as *(1)* Drikung, *(2)* Taklung, *(3)* Trophu, *(4)* Drukpa, *(5)* Martsang, *(6)* Yelpa, *(7)* Shuksep, and *(8)* Yamsang. Currently, the Shangpa lineage, itself of completely distinct historical origin, is considered to be a branch of the Karma Kagyu because its lineage has been held by some of the holders of the Karma Kagyu lineage; the Shangpa practices, however, are included through out the various Kagyu and Nyingma lineages. *See* KARMAPA, SHANGPA LINEAGE

Kalpa (Skt., Tib. *bskal.pa.* [kal pa]) A term referring to a very long period of time, sometimes tallied as being four thousand, three hundred and twenty million years. Sometimes thought to be even longer.

Kangyur (Tib. *bka'.'gyur.* [kan gyur]) The Tibetan collection of sūtras which was gathered, along with the *Tangyur*, by the great Buddhist scholar, Buton Rinchendrup (1290-1364) and by other teachers in subsequent editions. It contains one hundred and eight volumes.

Karma (Skt., Tib. *las.* [lay]) "Action," referring to the observation that all actions bear specific results, either wholesome, unwholesome, or neutral; that one's present situation is a product of one's past action; and that likewise one's present action produces the circumstances of the future. Buddhism does not confine the results to a single lifetime but recognizes the accumulation of actions reaped from past lifetimes as well. The law of karma is not considered absolute, and therefore negative karmic fruitions can be eliminated through applying correct purification methods, e.g., the practice of Vajrasattva.

Karmapa (Tib. *ka.rma.pa.* [kar ma pa]) Title given to the succession of reincarnated lineage holders of the Karma Kagyu branch of the Kagyu lineage. The first Gyalwa Karmapa was the successor and lineage holder of Gampopa, and during each of his recognized reincarnations, he has been the holder of the Karma Kagyu lineage. The most recent incarnation, the XVIth Gyalwa Karmapa Rangjung Rigpa Dorje, passed away in the fall of 1981. He and the other heads of the major orders are called *His Holiness* by Western students in an adaptation of the Catholic tradition. *See* FOUR EMINENCES, MAJOR ORDERS

Kleśa (Skt., Tib. *nyon.mongs.* [nyon mong]) Synonymous with poison, this refers to the five afflicted conditions, three of which are considered to be root poisons. Desire (or passion) (Tib. *'dod.chags.*, Skt. *ragā*), aversion (or anger) (Tib. *zhe.sdang.*, Skt. *dveṣa*), and ignorance (or bewilderment) (Tib. *gti.mug.*, Skt. *moha*) are the fundamental three, to which is added arrogance (or pride) (Tib. *nga.rgyal.*, Skt. *mānas*) and envy (or jealousy) (Tib. *phrag.dog.*, Skt. *īrṣyā*).

Kyirim (Tib. *skyed.rim.* [kyi rim], Skt. *utpattikrama*) The generation or developing stage of the anuttarayogatantra, also called the *arising yoga.* In this stage of meditation, the practice focuses upon identifying one's being with that of the yidam, thereby stabilizing vajra pride. *See* DZOGRIM, VAJRA PRIDE

Lama (Tib. *bla.ma.* [la ma], Skt. *guru*) The honorific term conferred by the tsaway lama that designates any person who has fulfilled a certain number of varying conditions. In the Karma Kagyu and Shangpa Kagyu traditions these include the completion of the traditional three-year retreat, the continual observation of several hundreds of vows of various ordinations, and the ongoing practice of vajrayāna sādhanas. This authorization gives the designated permission to give teachings and initiations as specified by the tsaway lama. *See* TSAWAY LAMA

Lhatong (Tib. *lhag.mthong.* [lha thong], Skt. *vipaśyanā*) This term refers to a stage of meditation usually practiced after the meditator has achieved proficiency in the zhinay meditation practice. On the basis of the stability of equipoise, the nature of mind is examined in an analytical manner. It is also called *insight meditation,* and as such relies upon the teachings contained in the *Prajñā Pāramitā Sūtra* regarding the emptiness of all phenomena.

Lung (Tib. *lung*. [lung]) The textual transmission which is required for the practice of tantrayāna yidam sādhanas. It consists of the reading of the instructions concerning the actual performance of the practice (including a recitation of the practice itself), in a rapid flow of speech that is instilled with the quality of attainment of the vajra master who is performing the transmission.

Mādhyamaka (Skt., Tib. *dbu.ma*. [wu ma]) This mahāyāna school employs the concept of dependent origination of all phenomena as its pivotal point of explanation, a theory that has caused it to become known as the middle way school. The focus of the *Prajñā Pāramitā Sūtra* serves as the main perspective in its approach. Its most famous expounder was Nāgārjuna, whose text *Mūlamādhyamakakārikās* is still considered to be the definitive explanation of the scope and breadth of the approach.

Mahā-Anu, Mahā-Ati *see* ANUTTARAYOGATANTRA, NINE VEHICLES

Mahāmudrā (Skt., Tib. *phyag.rgya.chen.po*. [chak gya chen po], in Kalu Rinpoche's dialect [cha ja chen po]) The state of attainment in which the principles of mādhyamaka are effortlessly put into practice. Term may refer either to an ordered set of meditations and instructions designed to prompt the attainment of enlightenment, or to the actual attainment itself. Its literal translation means "great seal" or "great symbolic gesture." *See* FOUR DEMONSTRATIONS OF MAHĀMUDRĀ

Mahāpaṇḍita *see* PAṆḌITA

Mahāsiddhās (Skt., Tib. *grub.chen*. [drup chen]) Great Indian tantric masters known for their simple and direct approaches to the transcendence of saṃsāra. Tilopa and Nāropa, the founders of the Kagyu lineage, are numbered among the famous mahāsiddhās. Persons who have mastered a given pathway, and have thus reached the attainment of an accomplished bodhisattva, are referred to as *siddhās*.

Mahāyāna (Skt., Tib. *theg.pa.chen.po*. [thek pa chen po]) "The greater vehicle," referring to the schools of Buddhist thought based on experiencing śūnyatā, employing compassion, and realizing the unimpeded nature of enlightened awareness. It holds as an ideal the bodhisattva way of life and the commitment to bringing all beings to a state of liberated clarity. Mahāyāna is one of the three yānas. *See* HĪNAYĀNA, VAJRAYĀNA

Major Orders of Vajrayāna Buddhism (Tib. *chos.lugs.bzhi*. [chö luk zhi]) The four major orders of vajrayāna Buddhism established in Tibet, beginning with the 'ancient ones' or Nyingma lineage, and followed by the Sakya, the Kagyu, and the Gelug lineages. Each has various traditions of both sūtra and tantra; each also has its own monastic tradition where the essential teachings of the triyānas is taught. Although their emphases may differ, because there is *no* difference in the final result, they are all *equally* considered to be the best path to enlightment. Other vajrayāna orders (outside the Tibetan cultural base) have developed in India, South-East Asia, Japan, and Korea. *See* RIME MOVEMENT

Mālā (Skt., Tib. *'phreng.ba.* [treng wa]) The name for the prayer beads that are used to count the number of recitations in vajrayāna practice; the standard number of beads, one hundred and eight, symbolize the number of volumes of the *Kangyur.*

Maṇḍala (Skt., Tib. *dkyil.'khor.* [chil khor]) Refers to the environment of an enlightened being, sometimes portrayed as a complex design which co-figures in ritual initiation and in meditation practices. Relating to the symbolic aspects of enlightened energy, maṇḍalas are often very beautiful in their symmetry and are traditionally painted either with colored sands or with paints made from gemstones.

Maṇḍala Offerings *see* FOUNDATION PRACTICES

Maṇḍala of the Hundred Peaceful and Wrathful Deities (Tib.*dam.pa.rigs. rgya.* [dam pa rig gya]) Externally, it is said to be the perfect representation of the embodiment of enlightened mind. Internally, it is said to be the realization of the yogi, in his dynamic state of awareness, of the liberation beyond saṃsāra. From a vajrayāna perspective, the maṇḍala is considered representative of the pure ālaya aspect of the five skandhas, so that the male buddhas of the maṇḍala represent the transformation of the five skandas into the five buddha families, while the female buddhas of the maṇḍala represent the transformation of the five elements into the same. Additionally, the forty-two peaceful deities embody the emptiness (Skt. *śūnyatā*) aspect of enlightenment, and the fifty-eight wrathful deities embody the luminosity (Skt. *prabhāsvara*) aspect of enlightenment.

Mañjuśrī (Skt., Tib. *'jam.dpal.dbyangs.* [jam pal yang]) The founder of all the sciences, the lord of knowledge, the bodhisattva of wisdom, this chief disciple of Lord Buddha has many manifestations and levels of being. Generally considered to be of the Vajra family (of Akṣobhya Buddha), his practice is said to be efficacious in increasing knowledge and learning.

Mantra (Skt., Tib. *sngags.* [ngak]) Sacred verbal expressions used to convey enlightened awareness, the numerous repetitions of which are part of the traditional sādhana practice.

Mantra, The Hundred Syllable (Tib. *yig.brgya.* [yik gya]) A term used to describe an unusually long mantra, regardless of the number of syllables it actually has. The practice of Vajrasattva employs a hundred syllable mantra; this is the mantra generally referred to when the term is used. *See* FOUNDATION PRACTICES

Mantrayāna *see* VAJRAYĀNA

Marpa the Translator (1012-1097) (Tib. *mar.pa.lo.tsa.wa.* [mar pa lo tsa wa]) Most famous as the teacher of Milarepa. Marpa made three grueling trips to India to seek the highest Buddhist teachings from the renowned teachers Nāropa and Maitrīpa. Having established many traditions of the mahāmudrā practice in Tibet, he became even more renowned through the success of his students and the subsequent Kagyu lineage that trace themselves back to his extraordinary efforts.

Meditation (Tib. *sgom.* [gom]) In vajrayāna, there are several styles of meditation. Those that are reflective (which still the mind or which consider the true nature of the mind) are termed *lhatong* and *zhinay*, which are employed in the mahāmudrā approach. Additionally, the vajrayāna contains purifying practices, accumulation of merit practices, and devotional practices, all of which use mantra recitation and visualization before beginning silent meditation. Generally, most vajrayāna practices employ the yidam sādhana, which is said to cultivate the enlightened awareness.

Mental Body *see* BODY OF THE BARDO EXPERIENCE

Merit, Accumulation of (Tib. *bsod.nams.tshogs.bsag.* [so nam tshok sag]) Considered to be an all-important aspect in the practice of vajrayāna and in the accomplishment of enlightenment. Traditionally, the practitioner dedicates the merit accumulated from any good deed and from the performance of any spiritual practice so that it will bring benefit to all sentient beings. One of the highest and most meritorious acts possible is the sponsoring of the gaṇacakra ritual; others include building stūpas, monasteries, or three-year retreat centers, supporting members of the saṅgha, and so forth. The accumulation of wisdom and of merit are referred to as the two accumulations.

Meru, Mt. *see* MT. SUMERU

Middle Path (or Way) *see* MĀDHYAMAKA

Milarepa (1040-1123) (Tib. *mi.la.ras.pa.* [mi la re pa]) The successor to Marpa the Translator, Milarepa became the most famous of the Tibetan yogis. Adhering to Marpa's instructions that he lead a solitary life, Milarepa wandered from cave to cave, shunning wealth and glamour. He taught many who came across him in the wilderness and, eventually, had a tight circle of ascetics around him, all of whom accomplished great degrees of attainment under his guidance. His teachings were given in the form of spontaneous songs, which are recorded in *The Hundred Thousand Songs of Milarepa, Drinking The Mountain Stream*, and *Miraculous Journey*. His successor was Lord Gampopa.

Mudrā (Skt., Tib. *phyag.rgya*. [chak gya]) Literally "gesture," or "symbol," referring to the specific characterization given in symbolic meaning to any sort of object, either real or abstract. For instance, the crystal mālā and the lotus are mudrās of Chenrezig. It may also refer to the hand gestures that traditionally accompany sādhana practices. The symbol of mudrā and the mudrā itself are considered to be inseparable.

Nāḍi(s) (Skt.) Subtle energy channel(s), of which there are said to be 72,000 in the human body. Three are primary: the central channel (Tib. *rtsa.dbu.ma*. [tsa u ma], Skt. *avadhūti nāḍī*), and the channels to the left (Tib. *rtsa.rkyang.ma*. [tsa kyang ma], Skt. *lalanā nāḍī*) and right (Tib. *rtsa.ro.ma*. [tsa ro ma], Skt. *rasanā nāḍī*) of the central channel. All course from below the navel to the head and are used in various breathing practices and visualizations of the vajrayāna traditions. *See* BINDU, CAKRAS

Nāga (Skt., Tib. *klu*. [lu]) A class of beings having the body of the snake, the wealth of the world, and the advantage of knowledge. They are said to live in marshy water areas and are thought to be hoarders of the treasures of the earth. Some are said to be quite spiritually advanced, due to the blessing of having guarded the *Prajñā Pāramitā* teachings of Lord Buddha Śākyamuni until the incomparable Nāgārjuna went to the nāga realm and brought them back.

Nāgārjuna (first or second century A.D.) (Tib. *klu.sgrub*. [lu grup]) Founder of the Mādhyamaka school, this Indian mahāsiddhā is also called the *second Buddha* for his penetrating insight into the *Prajñā Pāramitā Sūtra*. His major work was *Mūlamādhyamakakārikās*. *See* MĀDHYAMAKA

Namdok (Tib. *rnam.rtog*. [nam dok]) A term with many meanings, it is commonly used to refer to the unceasing and often disturbing flow of thoughts (including those that are wild, impulsive, imaginative, and fantastic) that bind one in saṃsāra.

Nāropa (1016-1100) (Tib. *na.ro.pa*. [na ro pa]) Renowned disciple of Tilopa and teacher to Marpa the Translator, this scholar from Bengal had became a monk in his early life and eventually served as the abbot of Nālandā, one of the greatest Indian Buddhist universities. He spent many years as a wandering yogi before finally meeting his tsaway lama, the incomparable Tilopa. He is also known as Nāropa, the North Door Keeper (Tib. *byang.sgo.bsrung.ba*.), an honor awarded his fame and position as one of

Vikramaśīla monastery's six famous professors in sitting.

Nidānas *see* TWELVE LINKS OF INTERDEPENDENCE

Nine Vehicles (Tib. *theg.pa.dgu.* [tek pa gu]) In the Nyingma tradition there are nine vehicles, or yānas. The hīnayāna is considered to be comprised of two, namely, the śrāvakayāna and the pratyekabuddhayāna. These, along with the mahāyāna, are considered to be the lesser yānas. The greater yānas are those of the lower level of tantric yoga, namely, kriyā, cārya (upa), and yoga yānas. The supreme yānas are considered to be the mahā-yoga, mahā-anu, and mahā-ati yānas. *See* TRIYĀNA

Nirmāṇakāya (Skt., Tib. *sprul.sku.* [tul ku]) The absolute compassion that demonstrates the essential nature of the form of the buddhas and accomplished bodhisattvas as undifferentiated from the inherent emptiness of phenomenal existence; the most notable manifestation being that of the historical Buddhas. Nirmāṇakāya sustains the demonstration of the five skandas within all phenomenal existence, displaying itself in an infinite array of manifestations, including that of the characteristics, features, and form of everyday life. Also, it is a term used in reference to the emanations of great artisans, reincarnated teachers, and historical Buddhas.

Nirvāṇa (Skt., Tib. *mya.ngan.las.'das.pa.* [nya ngen lay de pa]) Considered to be the pinnacle of accomplishment in the victory over saṃsāra, it represents the cessation of rebirth in saṃsāra and the end of suffering.

Nyingma Lineage (Tib. *rnying.ma.pa.* [nying ma pa]) The lineage that has remained unbroken since its eighth-century founder, Padma Saṃbhava, firmly established Buddhism in Tibet by subduing many opposing forces. Its literal meaning, "older ones," refers to its role in the historical establishment of Buddhism in Tibet. Today, there are five main lineage traditions within the Nyingma order, each representing untold volumes of texts, terma, and transmissions. *See* MAJOR ORDERS

Obscuration (Tib. *sgrib.pa.* [drip pa], Skt. *āvarana*) The description of the various degrees of obscurity that the deluded mind experiences in saṃsāra are said to number four levels or stages. In the first stage the mind does not see itself and so remains ignorant of its own true nature; it is termed the *obscuration of fundamental ignorance* (Tib. *ma.rig. pa'i.sgrib.pa.*). The second stage develops as the mind searches itself for something other than its true nature, and thereby defines a self; this is termed the *obscuration of habitual tendencies* (Tib. *bag.chags.kyi.sgrib.pa.*). The third is the stage of delusional development of the mind in which it reacts in its bewilderment with either clinging attachment or discriminatory aversion; the term for this level is *obscuration of emotional afflictions*

(Tib. *nyon.mongs.pa'i.sgrib.pa.*). And fourth, obscuration now breeds obscuration, as the endless mental, verbal, and physical reaction to the mind's emotional confusion (which was spawned from the mistaken concept of duality of self and other) is now bound to the law of karmic fruition; this has been termed the *obscuration of karma* (Tib. *las. kyi.sgrib.pa.*).

Padma Saṃbhava (c. 717-762) (Tib. *padma.sam.bha.ba.* [padma sam bha va]) Also known as Guru Rinpoche, this famous eighth-century teacher is credited with subduing the opposing spiritual forces that objected to the introduction and propagation of Buddhism in Tibet. Padma Saṃbhava, so named because he first appeared in the center of a lotus in the middle of a lake in Uḍḍiyāṇa, was called to Tibet by the king Trisong Detsen. He is the founder of the Nyingma lineage. *See* NINE VEHICLES

Paṇḍita (Skt., Tib. *pa.ndi.ta.* [pan di ta]) A term used to denote a scholar; also, a title given to one who has mastered the five sciences. The five sciences (Tib. *rig.pa'i.gnas.lgna.*) are language (Tib. *sgra'i.rig.pa.*), dialectics (Tib. *gtan.tshigs.rig.pa.*), spiritual thought (Tib. *nang.rig.pa.*), mechanical arts (Tib. *bzo'i.gnas.rig.pa.*), and medicine (Tib. *gso.ba.rig.pa.*). A truly great scholar is called a *mahāpaṇḍita*.

Parinirvāṇa (Skt., Tib. *yongs.su.mya.ngan.las.'das.pa.* [yong su nya ngen lay de pa]) The historical Buddha's departure from his physical form. Tibetan Buddhists observe the celebration of the historical Buddha Śākyamuni's birth, enlightenment, and parinirvāṇa on the fourth full moon of the Tibetan year, which can occur in either May or June.

Phowa (Tib. *'pho.ba.* [pho wa]) One of the six yogas of Nāropa, this training focuses on transferring the consciousness at the moment of death to the pure lands of Buddha Amitābha as a means of breaking the cycle of rebirth.

Poisons *see* KLEŚA

Prajñā Pāramitā (Skt., Tib. *shes.rab.kyi.pha.rol.tu.phyin.pa.* [she rab kyi pha rol tu chin pa]) A body of teachings contained in the mahāyāna sūtras that expounds upon the empty nature of phenomena. Often translated *perfection of wisdom*, this term is also used to name the female buddha who is representative of perfect wisdom.

Pratyekabuddha (Skt., Tib. *rang.sangs.rgyas.* [rang sang gye]) In the Tibetan tradition, this term symbolizes a specific stage or level of realization that is attained through the examination of the twelvefold chain of dependent origination. This stage of development, however, is not considered to be that of a fully realized buddha. In the early texts, the term referred to a sentient being who attains liberation without the benefit of a teacher and who does not teach others. It is also the name of the second of the nine yānas.

Precious Human Existence (Tib. *dal.'byor.lus.rten.* [dal jor lü ten]) A term that indicates a number of freedoms and opportunities associated with being human. The freedoms come from not having been born in any of the eight unrestful states. The opportunities refer to both one's personal condition and one's environment. The *five personal opportunities* include *(1)* being born human, *(2)* with one's senses and intelligence intact, *(3)* in a country where the Dharma exists, *(4)* as a person capable of having faith in the Three Jewels, and *(5)* without the karmic compulsions to commit evil deeds. The *five environmental opportunities* include *(1)* being born in an age in which a historical Buddha has appeared, and *(2)* has taught the Dharma, such that *(3)* the Dharma has not declined but is enduring; as well, being born *(4)* in a region where many practice the Dharma, and *(5)* where others are motivated by genuine faith and kindness to help one in one's practice. *See* EIGHT NON-FREEDOMS, EIGHT UNRESTFUL STATES

Primordial Consciousness *see* ĀLAYA-VIJÑĀNA

Primordial Wisdom *see* TATHĀGATAGARBHA

Pure Lands (Tib. *dag.pa'i.zhing.khams.* [dak pay zhing kham]) The sphere of activity of the buddhas; it is said of those sentient beings who have reached a stage of accomplishment while in a precious human body that they will mature their bodhisattva paths in this realm. Of all the pure lands, Dewachen (the pure land of Buddha Amitābha) is the best known, but pure lands of Vajrasattva and the other saṃbhogakāya buddhas are also considered to be obtainable rebirths.

Red Hat Lineage (Tib. *shwa.dmar.* [sha mar]) A designation applying to the Nyingma, Sakya, and Kagyu lineages to distinguish them from the reformed tradition of the Gelug, who are known as the yellow hat lineage (Tib. *shwa.ser.*).

Refuge *see* TAKING REFUGE

Relative Reality (Tib. *kun.rdzob.* [kun dzop]) A term used to describe the manner of phenomenal manifestation and of causality. *See* ABSOLUTE REALITY

Rime Movement (Tib. *ris.med.* [ri mey]) An ecumenical movement initiated by Jamgon Kongtrul the Great, Khyentse Wangpo, Mipham Rinpoche, Dechen Lingpa, and many others, to overcome the strongly sectarian atmosphere of nineteenth-century Tibet. This sectarianism had grown during four hundred years of political competition between the monasteries of the four major orders. By re-establishing individual practice as the basis of the Dharma and by skillfully acknowledging that all the schools were successful in their various approaches to attaining the one goal of enlightenment, the movement sought to encourage tolerance and forbearance toward all of the other orders, and to dispel the prevalent notions that denied the validity of other approaches.

Rinchen Terdzod (Tib. *rin.chen.gter.mdzod.* [rin chen ter dzö]) Called one of the *five great treasuries,* this is an extensive collection of terma initiations and pointing out instructions that were gathered by the vajra master Jamgon Kongtrul the Great. Consisting of over a hundred volumes of text, the collection takes several months to be fully transmitted. Kalu Rinpoche gave this great blessing in 1983 to thousands of practitioners at his monastery in Sonada, India.

Rinpoche (Tib. *rin.po.che.* [rim po che]) An honorific term meaning "precious one," it is usually conferred upon a lama by the tsaway lama in recognition of a degree of advancement in spiritual practice or of a person's being a reincarnation of a former great practitioner. It is also used affectionately to refer to persons considered to be quite holy.

Root Guru *see* TSAWAY LAMA

Rūpakāya (Skt., Tib. *gzugs.kyi.sku.* [zuk kyi ku]) Literally, "form kāyas," referring to the outer kāyas consisting of the body and the speech of all the buddhas. It is the counterpart to dharmakāya, and, together, they are termed the *two kāyas.* *See* NIRMĀṆAKĀYA, SAMBHOGAKĀYA

Sādhana (Skt., Tib. *sgrub.thabs.* [trup thap]) The vajrayāna meditation practice of a yidam, including the text used in the practice.

Sakya Lineage (Tib. *sa.skya.pa.* [sa kya pa]) A lineage of Tibetan Buddhism founded by Khon Kunchok Gyalpo, who was a contemporary of Marpa the Translator; the order combined elements from several lineages and has since evolved its own path of transmission. *See* MAJOR ORDERS

Samādhi (Skt., Tib. *ting.nge.'dzin.* [ting nge dzin]) Meditative absorption; (used alone, without any qualifying indication, the term contains no indication as to the level or degree of insight present in that absorption).

Samādhi of 'Elemental-Exhaustion' (Tib. *zad.pa.'byung.ba'i.ting.nge.'dzin.* [ze pa jung bay ting nge dzin]) In extremely advanced stages of yogic attainment, the yogi is able to control the prajñā-mind within his physio-mental complex, and is thus able to intentionally manifest the power of any of the five elements, and to use the five elements to create specific results. Milarepa's demonstration of this mastery is told by Kalu Rinpoche in the text.

Samantabhadra (Skt., Tib. *kun.tu.bzang.po.* [kun tu zang po]) Said to be both the primordial buddha nature that ultimately prevails in all sentient beings, and the essential seed of buddha nature present in all sentient beings; sometimes Samantabhadra is characterized as being the first buddha.

Samaya (Skt., Tib. *dam.tshig.* [dam tshik]) The bond of commitment that exists between the vajra master and the student of vajrayāna. Generally, samaya is incurred only when taking vajrayāna initiations. The extent of this commitment is detailed as fourteen major and eight minor vows, but may also be particular to the specifics of the oath requested by the vajra master. See VAJRA BROTHERS AND SISTERS

Sambhogakāya (Skt., Tib. *longs.spyod.rdzogs.pa'i.sku.* [long cho dzok pay ku] or *longs.sku.* [long ku]) Known as the illuminating mind potential, this is the quality of the Buddha's speech that is empty like the echo, yet said to be full of all the wisdom of all the Dharmas. Additionally in this text its usage sometimes refers to the dreamlike quality of reality; other times it refers to the path emanated from the dharmakāya that serves as a demonstration that enlightenment is an attainable goal.

Saṃsāra (Skt., Tib. *'khor.ba.* [khor wa]) The cyclic nature of phenomenal manifestation and existence; refers to the concept of the beginningless and endless process of birth, death, and rebirth to which sentient beings are bound until they are liberated through enlightenment. See SIX REALMS OF SAMSĀRA

Saṅgha (Skt., Tib. *dge.'dun.* [gen dun]) The Sanskrit term used to denote the followers of Lord Buddha's teachings. It may refer specifically to those with monastic ordination, or, more generally, it may be used to refer to both lay and monastic practitioners. It may also refer to the community of accomplished arhats and bodhisattvas.

Seed Syllable (Tib. *rtsa.sngags.* [tsa ngak]) The primal embodiment of the enlightened mind, these sacred letters play an important part in the developing stage of meditative visualization. Each yidam has its own seed syllable, as well as its own mantra. See KYIRIM

Sentient Beings (Tib. *sems.can.* [sem chen]) All beings, in all the six realms of samsāra, who possess (to any degree) the ability to perceive or to feel, which is considered indicative of their having consciousness.

Seven Offerings (Tib. *yan.lag.bdun.pa.* [yan lak dun pa]) A popularization of seven out of the ten vows of the Bodhisattva Samantabhadra, as recorded in the *Avataṃsaka Sūtra,* which are considered to be exemplary of seven of the bodhisattva's ten actions. These are: *(1)* paying homage to all the buddhas and bodhisattvas in all the ten directions; *(2)* making offerings to all the assembly of enlightened ones; *(3)* expressing contrition and resolve concerning one's non-virtuous actions; *(4)* delighting in the joyous good fortune and virtues of others; *(5)* beseeching the buddhas and bodhisattvas to teach the Dharma; *(6)* imploring the accomplished bodhisattvas and the buddhas not to abandon sentient beings drowning in the ocean of saṃsāra; and *(7)* dedicating the accumulation of merit generated from this recitation, and from all actions, so it may serve to benefit all sentient beings in their attainment of enlightened awareness. Also the seven offerings may be either visualized or actualized in the use of shrine bowls containing the seven offerings of drinking water, water to wash the feet, flowers, incense, light, scented water to drink, and food.

Seven Postures of Vairocana (Tib. *snyam.snyang.chos.bdun.* [nyam nyang chö dun], Skt. *saptadharma Vairocana*) This term refers to the ideal posture of the Buddha Vairocana, illustrative of the posture the meditator should ideally assume. The various aspects of this bodily positioning are: *(1)* holding the torso up-right in a stable but relaxed manner, *(2)* gazing at a point in space four or more inches in front of the nose, with the chin and neck held upright, *(3)* settling the shoulders back, (in the manner of a vulture flexing its wings), *(4)* holding the lips lightly closed and keeping the tongue touching the front of the upper palate, *(5)* tucking the chin in slightly, *(6)* crossing the legs either tightly or loosely in the vajrasana or padmasana postures, and *(7)* resting the hands at the navel in the mudrā formed by placing the upturned right hand on top of the upturned left hand, with the tips of the thumbs lightly touching.

Śamatha (or Shamatha) *see* ZHINAY

Shangpa Lineage (Tib. *shangs.pa.* [shang pa]) Founded by the incomparable Khyungpo Naljor in the eleventh century, the lineage draws its name from the place where its main monastery was located. Khyungpo Naljor lived to be 150 years old, and had over 150 teachers and tsaway lamas, including some of the most famous enlightened women in the history of vajrayāna. The lineage mainly draws from the teachings given to Khyungpo Naljor by these women, as well as its highly respected tradition of protector practices. Most lineage traditions of the protector Mahākāla trace themselves back to the Shangpa lineage. The Shangpa lineage is now considered a branch of the Karma Kagyu tradition. Bokar Tulku Rinpoche is the present lineage holder, having received this authority from Kalu Rinpoche, who received his authority from the former retreat master of Palpung Monastery, Norbu Döndrup Rinpoche.

Śrāvakas (Skt., Tib. *nyan.thos.* [nyen tho]) Beings who have obtained the śrāvakayāna, the first level of the nine yānas, where the realization of full awareness begins to dawn, a stage that is often compared to infancy in the human life cycle. Śrāvakas are characterized as listeners who rely wholly upon spiritual discourses and the advice of their teacher. They are said to have grasped the essential truth concerning the emptiness of self but not the emptiness of phenomena other-than-self characteristic of the following stage of the pratyekabuddhas.

Śūnyatā (Skt., Tib. *stong.pa.nyid.* [tong pa nye]) Although often misconstrued to mean nothingness (in the sense of absence or extinction), this term actually refers to the interdependence of phenomenal existence which precludes any self-existence, inherent or otherwise. It is also used to describe the experience of the dharmakāya, the essential quality of enlightened mind, which is said to be beyond any delusion.

Siddhās *see* MAHĀSIDDHĀS

Six Consciousnesses (Tib. *rnam.shes.tshogs.drug.* [nam shi tshok druk]) The perceptions and experiences of the five sensory organs together with the thought process, thereby totalling six. Its components, the six sense objects, comprise form, sound, smell, taste, touch, and dharma (ideas).

Six Elements (Tib. *'byung.ba.drug.* [jung wa druk]) Considered in Buddhist thought to be the elements of earth, water, fire, wind (air), space, and consciousness. All six elements are at play in the human realm; however, other realms are said to be lacking in some of the elements, *i.e.*, the form heavens of the gods' realm lack earth, water, and fire, the formless heavens of the gods' realm have only the manifestation of consciousness, and the animal realm, by contrast, has all the basic five elements but lacks the overt quality of consciousness known as wisdom (Tib. *ye.shes.*, Skt. *jñāna*).

Six Pāramitās (Skt., Tib. *pha.rol.tu.phyin.pa.drug.* [pha rol tu chin pa druk]) Literally "to cross to the other side," referring to the transcendent actions that lead to the other shore of enlightenment that is self-existent beyond the shore of karmic entanglements, these virtuous practices or perfections of the mahāyāna path are: *generosity* (Tib. *sbyin.pa.*, Skt. *dhāna*), *discipline* (Tib. *tshul.khrims.*, Skt. *śīla*), *patience* (Tib. *bzod.pa.*, Skt. *kṣānti*), *exertion* (Tib. *btson.'grus.*, Skt. *vīrya*), *meditation* (Tib. *bsam.gtan.*, Skt. *dhyāna*), and *wisdom* (Tib. *shes.rab.*, Skt. *prajñā*).

Six Realms of Saṃsāra (Tib. *'gro.ba.rigs.drug.* [dro wa rik druk]) In order of ascension, the three lower realms are: the *hell realms* (Tib. *dmyal.ba.*,

Skt. *naraka*), where beings suffer the consequences of past wrong actions of anger in extreme settings of heat or cold; the *hungry ghost realms* (Tib. *yi.dwags.*, Skt. *pretā*), where beings suffer the consequences of past greed in extreme hunger, having either an inadequate food source or an inappropriate consumptive organism; and the *animal* realms (Tib. *dud.'gro.*, Skt. *tiryañca*), where beings suffer the consequences of past ignorance in the extreme conditions of having always to seek shelter, protection, and food. The three higher realms are: the *human realm* (Tib. *mi.*, Skt. *manuśya*), where beings suffer the consequences of past pride in extremes of weather, environment, and societies; the *demi-gods' realms* (Tib. *lha.ma.yin.*, Skt. *asura*), where beings suffer the consequences of past jealousy in the extremes of warlike situations and settings; and the *gods' realms* (Tib. *lha.*, Skt. *deva*), where beings suffer the consequences of past laziness in the extremes of pleasures that eventually come to an end.

Six Yogas of Nāropa (Tib. *na.ro.chos.drug.* [Naro chö druk]) The practices given by Nāropa to Marpa the Translator. These include: tummo (or psychic heat) yoga (Tib. *gtum.mo.*); illusory (or apparition) body yoga (Tib. *sgyu.lus.*); dream yoga (Tib. *rmi.lam.*); radiant light (or clear light) yoga (Tib. *'od.gsal.*); bardo yoga (Tib. *bar.do.*); and transference yoga (Tib. *'pho.ba.*). Considered a basic part of the Kagyu traditions of training, they are usually taught within the three-year retreat cycle.

Skandhas *see* FIVE SKANDHAS

Storehouse Consciousness *see* ĀLAYA-VIJÑĀNA

Stūpa (Skt., Tib. *mchod.rten.* [cho ten]) The structures that serve as reliquaries for the Buddha Śākyamuni's remains, constructed by devoted followers in symbolic memory of his body, speech, and mind. Later, other saint's relics were also placed in stūpas, as were scriptures, statues, etc. Traditionally, very large ones are circumambulated in a clockwise direction, while smaller versions are used to decorate shrines, etc. Stūpas are said to be symbolic representations of the world in the mind of the Buddha, and, likewise, representative of the Buddha's mind in the world.

Sufferings (Tib. *sdug.bsngal.* [duk ngal], Skt. *dukha*) Generally considered to be of either three or four types. The three sufferings are thought of as the *fundamental, all-pervasive suffering* (Tib.*rkyab.pa.'du. byed. kyi. sdug. bsngal.*), the *suffering of change*, (Tib. *'gyur.ba'i.sdug.bsngal.*), and the *suffering of suffering* (Tib. *sdug.bsngal.kyi.sdug.bsngal.*). The *four sufferings* are those of sentient existence, namely, birth, aging, ill-health, and death. These four are sometimes referred to as the four devils (Tib. *bdud.bzhi.*).

Sumeru, Mt. (Skt., Tib. *gling.bzhi.ri.rab.* [ling zhi ri rab]) Also known as Mt. Meru or the legendary center of the universe, thought of as being made of precious gems and arising from an ocean resting on the golden ground of the universe and bound by a ring of iron mountains. Various islands and smaller continents surround it. According to Buddhist legends, the world as we know it is contained in that sectional division of the ocean surrounding Mt. Sumeru known as South, where there is a continent which enjoys blue seas and skies. Other sectional directions have seas and skies in red, white, and gold, respectively.

The four continents are: to the South, Jambudvīpa (Skt., Tib. *lho.'dzam.bu.gling.*); to the West, Aparagodānīya (Skt., Tib. *nub.ba.glang.spyod.*); to the North, Uttarakuru (Skt., Tib. *byang.sgra.mi.snyan.*); and to the East, Pūrvavideha (Skt., Tib. *shar.lus.'phags.pa.*).

Sūtra(s) (Skt., Tib. *mdo.* [do]) The discourse(s) of the historical Buddha Śākyamuni; originally written in Pali, they have been translated into several languages.

Svabhāvikakāya (Skt., Tib. *ngo.bo.nyid.sku.* [ngo bo nye ku]) The fourth kāya, referring to the coemergence of the trikāya with the body, speech, and mind gates of the precious human existence.

Taking Refuge (Tib. *skyabs.su.'gro.ba.* [chap su dro wa], Skt. *sāraṇa*) The formal commitment taken before a lama that indicates the student has determined to become free from saṃsāra by attaining the fully liberated state of buddhahood. It also indicates that the person receiving the refuge vow accepts the Lord Buddha's teachings (the Dharma) and his close followers (the Saṅgha). In vajrayāna, one also takes refuge in the Three Roots — Tsaway Lama, Yidam, and Dharmapālas.

Tangyur (Tib. *bstan.'gyur.* [tan gyur]) Part of the Tibetan scriptural compilation by the great Buddhist scholar, Buton Rinchendrup (1290-1364), with later redactions by others, this is the collection of commentaries made by authoritative Indian Buddhist masters. *See KANGYUR*

Tantra (Skt., Tib. *rgyud.* [gyü]) Literally "thread" or "continuity," it is a term used to describe the esoteric pathway assumed by the followers of vajrayāna. Also refers to a collection of many writings joined as texts, called *tantras* (Tib. *brgyud.*), that serve as sādhanas and commentaries on the basic teachings of the triyānas, with special emphasis on the vajrayāna.

Tantrayāna *see* VAJRAYĀNA

Tārā (Skt., Tib. *sgrol.ma.* [drol ma]) The embodiment of the female aspect of compassion, Tārā is an emanation of Chenrezig, said to have arisen from his tears of compassion. Traditionally, the Green Tārā practice is considered useful in overcoming obstacles and promoting prosperity, and the White Tārā practice is said to help promote long life and a successful spiritual practice.

Tathāgata (Skt., Tib. *de.bzhin.gshegs.pa.* [de zhin shek pa]) An epithet for the Buddha implying that he is the nature of suchness. Controversy over the translation has produced learned commentary from the third century B.C. up until today. It stems from how the compound word is analyzed: if it is broken into tātha⌢gata, it means thus gone; if it is broken into tathā⌢agata, it means thus come. Given the nature of Sanskrit phonetics, the word could be translated either way. *See* BUDDHA ŚĀKYAMUNI, EMPTINESS

Tathāgatagarbha (Skt., Tib. *de.bzhin.gshegs.pa'i.snying.po.* [de zhin shek pay nying po]) The potential considered to be inherent in all sentient beings, that of the pure ālaya of enlightened awareness. Thus, it is said that a buddha is one who has re-discovered his or her true nature.

Ten Levels of Bodhisattva *see* BHŪMI

Ten Non-Virtuous Actions (Tib. *mi.dge.ba.bcu.* [mi ge wa cu], Skt. *akuśala*) The opposites of the ten virtuous actions, they include killing, stealing, committing adultery, lying, divisive speech, using course language, talking nonsense, being covetous, exhibiting anger, and stubbornly holding wrong views.

Ten Virtuous Actions (Tib. *dge.ba.bcu.* [ge wa cu], Skt. *daśa kuśala*) These actions are divided into three of body: protecting life (Tib. *srog.skyob.pa.*), generosity (Tib. *sbyin.pa.*), preservation of moral conduct (Tib. *tshul.khrims. srung.ba.*); four of speech: truthful speech (Tib. *bdeny. par.smra.ba.*), reconciliation (Tib. *'khon.sdum.pa.*), pleasant speech (Tib. *ngag.'jam.por.smra.ba.*), worthwhile speech (Tib. *don.dang.ldan.pa'i.gtam.*); and three of mind: contentment (Tib. *chog.shes.*), bodhicitta aspiration (Tib. *phan.sems.*), and abandoning wrong views (Tib. *log.lta.spong.ba.*).

Textual Transmission *see* LUNG

Thirteenth Stage of Enlightenment (Tib. *bcu.sum.rdo.rje.'dzin.pa'i.sa.* [cu sum dor je dzin pay sa]) Considered to be the full realization of the absolute truth within the vehicle of the vajrayāna, this stage is accomplished only after having crossed the ten bhūmis (or stages) of bodhisattva development.

Three Gates (Tib, *sgo.gsum* [go sum]) Body, speech, and mind are thought of as being the openings (or gates) of the trikāya.

Three Jewels (Tib. *dkon.mchog.gsum.* [kon chok sum], Skt. *triratna*) Lord Buddha Śākyamuni, his teachings (known as the Dharma), and his followers (or Saṅgha), which are considered so precious that they are known as the Three Jewels. *See* BUDDHA ŚĀKYAMUNI, TAKING REFUGE, THREE ROOTS

Three Roots (Tib. *rtsa.ba.gsum*. [tsa wa sum]) The essential ingredients of vajrayāna practice, namely, the Tsaway Lama, the Yidams, and the Dharmapālas. *See* TAKING REFUGE, THREE JEWELS

Three Times (Tib. *dus.gsum*. [dü sum]) The past, the present, and the future; a reference meaning throughout the whole of time.

Three-Year Retreat (Tib. *lo.gsum.phyogs.gsum*. [lo sum chok sum]) Also called the *three-year, three-month, three-day retreat,* it is held in total isolation and is organized in such a way so as to allow the progressive development of the traditions of vajrayāna approach, i.e., foundation practices, yidam practices, the mahāmudrā, etc. On several occasions, Kalu Rinpoche sought to dispel some of the confusion concerning the titles associated with persons who have completed such a retreat. He clarified that persons who complete it and who no longer desire to continue their vows of being either a nun or a monk are traditionally called *yoginī* or *yogi,* respectively (Tib. *rnal.'byor.ma.* and *rnal.'bjor.*). Those monks that do retain their vows are usually called *lama* to distinguish their level of discipline from that of the normal monk. A woman who keeps her vows following the retreat is referred to as ani, meaning nun. (Although this is not a title specifically designating the distinction of having completed the retreat, according to Kalu Rinpoche, this is neither a slight nor an oversight. He explained that when the lineage transmission for full bhikṣuṇī ordination is reinstated in the Tibetan tradition, which will require ten women to take full ordination in other mahāyāna lineages and to keep these vows for at least ten years, then there was a strong likelihood if enough requests are received from fully ordained nuns wishing to distinguish themselves from other nuns as having completed the three-year retreat that a distinguishing title may be designated, presumably by the reigning holder of the Kagyu lineage). *See* LAMA, TSAWAY LAMA

Tilopa (988-1069) (Tib. *ti.lo.pa*. [ti lo pa]) This Indian mahāsiddhā was the teacher of Nāropa, and is noted for his lineage of the mahāmudrā, which he is said to have received directly from Dorje Chang. He is the original founding father of the Kagyu lineages.

Tonglen (Tib. *gtong.len*. [tong len]) A practice promulgated by Atīśa while he was in Tibet, it focuses on expanding the consciousness of the meditator through the application of compassion and loving kindness. The practice involves the meditator visualizing that the in-breath draws in all the suffering of sentient beings, which is transformed by the meditator's heartfelt prayer for the cessation of all suffering. The out-breath bestows a blessing of purity that is of great benefit to all sentient beings. It is considered to be an excellent way to increase and develop bodhicitta.

Tri (Tib. *'khrid.* [tri]) The instructions that are given following the vajrayāna tradition of initiation and textual transmission, which clarify the procedural approach to accomplish the yidam practice. Considered the necessary third ingredient before a yidam practice of the tantrayāna tradition can be commenced.

Triyāna (Skt., Tib. *theg.pa.gsum.* [tek pa sum]) Collectively, the manifestation of the clear luminosity of the unimpeded emptiness of the mind of the buddhas. Known as the *vehicle of expression of the experience of transcendence,* it has three facets, that of the hīnayāna, the mahāyāna, and the vajrayāna.

Tsaway Lama (Tib. *rtsa.ba'i.bla.ma.* [tsa way la ma], Skt. *mūlaguru*) Literally "primary guru," often translated as source or root guru. It is thought that the physical form and activities of a vajra master (in performing vajrayāna initiations and giving teachings on the four levels of tantric yoga) are the nirmāṇakāya form of the Lord Buddha Śākyamuni and that the connection formed between students and the tsaway lama allows the students an opportunity to develop their bodhicitta in full certainty of the unbroken connection with that of Lord Buddha himself, as established by the tsaway lama's unbroken lineage. Also one of the Three Roots of vajrayāna, in which usage the term refers to the absoluteness of the union of wisdom and skillful means that is the mind of enlightened awareness (on a dharmakāya level), that is the path of enlightened recognition (on a saṃbhogakāya level), and that is the form of enlightened teaching (on a nirmāṇakāya level). Thus, this Root takes the nirmāṇakāya form of that of the physical teacher, has the saṃbhogakāya manifestation of that of the yidam, and demonstrates dharmakāya in both absolute and relative reality.

Twelve Links of Dependent Origination (Tib. *rten.'brel.bcu.gnyis.* [ten drel cu nye], Skt. *dvadaśa pratītya samutpāda*) The successive stages (Skt. *nidānas*) of ignorance (Tib. *ma.rig.pa.*) of the formation of karmic consequences of habitual tendencies (Tib. *'du.byed.*) thereby producing a dualistic consciousness (Tib. *rnam.par.shes.pa.*) that naturally spawns the sense of embodiment (Tib. *ming.gzugs.*) which is enlivened through the recurring differentiation of sense fields (Tib. *skye.mched.*) that produce contact (Tib. *reg.pa.*) which in turn creates longing sensation (Tib. *tshor.ba.*), leading to craving (Tib. *sred.pa.*) that can turn to grasping (Tib. *len.pa.*), and, as the delusion of self and other now produces becoming (Tib. *srid.pa.*), then the sentient being experiences birth (Tib. *skye.ba.*), aging, and death (Tib. *rga.shi.*). Thus, these links of dependent origination endlessly intertwine in space and time.

Two Gates (Tib. *zin.chad.tshan.med.* [zin che tshen mey]) Designates the developing practice, known as the yoga with form (Skt. *sanimittayoga*), and the completing practice, known as the yoga without form (Skt. *animittayoga*). See DZOGRIM, KYIRIM

Two Kāyas (Tib. *sku.gnyis.* [ku nye]) Reflects the view that reality is composed of rūpakāya and dharmakāya. See TRIKĀYA

Two Truths (Tib. *bden.pa.gnyis.* [den pa nye]) The absolute truth and the relative truth.

Uḍḍiyāṇa (Skt., Tib. *o.rgyan.* [Ö gyen]) Birthplace of Padma Saṃbhava and also thought to be a place Tilopa resided, it is considered to be either in the region surrounding Paghman, Afghanistan, or in the northern reaches of Swat Valley, Pakistan; more generally, it is considered to lie somewhere in between the Hindu Kush, the Pamirs, and the Himalayas. The term is also used to designate the realm of dakinis.

Unimpededness (Tib. *ma.'gag.pa.* [man gak pa]) Corresponding to the nirmāṇakāya aspect of enlightenment, it is considered to be one of the three basic qualities of the nature of the mind, giving the manifestation of inseparable union of the natural clarity and the essential emptiness of the mind. See CLARITY, EMPTINESS

Vajra Brothers and Sisters (Tib. *rdo.rje.lcam.dral.dang.rdo.rje.mched.lcam.dral.* [dor je cam trel dang dor je chay cam trel]) An important concept in vajrayāna, forming the basis of one of the root samaya vows. Those who share the same tsaway lama and maṇḍala of initiation are considered to be in the closest active relationship, those who share the same tsaway lama are considered to be in a close relationship, and those who share the same mandala are considered to be in an active relationship. The vow requires that each student respect the others of the maṇḍalas which they have shared to the degree indicated above, and that unforgiving anger and recriminatory actions (taken as a result of jealously or resentment, etc.) towards one's vajra brother or sister (regardless of the degree of the proximal relationship) not exist in any form because it is considered that to behave in such a manner breaks the samaya with the tsaway lama. See SAMAYA

Vajradhāra (Skt., Tib. *rdo.rje.'chang.* [dor je chang]) Considered to be the ultimate source of all Buddhist tantric teachings, Vajradhāra is the form in which the Lord Buddha appeared when giving vajrayāna teachings and initiations.

Vajra Master (Tib. *rdo.rje.slob.dpon.* [dor je lop pon], Skt. *vajracārya*) An accomplished meditator who has the transmissions of lineage, yidams, tantras, and teachings of the vajrayāna, and who has the authority and capability of transmitting them to others. *See* TSAWAY LAMA

Vajra Pride (Tib. *rdo.rje.nga.rgyal.* [dor je nga gyal]) Also known as pride of the deity (Tib. *lha'.nga.rgyal.*), it refers to the meditator becoming fully aware of the qualities associated with the yidam. The sense of completeness of being that arises while realizing the nature of the yidam is considered indicative of the aspirant's merging his or her body, speech, and mind with those of the Three Roots. Not to be confused with the kleśa of pride.

Vajrasattva (Skt., Tib. *rdo.rje.sems.dpa'.* [dor je sem pa]) The buddha of the eastern direction, whose elemental association is water, whose wisdom is mirror-like, and whose practice is used as an antidote to the poison of anger; the foundation practice of purification is performed by reciting the hundred-syllable mantra associated with the Yidam Vajrasattva. *See* BUDDHA FAMILIES

Vajrayāna (Skt., Tib. *rdo.rje.theg.pa.* [dor je thek pa]) Literally "the diamond-like, indestructible vehicle." It is considered to be the most esoteric of the three yānas, and is alternatively termed *mantrayāna* (Tib. *sngags.kyi.theg.pa.*) because of its heavy reliance upon mantra recitation, or *tantrayāna* because it works to bring about the union between wisdom and skillful means. Essential to the tradition of vajrayāna are the yidam practice and the study of mahāmudrā, mahā-anu, and mahā-āti. *See* HĪNAYĀNA, MAHAYĀNA, NINE VEHICLES

Vipaśyanā *see* LHATONG

Wang (Tib. *dbang.* [wang], Skt. *abhiṣeka*, one of several Sanskrit equivalents.) Ritualistic initiation or empowerment (with many varieties of formats, components, and ritual objects) given by a vajra master to confer the blessing of the yidam(s) and enable vajrayāna students to perform yidam sādhanas.

Waves of Grace (Tib. *byin.rlabs.* [jin lap], Skt. *adhiṣṭhāna*) The blessing power that emanates from the tsaway lama to the student, said to be one of the determining factors in the student's success in his or her devotion. It is said that the speed of the student's accomplishment is directly proportional to the amount and intensity of the grace-waves the student is capable of receiving from the tsaway lama.

Wisdom and Means (Tib. *thabs.dang.shes.rab.* [thap dang she rab], Skt. *prajñā* and *upāya*) According to the mahāyāna school of thought, the union of wisdom (or transcendental understanding) and means (or skillful methods) brings about the highest stage of realization.

Yānas *see* HĪNAYĀNA, MAHAYĀNA, VAJRAYĀNA, NINE VEHICLES

Yidam (Tib. *yi.dam*. [yi dam]) Meditational deities taught by Lord Buddha Śākyamuni as being the embodiment of the various aspects of enlightenment. He himself demonstrated the yidams of Guhyasamaja (to King Indrabodhi) and of Kālacakra (to the King of Śambhala). Following his parinirvāna, the demonstration of other yidams occurred through his sambhogakāya form to many different yogis and mahāsiddhās. Therefore, hundreds of yidams are known today. Each has a tradition or lineage within the human realm, and each is capable of bringing the practitioner to the state of full awareness. Examples of commonly practiced yidams are Chenrezig, Green Tārā, White Tārā, and Vajrasattva.

Zangthal (Tib. *zang.thal*. [zang thal]) Also called *freedom from obstacles*, this refers to the advanced stage of accomplishment on the yogic path that enables the yogi or yoginī to pass through all concrete, material objects without hindrance or difficulty.

Zhinay (Tib. *zhi.gnas*. [zhi nay], Skt. *śamatha*) Usually translated as tranquility, the two syllables of the Tibetan word mean pacification and abiding. Denotes a specific style of meditation in which the mind is held in tranquility following the pacification of the mental afflictions or emotions, termed *tranquility meditation*. The meditation conveys an all important concept reflected in the Buddhist teachings that when one rests in the mind's emptiness one does not abide in nothingness. Rather, the teachings assert that there is a quality to all phenomenal existence which reflects the suchness of the absolute nature of reality in each passing moment. If one abides in recognition of the true nature of mind, then the individual experiences tranquility even while performing the activities of daily life.

BIBLIOGRAPHY

Chang, Garma C.C. *The Hundred Thousand Songs of Milarepa*, Vols. I & II. Boulder & London: Shambhala, 1977.

"Drinking the Mountain Stream," *New Stories & Songs by Milarepa*. Translated by Lama Kunga Rinpoche and Brian Cutillo. Novato: Lotsawa, 1978.

Heruka, Tsang Nyon. *The Life Of Marpa the Translator*. Translated from the Tibetan by the Nalanda Translation Committee under the direction of Chögyam Trungpa Rinpoche. Boulder: Prajna Press, 1982.

Inada, Kenneth K. *Nagarjuna, A Translation of his "Mulamadhyamakakarika" with an Introductory Essay*. Tokyo: The Hokuseido Press, 1970.

'Jam-mgon Kong-sPrul. *A Direct Path To Enlightenment*. Translated from the Tibetan by K. McLeod. Vancouver: Kagyu Kunkhyab Chöling.

Johnson, Russell, and Moran, Derry. *"The Sacred Mountain of Tibet,"* *On Pilgrimage to Kailas*. Rochester, Vermont: Park Street Press, 1989.

Luk, Charles. *"Surangama Sutra" by Sakyamuni Buddha as rendered in Chinese by Master Paramiti in 750 A.D.* New York: Charles Tuttle & Co., 1969.

Maitreya, Arya & Asanga, Acarya. *The Changeless Nature*. Translated by Kenneth Holmes and Katia Holmes, with commentary by Khenchen Trangu Rinpoche. Scotland: Karma Drubgyud Darjay Ling, 1985.

Maintaining The Bodhisattva Vow and The Bodhicitta Precepts. Translated by Karma Tenpei Gyeltsen. San Francisco: Kagyu Droden Kunchab, 1980.

McLeod, Kenneth I. *"The Chariot for Travelling the Path To Freedom," The Life Story of Kalu Rinpoche.* San Francisco: Kagyu Dharma, 1985.

"Miraculous Journey," New Stories & Songs by Milarepa. Translated by Lama Kunga Rinpoche and Brian Cutillo. Novato: Lotsawa, 1986.

Namgyal, Takpo Tashi. *"Mahamudra," The Quintessence of Mind and Meditation.* Translated and annotated by Lobsang Lhalungpa. Boston and London: Shambhala, 1986.

"The Rain of Wisdom," The Vajra Songs of the Kagyu Gurus. Translated by the Nalanda Translation Committee. Boulder & London: Shambhala, 1980.

Rinpoche, Kalu. *The Crystal Mirror.* New York: Kagyu Thubten Chöling, 1982.

Rinpoche, Kalu. *"The Dharma," That Illuminates All Beings Impartially Like the Light of the Sun and the Moon.* Albany: State University of New York Press, 1986.

Rinpoche, Kalu. *The Ocean of Attainment.* Vancouver: Kagyu Kunkhab Chöling, 1974.

Snellgrove, David, and Richardson, Hugh. *A Cultural History of Tibet.* Boulder: Prajna Press, 1980.

Snellgrove, D.L. *"The Hevajra Tantra," A Critical Study, Part I.* London: Oxford University Press, 1980.

Sprung, Mervyn. *Lucid Exposition of the Middle Way.* English translation of the Sanskrit in collaboration with T.R.V. Murti and U.S. Vyas. Boulder: Prajna Press, 1979.

Thinley, Karma. *The History of the Sixteen Karmapas of Tibet.* Edited by David Stott. Boulder: Prajna Press, 1980.

The Tibetan Book of the Dead. Translated with commentary by Francesca Fremantle and Chögyam Trungpa Rinpoche. Boulder: Shambhala, 1975.

Tsong-Ka-Pa. *"Tantra in Tibet,"* The Great Exposition of Secret Mantra. Translation by Jeffery Hopkins. London: George Allen & Unwin, 1977.

Willis, Janice Dean. *The Diamond Light.* New York: Simon and Schuster, 1972.

The Writings of Kalu Rinpoche. Translated by Kenneth McLeod. Vancouver, B.C.: Kagyu Kunkhyab Chöling, 1976.

Kalu Rinpoche, fond of domestic animals, usually had a cat for a pet. (Photograph J.G. Sherab Ebin)

INDEX

Absolute reality. *See* Reality, absolute

Absolute truth. *See* Truth, absolute

Absolute view, 127

Adultery, among Tibetans, 54

After-death experience, 78-82, 130-131; attachment to wealth, 81; and clinging, 80; of perceiving the living, 81; projections of mental body in, 130-131; reality to consciousness, 68-69

Air element, 85; breakdown of element in dying process, 73-74

Alaya: coursing through physical channels, 106-107; elimination of impure, 180; pure, 27-30; pure, recognizing, 145-146; and samadhi, 34; sensory organs, base consciousness of, 92-93; why pure is impure, 43

Allegories. *See also* Metaphors; Stories

— using animals: tortoise and yoke, 4

— using electricity: broken wire and broken lineage, 172; connection to tsaway lama and wire, 172; light and dzogrim, 102; T.V. remote control, 79

— using luminaries: absence of luminaries, 7; moon and path of vision, 178; radiating sun shine and enlightenment, 156-

157, 179-180; sunlight and clouds, 3, 18; sunrise and dawning awareness, 86

— using people: babes in path of Dharma and nurturing teachers, 147; inability to see another's mind, 8; people's mental discursiveness, 8

— using places: comparing cities, like Bodh-Gaya, 148; distance between two places, like New York and Los Angeles, 6-8

— using plants: planting seeds and seed of Dharma, 138

— using sleep: darkness and stupor of ignorance, 102; six hour conversation and sleep, 101

— using societal circumstances: living on credit and disparaging tsaway lama, 176; three story building and three yanas, 11-16

Altruism: and bodhisattva ideal, 138

Amitabha, Buddha. *See* Buddha Amitabha

Anger, 52; and bodhisattva commitment, 139; during breakdown of consciousness (space), 75; meditation on, 62; at the mercy of, 57; turned into compassion, 14; what is really taking place, 58, 60

Animal realms: being of direct benefit to, 4; birth into, 71; suffering in, 125; way it differs from human realm, 86

Animals: unable to practice vajrayana, 118; ways to seed Dharma in them, 4-5

Antidote: to anger, 14; to clinging to reality, 66; of dzogrim, 102; to ignorance, 102; of kyirim, 102; to laziness, 162; for unconsciousness in after-death, 79

Antidotes: in mahayana, 14; in vajrayana, 15

Arhat: attainment stage of hinayana, 89; path of, 88; realization of, by Arya Katayana, 126-127

Arya Katayana. *See* Stories: Arya Katayana

Asian Cultures: contrasted to Western, 51, 53-55

Attachment: in bardo of possibilities, 80-81. *See also* Desire

Attraction, 26, 29; and anger, 64; between sexes, 64; in conception process, 72; meditation on, 61-64

Avalokiteshvara. *See* Chenrezig

Aversion, 26, 29, 52; in conception process, 72; meditation on, 61-64

Awareness: bare, in meditation, 163; and ignorance, 149; key to enlightenment, 166; of mind, 150; spacious, defined, 165; unimpeded, 153

Awareness, unobstructed. *See* Unimpededness of mind

Bardo, after-death, 2; defined, 67; liberation in, 16

Bardo of the dying process, 68, 73-76

Bardo of possibility, 68, 71-72, 78; earlier and later phases, 81-82; experience of, 80-82; hallucinations in, 68; liberation from, 79; shock while in, 81-82

Bardo of the ultimate nature of phenomenal reality, 68

Bardo practice, 79

Bardos, six, 67-68

Bardo Thödol, 78

Bell. *See* Stories: bell, hell, and mantra

Bhumis. *See* Bodhisattva, accomplished, levels of

Bindu, defined, 75

Bindus, red and white, 75-76

Birth, human. *See* Human birth

Birth, into various realms. *See* Samsara, six realms: birth into

Bodh-Gaya, India. *See* Allegories: using cities

Bodhicitta, 113; of actualization, 127-128; for bodhisattva prayer/vow, 133; of intention, 127-128

Bodhicitta, absolute, 43, 127-128; defined, 131

Bodhicitta, relative: matured to absolute, 129

Bodhisattva. *See also* Bodhisattva, accomplished; Vow, bodhisattva

— approach: boundless concern for sentient beings, 123; giving rise to absolute bodhicitta, 131; of love and compassion, 127

— attitude: absolute, 127-128; ideal and altruism, 138

— path: 88; progressive stages in 107-108; stages of, 15; strengthening commitment, 140

— vow: benefits of vow, 140; how

to break vow, 139; keeping and maintaining vow, 138-139; means in everyday life, 138

Bodhisattva, accomplished.
— attainment of: attained by yidam practice, 88; first level attainment, 145; irreversibility of attainment, 178
— connection to, 46
— levels of: first level of, 80; ten levels of, 77
— powers of: eighth level 107-108; first level, 107, 141; ninth level, 108; powers multiplied tenfold, 107; second level, 107; seventh level, 107; tenth level, 108

Body, fully ripened, 1, 15

Body, mental, 1-2, 15, 81, 93, 129; experiences in bardo of possibilities, 81; obscurations of, 69; projections of in after-death, 130-131; reality to consciousness, 68-69

Body of habitual tendencies, 1, 15, 93, 129-130

Body of karmic fruition, 1, 93; projection of mind, 129-130. See also Five elements

Branches of learning, inner and outer. See Introduction

Buddhas. See also Historical Buddhas; Tathagata
— compassion of: degree of, 88; boundless concern for sentient beings, 123; giving rise to absolute bodhicitta, 131
— defined: meaning of term in Tibetan, 44, 87
— nature: reasons not to doubt, 35
— pratyeka, 88
— qualifications for being, 18
— qualities of: body, 87; how they manifest in nirmanakaya, 151; of mind, 87; of speech, 87

— sambhogakaya, 113

Buddha Amitabha, 79-80

Buddha Kashyapa. See Historical Buddhas

Buddha Sakyamuni, 159; as object of refuge, 46; demonstration of vajrayana path, 103; fourth buddha of kalpa, 91; manifested all paths to liberation, 88; manifested mantras and dharanis, 108; reason for giving Dharma, 6; teaching on rebirth, 8

Buddha Vairocana, 172

Buddhadharma: eighty-four thousand collections of, 154; fundamental approach of, 29; inner teachings of, 171; love of, 138; and obscurations, 2-3; reason to practice, 11; whole point of, 43

Buddhahood: and absolute reality, 157-159; and absolute truth, 157-158; attainment defined, 179; attainment of, 15; experience of mind in, 153; four activities of, 179-180; lacking any limitations, 179; methods for attaining, 13-18; nature of state of, 154; realization of, 9-11, 108; seed of, 2

Buddhism. See also Buddha Shakyamuni; Historical buddhas
— in India, 171
— in West, 169-170; problems in coming to West, 172
— Tibetan: came to Tibet due to Marpa, 173; first step in, 43-44; names of major orders of, 171-172; origin of, See Introduction; the "quick path" of, 48; reason for path chosen, 43-44; reason for practices in, 177; reason for practicing, 11; specialization in

purification, 98; various line-
ages of, 176
Buddhist traditions, similarities of.
See Introduction
Bugs, seven. See Stories: seven
bugs and stupa
Cakras, five, 106
Calming the mind. See Nature of
mind, calming
Cause and effect, fundamental to
Buddhism, 34
Cave. See Student, Western
Celibacy, 54-55; among Tibetans,
standards of, 54
Chakja chenpo, syllables explained,
93, 154-155
Chakras. See Cakras
Change, 149; of mind, 150
Channels: discursive consciousness flowing in, 107; needle-
point openings, 106; number in
human body, 106; in physical
body, 106
Characteristics, three, 109
Chenrezig. 112 See also Appendix
B
— benefits of: blessings, 111;
compassion of, 111; meditation
on in after-death bardos, 79
— Bodhisattva: and demoness, 124
— introduced by Buddha
Shakyamuni, 110
— meaning of name, 111
— sadhana: benefits of doing, 111;
practice of, 150; recitation of
fulfills all samayas, 111
— visualization of: 113-114; during
mantra recitation, 115; stabiliza-
tion of, 143-144
— Yidam: 110; symbolism of, 177
Christian traditions and
Buddhadharma. See Introduction
Chungawa. See Stories:

Chungawa's
Circumambulation of stupa: by
seven bugs on leaf, 5
Cities, distance between. See
Mind, insubstantial nature of
Clarity, 109; illustration of, 7-9;
inseparable from emptiness,
153; and luminosity, 165-166;
of mind, 61, 151, 153
Clinging. See also Insubstantialness
— antidotes to: clinging to reality,
66; and kyirim, 102
— to duality: 44; difference
between samsara and nirvana,
2; dualistic, eliminated, 108;
habitual, 25
— liberation from, 16
— to phenomena: in after-death
experience, 80; to external
appearances, 1; to impermanence, 89; to the past, 82; to
sensory experiences, 92-93; to
suffering as pleasure, 89
— to self: 11; and other, 2; self-
ego, three states of, 144-145
Clouds, manifestation of space, 63.
See also Metaphors: clouds
Commitment, bonds of. See
Samaya
Compassion, 158; and alaya, 29; as
antidote to anger, 14; of a
buddha, 44-45; of buddhahood,
179-180; of Chenrezig, 111;
complete and impartial, 159;
giving rise to it, 125-126; reason
for engendering, 131; of Three
Jewels at work, 97; and virtuous
actions, 3
Conception, human: according to
Buddhist tradition, 71-72
Confidence, development of, 158
Confusion, 23
Consciousness: in after-death
state, 68-69; base (or Primor-

dial), 1-2; discursive, 28, 87; discursive, flowing in channels, 107; and emptiness, union of, 117; physical basis for expression of, 72; sensory, 90, 92-93

Consciousness transference. *See* Phowa

Consciousnesses, five (or six), 92-93

Corporal existence, fully ripened. *See* Body, fully ripened

Dakini realms: rebirth in, 64

Dakinis, speech of, 172; work of, 99

Dark times: fortune in, 105

Death: and moral codes, 21; the process of, 73-76; three days following, 2. *See also* After-death experience; Bardo of possibility

Dedication, of merit, 141, 180

Deer and mirages, 16

Definitions, all our, 154

Deities, peaceful and wrathful, mandala of, 77-78

Deity. *See* Yidam

Delusion, 26-27, 150-151

Desire, 52; during breakdown of consciousness (space), 75-76; expression of, 55; sexual, 54, 55; sexual, meditation on, 61-62; what is really taking place in, 60, 61-62

Devotion, developing unshakable, 99; inconceivable, 159

Dewachen. *See* Pure land of Buddha Amitabha

Dharanis, 107, 108

Dharma. *See also* Introduction
— defined: 45-46; door of, 132
— eighty-four thousand texts: reason given, 6
— interest in: auspiciousness of, 91; reason for, 23

— name, 47
— practice: based in hinayana, 12; obstacle of discursive consciousness, 86; purifies four veils, 87

Dharmakaya, 101; all-pervading, 157; of buddhahood, 157-158; defined, 153; inherence of, in sambhogakaya, 106; and nature of mind, 151; and thought, inseparability of, 150-151. *See also* Trikayas

Dharmapalas: as object of refuge, 46; root of all buddha activity, 96; speech of, 172

Dharmata, 90

Dhyana heaven: birth into, 71

Dog. *See* Stories: Arya Katayana

Dorje Chang, *100*; Dharmakaya, 173; essential tsaway lama, 99. *See also* Vajradhara

Dorje Sempa practice: benefits of, 98. *See also* Foundational practices

Dream body, *See* Body of Habitual Tendency

Dreams: ability to change phenomena in, 156; and duality, 1; and emotions, 10; environment, and waking state, 129-130; illusion of, 2; projections, 1, 10; validity of for dreamer, 25

Dream state experience, 14; memories of, 129-130; nightmares, 156; sensory experiences in, 93; total environment in, 14

Drolma, Jetsün. *See* Green Tara

Duality, illusion of, 155; resolution of, 93-94

Dullness of mind, 26-27. *See also* Metaphors: darkness; sleep

Dying Process. *See* Bardo of the dying process

Dzogrim, 171; antidote of, 102

Ears, 90; consciousness of, 92-93

Earth, breakdown of element in
    dying process, 73-74
Earth element, 85
Echo, 16
Ego: clinging to, 145-146; empty,
    64; three states of clinging to,
    144-145
Elements, five (or six), 1, 73-74,
    85. *See also* Earth, Water, Fire,
    Air, Space
Emotionality. *See also* Emotions
— in the after-death bardos, 68
— antidote to: emotional energy,
    transforming, 52; emotional
    expression, controlling, 55
— approach to: 52, 60-62, 63;
    benefits of conquering, 66
— conflict of: 66; and confusion,
    51-52; and mahayana path, 103;
    resolution of, 62-63
— habituation of: 18, 56; reality,
    57-58; subjectivity, 51-60, 62-66;
    tendencies, different cultural
    expressions of, 53
— and hinayana: 11; methods of
    confronting, 56
— and mahayana: methods of
    confronting, 56
— and vajrayana: methods of
    confronting, 56-57
Emotions, 101-102; comprehend-
    ing them, 60; discussion on
    non-reality of, 57-60; and
    dreams, 10; examination of
    solitary emotion, 59-62; how
    not to feel at their mercy, 59;
    and ignorance, 3;
    insubstantialness of, 65-66;
    manifestation of mind, 63; in
    meditation, 152; meditation
    upon, 151, 148-150; negative,
    55; origin of, 52; overcoming
    them, 64; right and wrong of
    60; six primary, 52; of sleep, 53

Emptiness, 7-9, 13; authentic
    experience of, 61; and emotions,
    59; of hearing, 90; how to
    experience, 165; illustration of,
    7-9; inseparable from clarity,
    153; of mind, 58; path of
    mahayana, 89; and path of
    vajrayana, 89-90; of personality,
    13; recognizing truth of, 144;
    and self-conceptualization, 131;
    of sight, 90; view in hinayana,
    13. *See also* Mind, insubstantial
    nature of
Enemies, and bodhisattva commit-
    ment, 139
Enlightenment: blessing of yidam,
    16; complete, experience of 179;
    defined, 14, 29, 179; easiest
    path to, 132; guarantee of, 45;
    and mind's nature, 22; most
    accurate statement about, 158;
    nature of state of, 154; not
    elimination of mind, 166; object
    of taking refuge, 44; "quick
    path" to, 48; why it is libera-
    tion, 9; why not to reject idea
    of, 35; why omniscient, 154. *See
    also* Buddhahood
Eyes, 90; consciousness of, 92-93
Faith, development of, 158
Fighting. *See* Violence, physical
Fire element, 85, breakdown of
    element in dying process, 73-74
Fish. *See* Stories: Arya Katayana
Five paths. *See* Paths, five
Fog. *See* Allegories: clouds and
    weather
Form: and emptiness, union of,
    117; as union of wisdom and
    means, 90
Form, realm of, 92. *See also*
    Phenomena
Foundational practices, 18; bene-
    -fits of doing, 95-96; elaborated,

98-99

Four noble truths. *See* Noble truths, four

Four obscurations. *See* Obscurations, four veils of

Four Veils of Obscurations. *See* Obscurations, four veils of

Freedom, mental, 143-144

Fruition, Karmic *See* Karmic fruition

Ganachakra, sponsoring, 132

Gates of body, speech, and mind. *See* Gates, three

Gates, three: and liberation, 11

Generosity, 32-34; antidote to non-virtuous actions, 97-98; correct motivation for, 34; how to defeat rewards of, 38; moral quality to it, 32

Genyen vows. *See* Vows, genyen

Giving and receiving. *See* Tonglen

Gods' realms: birth into, 71; Chungawa's experience in, 121; compared to 'heaven', 35; Heaven of the Thirty-Three, 121, 122, 123; to obtain rebirth in, 124; reason why human realm better than, 37; rebirth in, 42; rebirth in, result of generosity, 33; temporary existence in, 30

Golden ground of universe, 96

Green Tara, benefits of prayer to, 117-118; introduced by Buddha Shakyamuni, 110

Guilt, 38-39; about sexuality, 54

Guru. *See* Tsaway lama

Guru yoga, 99. *See also* Foundational practices

Gyaltshap Rinpoche, 99, 175

Hallucinations, in bardo, 78; *See also* Bardo of possibility

Hearing, emptiness of, 90

Hell realms: birth into, 70-71,

Chungawa's experience in, 122-123; cold, experience in, 124-125; hot, experience in, 124; iron pavement in, 10

Hevajra Tantra, 18

Hinayana: applicability of in former times, 103; behavior of practitioners, 11-13; different from mahayana, 14; methods in confronting emotionality, 56

Historical Buddhas: Buddha Kashyapa, 5; giving vajrayana path, 103-104; one thousand in kalpa, 91; only three teach it, 91; qualities of body, speech, and mind, 87; third, of this kalpa, 5

Hook of compassion, 44-45, 97; symbolized, 177; disengaging of, 48

Householder vows. *See* Vows, genyen

HRI, sacred letter, *112*; visualized in Chenrezig sadhana, 113, 116

Human birth, 71

Human conception, according to Buddhist tradition, 71-72

Human experience, 93

Human realm: causes of suffering in, 23-24; compared to gods' realm, 33; reason why better than gods' realm, 37

Human rebirth: average existence in, 92; excellent existence in, 92; inferior existence in, 91-92

Hungry ghost realm, 33; birth into, 71; suffering of, 125

Hunters. *See* Stories: Milarepa and hunters

Ignorance, 22, 52, 101-102; and awareness, 149; basis for samsara, 15; basis of sentient obscuration, 18; defined, 26; of self, 144-145; veil of, and samsaric experience, 9-10

Illusory nature of phenomena. *See* Phenomena, illusory nature of

Impermanence; clinging to, 89; of human life, 161

India, 78; source of Buddhism, 173; source of teachings in Buddhism, 171

Insubstantiality: of emotions, 65-66; of phenomena in after-death, 130-131; of reality, 57, 59; of thoughts, 149

Insubstantiality of mind. *See* Mind, insubstantial nature of

Interdependent arising, 97

Interdependent origination, 6-8

Iron mountain, of Mt. Sumeru, 98. *See also* Mount Sumeru

Iron pavement of hell realm, 10. *See also* Hell Realms

Islamic tradition of charity and Buddhadharma. *See* Introduction

Jambudvipa. *See* Mount Sumeru

Jamgon Kongtrul Rinpoche, 175; letter of, *See* Appendix B; requests of, *See* Preface

Jealousy, 55, 57

Jewel, wish-fulfilling, symbolism of, 177

Jewels, Three, 45-46; confidence in, 48; faith and devotion in, benefits of, 96-97; karmic connections to, 3; undifferentiated from tsaway lama, 172

Kagyu tradition, 150. *See also* Karma Kagyu lineage

Kalpa: and current state of darkness, 103; of one thousand buddhas, 91

Kalu Rinpoche, his life in Tibet. *See* Introduction

Karma. *See also* Alaya; Karmic

accumulations

— accumulation of: and duality, 2, 155; results in human birth, 69

— collective, 23-24, 69-70

— experience of: 23-30, 32-36, 155; by sentient beings, 9-11

— fruition of, 11

— how it can be invalidated, 155

— individual, 69-72, 155

— meritorious, 132

— most fundamental understanding in Buddhadharma, 34

— nature of: and nature of mind, 9

Karma Kagyu lineage, 99, *174;* listed and explained, 173, 175-176; tradition, 167. *See also* Lineage

Karmapa, Gyalwa: lineage of, 175; the XVIth, 167; Third Gyalwa, on illusory nature of phenomena, 9, 14

Karmic accumulations, 82. *See also* Karma; Alaya

— acts of: committed by mind, 129

— fruition of: and bardo of possibilities, 82; and empty, clear, unobstructed awareness, 9; lack of empirical proof, 25; and nirvana, 28; voidness of, 17

— predisposition to: path taken, 88

— process of, 70-72, 155-156; focus on fruition, 31; ultimately not real, 155

— tendencies in, 24, 38, 44; and duality, 27; and reincarnation, 69-72. (*See also* Virtuous actions)

Kyang-ma. See Channels

Kyirim, 31, 171; antidote of, 102

Lama. *See* Tsaway Lama

Law of karma, 9, 24; defined, 24; its infallibility, 32. *See also* Karmic fruition

Laziness, 161-162
Learning, branches of. *See* Introduction
Leopards. *See* Dreams, nightmares
Letters, sacred, 106-107. *See also* HRI, sacred letter
Lhatong, 30-31; darkness during practice, 152-153; reason to practice, 11-12
Liberation: assurance of, 67; in bardo of possibility, 79; by hearing explanation of mahamudra, 94; of clinging, 16; and development of wisdom, 30; instantaneous, 80; keys to, 159; means of obtaining, 22; and three gates, 11; through yidam practices, 88. *See also* Enlightenment
Light, spheres of. *See* Meditation, on spheres of light
Lineage, defined, 173; unbroken, benefits of, 101; unbroken, most important quality of teacher, 99
Lions. *See* Dreams, nightmares
Los Angeles. *See* Mind, insubstantial nature of
Lotus, symbolism of, 177
Love, giving rise to it, 125-126
Loving kindness, 159
Lower realms, how to escape from, 4-5
Luminosity. *See also* Meditations
— illustration of, 7-9
— and intangible awareness, 153
— of mind, 7-9, 61, 165-166; luminous nature of mind, 14
— one of six yogas of Naropa, 76-77
— and rainbows, 58-59
Mahamudra, 18, 94-95. *See also* Zhinay; Lhatong
— benefits of hearing teaching, 160
— explanation of: defined, 31; resting the mind in, 163; studied in retreat, 168; term, 94
— fruition of: 95, 154; bringing to, 152; ground, 154; maturing experience of, 150; path, 154
— Karma Kagyu lineage of, 173, 175-176
— practice of: and guru yoga, 99; and kyirim, 102
— signs of: in beginning progress, 153; realized by zhinay or lhatong, 18-19; seal of voidness, recognizing, 155
— three stages of, 154
— Tilopa's teaching on, 151-152
Mahayana, 13-15; and Japanese Buddhist orders, 13; path of, recognition of emptiness, 89; path, suitable in today's times, 103; transformation as antidote, 14; usefulness of view, 93
Mala, crystal: symbolism of, 177
Mala, symbolism of number of beads, 115
Mandala of peaceful and wrathful deities, 77-78
Mandala Offerings. *See* Foundational practices
Manjushri: benefits of devotion to, 128-129; mantra of, 128
Mantra. *See also* Om Mani Padme Hung; Foundational practices
— as nature of all sound, 16
— benefits of: liberation in after-death bardo, 16; recitation of, 106; recitation, anytime/where, 117
— power of: 16; specific powers of, 108
— preservation of: tradition of in Tibet 108-109
— syllables in: one hundred syllable, 98, 109; six-syllable, 109

Mantrayana, discussion of, 106-107

Marriage, among Tibetans, 54

Matricide, purification of, 42. *See also* Stories: of matricide

Means, skillful, 15; defined, 90. *See also* Wisdom

Meditation, 19. *See also* Dzogrim; Kyirim; Visualization practice

— and awareness: 149; awareness important in, 166; bare awareness in, 163; levels of alertness in, 162-163

— on Chenrezig: in after-death bardos, 79; sadhana introduced, 111-117. (*See also* Appendix B)

— emotions and thoughts during: 152; in mahayana for combatting emotions, 56; on nature of thoughts, 148-150; techniques for analyzing emotions, 64-65; what to do with thoughts in, 151

— Jetsün Milarepa's: with hunters, 17; instructions to Paldenbum, 63-64

— made easy, 19-20

— on mahamudra: 148-150; in dying process, 76-77; on trees and ground, 149-150. (*See also* Mahamudra, Tilopa's teaching on)

— on nature of mind: 8, 60-64, 63; and clarity, 63; and emptiness, 116; and luminosity, 63; on true, 159; a state of mind, 150-151

— and obscurations in: darkness in, 152-153; sleep-like state in, 152-153; of stupidity, 163; stupor in, 152

— on ocean, 63; and waves, 149

— practices: on attraction/aversion, 61-64; bardo practice, 79;

beginning practice of, 111; practice in mahayana, 13

— problems: pitfalls along path of, 152

— on selflessness, 144-145

— on space, 7, 63

— on spheres of light, 145

— stages of. (*See* Zhinay; Lhatong)

— tantric, 31

— tonglen visualization, 140

— transcendental, 30

— on tsaway lama, 152

— on yidam: three characteristics of, 109-110

Meditative absorption, 145. *See also* Dzogrim; Kyirim

Mental body. *See* Body, mental

Mental constructs. *See* Definitions

Mental discursiveness, 8

Mental phenomena. *See* Phenomena, mentally projected

Merit, 30; accumulation of, 146; accumulation of, key to realizing mahamudra, 95; dedication of, 50, 160, 180; how to accumulate, 95-96, 132

Meritorious tendencies, 23

Metaphors. *See also* Allegories; Stories

— using animals: bird down and touch, 92; insect brains and mind, 150

— using electricity: T.V. remote control and interdependent arising, 97

— using food: milk tea and Chenrezig, 116; nectar and one hundred syllable mantra, 98; restaurant menu and variety of spiritual paths, 88

— using light/darkness: darkness and obscuration, 86

— using luminaries: full moon and enlightenment, 179; moon

and levels of accomplished bodhisattva, 178; moon and tongue, 92; space, sun, rain bows, and trikaya, 157
— using physical objects: burning paper and tsaway lama, 172-173; clay pot and obscurations of buddhahood, 146, 147; copper tubes and nose, 92; deposit of gold and unexcelled teachers, 99; key in hand and mahamudra instructions, 159; mirror and mind, 92; ultimate jetsetting and bardo experience, 78; windows of house and sensory functions, 92
— using plants: lotus flower and actualized awareness, 158; tree bark and ears, 92; flowers and eyes, 92; seed germination and karma, 32
— using senses: sensory organs in Tibetan view, 92
— using sleep: levels of discursiveness and alertness, 162-163; sleep and bad meditation, 163; sleep of ignorance and enlightenment, 158
— using space: sky and mind, 150; space and mind, 153
— using water: agitated emotions and boiling water, 65; cleaning cloth and purification practices, 98; crossing ocean and vajrayana, 105; ocean and emotions, 58; pure water and enlightenment, 27; rivers and emotions, 59, 65; water and buddha nature, 85; waves in ocean and thoughts, 149
— using weather: clouds and emotions, 64; clouds and four veils disappearing, 87; snow in summer and excellent

students, 147
Milarepa, Jetsün, 16-17; life compared to Western students, 164; life story example, 140; meditation instructions of 63-64
Mind: consciousness of, 92-93; insubstantial nature of, 6-9; resting in no awareness, 149; three qualities of, 7-9. See also Nature of mind
Mind, luminosity of. See Luminosity of mind
Mirage, 16
Mirror, reflection in, 14, 16
Monastic lifestyle, 54-55
Moon, reflection in water, 16. See also Allegories: moon and path of vision
Moral development, 39
Morality, 29-30; similarity between various traditions, 35
Mothers, as limitless as space, 126, 139
Motivation: correct, results of, 34; for making use of precious human existence, 42; proper framework of, 162
Mount Meru. See Mount Sumeru
Mount Sumeru, 98; Southern continent of, 164
Mudra, 109-110
Nadis. See Channels
Namdok. See Thought
Name, bodhisattva, use of, 138
Naropa, six yogas of. See Six yogas of Naropa
Nature of mind. See also Liberation
— analytic meditation: and laziness, 161-162; on thoughts, 148-150; why not to doubt, 35
— antidote of vajrayana, 15-16
— benefits of: understanding true, 145-146
— calming, 145

— and emotions: origin of, 52;
understanding of conquers
emotionality, 57
— and emptiness: 58; of self, 144-
145
— essence of: clarity, seat of
sambhogakaya, 151; devoid of
descriptive characteristics, 13;
and nature of karma, 9; and
realization of mahamudra, 94;
and reincarnation, 25; seat of
dharmakaya, 151; unimpededness, seat of nirmanakaya, 151
— experience of: complete enlightenment, 179; direct experience
of irreversible, 178; how to
experience, 148-150; mind in
buddhahood, 153; sentient
beings', 155
— freedom in knowing true, 144
— illustration of: 6-7; likened to
mirror, 14; likened to rainbow,
14
— meditation on, 7-9, 8, 60-64, 159
— qualities of: deathlessness of
mind, 67; continuity of mind,
21
— and samaya: pure, 177; and
vajra pride, 177
— when enlightened: 166-167; not
disappearing in liberation, 166-
167
— wisdom, reason it can be
recognized, 86
New York. See Mind, insubstantial
nature of
Nidanas. See Links of dependent
origination, twelve
Nightmares, 156
Nirmanakaya: and nature of
mind, 151; physical manifestation of buddhas, 157; rainbow
manifestation of, 58. See also
Trikayas

Nirvana: continued experience of,
167; dawning of, 156; devoid of
karmic fruition, 28; has "one
taste" with samsara, 109;
recognition of from vajrayana
view, 89-90
No meditation. See Mahamudra,
Tilopa's teaching on
Noble truths, four, 118
Non-distraction, state of, 152. Also
see Mahamudra, Tilopa's
teaching on
Non-interdependence: and mind,
6-7; of reality, 10
Non-virtuous actions, 39; cause of
pain and suffering, 32; defined,
32; reinforced by confusion, 27;
See also Virtuous actions
Nose, consciousness of, 92-93
Nothingness, not emptiness, 14
Obscurations: dispelling of, 18; of
mental body, 69; of nature of
mind, 3; purification of, and
realizing mahamudra, 95. See
also Obscurations, four veils of
Obscurations, four veils of, 2-3,
18, 29; Dharma practice purifies, 87; dispelling, 146; expression of Tathagata beyond, 44;
fourth level, 27-29; purified in
path of application, 178
Ocean. See Meditation: on water;
Metaphors: ocean and emotions
Offerings, seven, 111
Om Mani Padme Hung, 108, power
of recitation of, 113; recitation
at sound of bell, 130
Omniscience, 154; and enlightenment, 179
One hundred syllable mantra, See
Mantra
Ordination, 56; Chungawa's
lesson concerning, 121-123; of
Shariputra, 41. See also Vows,

full ordination
Paldenbum, 63-64
Palmo, nun named, 114
Paramitas, six, 128; listed, 15; "wings" of mahayana path, 89. *See also* Mahayana path
Path: of accumulation, 178; of application, 178; easiest to enlightenment, 132; easy, 159; to liberation, karmic predisposition to, 88; of vision, 178
Paths, five, 149, 178-179
Perfections, six. *See* Paramitas, six
Phenomena: ability to change in dreams, 156; in after-death state, 130-131; antidote to clinging to, 66; attractions and aversions to, 13; delusions caused by, 26-28; and delusion of reality, 155-156; falseness of, 59; from hinayana view, 13; illusory nature of, 9-11; insubstantial like rainbow, 14; insubstantialness of, 131; like mirror reflection, 102; mentally projected, 1-3; nature of, 13; non-reality of emotions, 57-60; sensory, 13
Phowa, practice of, 76
Physical violence. *See* Violence, physical
Powers, associated with accomplished bodhisattva, 107, 141; ten, 108
Prajna Paramita Sutra, 13-14, 155; statement on voidness, 14
Pratyeka buddha, path of, 88
Prayer, bodhisattva, 134-135; prayer in Tibetan transliteration, 136-137
Prayer, Refuge. *See* Refuge prayer
Preceptor, in hinayana, 172
Precious human existence, 3-5, 17, 43; meaningful use of, 118;

most significant about it, 82-83; not to be wasted, 103-104; only context to liberation, 82-83; rarity of, 92; reasons to develop, 42
Pretas. *See* Hungry ghost realm
Pride, leads to obscurations, 144; vajra, pure, 176
Projections, in after-death state, 130-131; always changing, 22; in bardo of possibilities, 80-82; in dream, 14; of duality, 3; mental, 10; of the mind, 57; of reality, 28; result of confusion, 28. *See also* Phenomena, mentally projected
Prostrations, 111; benefits of doing, 96. *See also* Foundational practices
Psycho-therapists (various), discussion of techinques used, verses meditation of nature of mind, 65-66
Puja. *See* Sadhana
Pure land: of Amitabha Buddha, 102; practices, 79-80; pray to be reborn there, 117; of yidam, 102
Purification practices. *See* Foundational practices
Quick path. *See* Buddhism, Tibetan
Radiant light yoga, 76-77
Rainbow: and clarity of and body, 15-16; insubstantialness of, 58-59; and nirmanakaya, 58-59. *See also* Phenomena, insubstantial
Reality. *See also* Phenomena
— absolute: and bardo, 2; defined, 157; and emptiness, 14, 17; viewpoint on samsara, 10
— ascribing to experiences, 156
— conceptual, 11
— relative, defined, 157
Realms, lower, 35; liberation from

97. *See also* Samsara, six realms of

Rebirth: what is reborn, 8; *See also* Reincarnation

Red and white bindus. *See* Bindus, red and white

Refuge. *See* Taking Refuge

Refuge prayer, 50; benefits of recitation, 46. *See also* Appendix B

Refuge, principle source of: in triyanas, 46

Refuge tree, *49*

Refuge vows. *See* Vows, of refuge

Regret, 39; compared to guilt, 39; virtue of, 42

Reincarnation, ability to know past and future, 107; continuity of mind in, 161-162; endless cycle of, 67; guarding against, 45; how to obtain rebirth in gods' realms, 124; infinite series of, 22; and karmic tendencies, 69-72; limitless as space mothers, 139; in lower realms, 42-43; and mind's emptiness, 25; reasons for rebirth in gods' realm, 33; reasons for rebirth in hungry ghost realm, 33; and samsara, 82

Retreat, three-year: locations of, 167-168; and merit for, 132; practices given in, 168

Rinchen Terdzod. See Preface

Ring of faith, 44-45, 97; disengaging of, 48

River, flowing. *See* Metaphors: rivers and emotions

Rivers. *See* Metaphors: rivers

Robes, reason for wearing, 12

Ro-ma. See Channels

Root Guru. *See* Tsaway lama

Roots, Three: faith and devotion in, benefits of, 96-97; manifestation of, blessing of Lord Buddha, 95-96; taking refuge in, 46; undifferentiated from tsaway lama, 172

Sacred letters. *See* Letters, sacred

Sadhana: Chenrezig of, benefits of doing, 111; individual to yidam, 106. *See also* Chenrezig sadhana, Appendix B

Samadhi, 17; mundane, 30; transcendental, 30

Samadhis, one hundred, attaining, 145

Samaya, 176; vajrayana commitments, 111

Sambhogakaya: direct experience of, 79; inherence of, in nirmanakaya, 106; luminosity of, 157; and nature of mind, 151. *See also* Trikayas

Sambhogakaya buddha. *See* Buddha, sambhogakaya

Sampannakrama. *See* Dzogrim

Samsara. *See also* Animal realms, Gods' realms, Hell realms, Human realms, Hungry ghost realms

— continuity of: mind in, 21; experience of, 167; endlessness of, 22

— defined: 82; temporary state and primal confusion, 23

— and nirvana: has "one taste" with, 109; only way out, 37; possibility of ending it, 23; recognition of from vajrayana view, 89-90

— six realms of: birth into, 70-72; liberation through vajrayana, 16; number of sentient beings in, 127; and reincarnation, 67; suffering in, 124-125

— three bodies in, 93

Sangha, taking refuge in, 45
Sangye, meaning explained, 44, 87
Secret mantra vehicle
  (mantrayana). *See* Vajrayana
Seeds. *See* Metaphors: seed
  germination
Self. *See also* Void, Voidness
— basis for karmic process, 155
— clinging to: 11, 13; elimination
  of, 19
— conceptualization, 131
— existence, 60
— and other: 157; dualistic framework of, 26; duality of, 2, 3
— voidness of, 144-145
Sense organs, five: emptiness of,
  90; termination of, 123
Sensory appearances. *See* Phenomena, sensory
Sensory consciousness, emptiness
  of objects of, 90
Sensory experience, mediation
  upon, 148-150, 151
Sentient beings. *See also* Samsara,
  six realms of
— all possess: body, speech, and
  mind, 5; mind, 144; qualities of
  buddhas, 145-146
— catagories of, 88, 91-92; number
  of, 127
— and emotions, 60
— experience of mind, 155
— mothers: our mothers, 126; to
  one another, 139
— qualities of, 144
— reasons for: experience of
  samsara, 28; suffering, 25-27
Seven branch offering prayer, 114
Sex determination: during conception, 72
Shakyamuni, Lord Buddha. *See*
  Buddha Shakyamuni
Shamatha. *See* Zhinay
Shangpa Kagyu tradition, 168

Shariputra. *See* Stories: Shariputra
  and mother
Sharmarpa Rinpoche, 99, 175
Sheik: and thirty wives, 62-63
Shock, while in bardo of possibili-
  ties, 81-82
Shrine, arrangement of, 110-111
Signs of perfection: of historical
  buddhas, 87-88
Six Bardos. *See* Bardos, six
Six primary emotions. *See* Emo-
  tions, six primary
Six realms of samsara. *See*
  Samsara, six realms of
Six yogas of Naropa, 76-77; bardo
  practice, 79; studied in retreat,
  168
Six-syllable mantra. *See* Mantra,
  six-syllable
Skandas: void of causal reality, 16
Skillful means. *See* Means, skillful
Sleep, emotional activity of, 53
Sound: as union of wisdom and
  means, 90; and emptiness,
  union of, 117; insubstantial like
  echo, 16; reason able to express
  with it, 107; vajrayana view on,
  16
Southern continent. *See* Mount
  Sumeru
Space, element, 85; breakdown of,
  in dying process, 73-76
Space, meditation upon, 7. *See also*
  Meditation, on space
Space, ten directions of, 131. *See
  also* Consciousness
Speech, vajrayana view on, 16
Sphere of consciousness. *See*
  Consciousness, discursive
Spiritual development, 35, 38-39,
  42, 159; necessary elements of,
  158; progress in path of, 44;
  uselessness of guilt in, 38
Spiritual friend, in mahayana, 172

Spiritual practice: basis for, 35; making it effective, 158

Stories: Arya Katayana and angry woman, 126-127; bell, hell, and mantra, 130; Bodhisattva Chenrezig and demoness, 124; of building monastery, 39-42; Chungawa's, 119-123; dakini and dull-witted husband,128-129; of Manjushri's powers, 128-129; of marriage desires, 39-42; of matricide, 39-42; Milarepa and hunters, 17; seven bugs and stupa, 5; Shariputra and mother, 39-42; sheik and thirty wives, 62-63; tortoise and stupa, 5

Students. *See also* Tsaway lama
— average, opportunities of, 95
— benefitted by explicit/implicit teachings, 147
— doubting tsaway lama, 176
— excellent: capabilities of, 146-147; opportunities of, 94
— inferior, difficulties of, 95
— qualities of, 176
— Western: becoming like Milarepa, 164; demonstrating commitment to Dharma, 169; with Dharma interest, 169-170

Stupa, construction of, 132
Stupidity. *See* Dullness of mind
Stupor: in meditation, 152
Suffering, 179; clinging to as pleasure, 89; how to end, 36; mental and emotional, 51; reasons for, 25-27
Suicide, 66
Sun. *See* Allegories; Metaphors
Sunlight. *See* Allegories: luminaries
Surangama Sutra. See Preface
T.V. remote control. *See* Metaphors: T.V. remote control

Tai Situ Rinpoche, 175; the XIIth, letters of, *See* Appendix A, Foreword, Preface

Taking refuge: benefits for children, 47; benefits of, 48; Dharma name, 47; first step in Tibetan Buddhism, 43-44; and maintaining other spiritual traditions, 48; objects of, 45-46. *See also* Vow of refuge

Tantrayana. *See* Vajrayana; Visualization practices
Taste, one, 109
Tathagata, 22; free expression of, 44
Teacher: most important quality of, 99; rarity of finding superior, 146
Teachings, explicit/implicit, 147
Thoughts: arising of, 148-150; manifestation of mind, 63; meditation upon, 148-150; reason they arise, 149
Thoughts, discursive, 8-9, 60, 101-102; inability to control, 143; and mahayana path, 103; stages of, 162-163
Three gates. *See* Gates, three
Three Jewels. *See* Jewels, Three
Three kayas. *See* Trikayas
Three Roots. *See* Roots, Three
Three story building. *See* Allegories: three story building
Three Yanas. *See* Triyanas
Three-year retreat. *See* Retreat, three-year
Tibetan Book of the Dead, 77-78
Tibetan Buddhism. *See* Buddhism, Tibetan
Tigers. *See* Dreams, nightmares
Tilopa. *See* Mahamudra
Tonglen, 140
Tongue, consciousness of, 92-93
Tortoise. *See* Allegories: tortoise

and yoke

Tortoise and stupa. See Stories: tortoise and stupa

Touch, consciousness of, 92-93

Transformation, obstacles to complete, 81; See also Mahayana, transformation

Trikaya, illustrated qualities of, 157

Triyanas, 11; gradual progressive development, 89-90; mastery of, 16; paths explained, 11-16; principle source of refuge, 46; See also Hinayana; Mahayana; Vajrayana

Truth, absolute, 131; of co-emergent wisdom, attaining, 95

Truth, relative, 131, 158

Tsaway Lama. See also Dorje Chang; Mahamudra
— as object of refuge, 46
— benefits of having, 148, 172-173
— blessings of: 146; kindness of, 159
— disparaging of: difficulties it causes, 176
— doubts about, 176
— in Karma Kagyu lineage, 99, 174-177
— meditation on 152
— qualities of: 176; good, 146; root of all blessings, 95
— and students, various capacities of, 94-95
— vajrayana idea: 172; undifferentiated from Three Jewels/Roots, 172

Tsu-u-ma. See Channels

Twelve links of dependent origination. See Links of dependent origination, twelve

Unconsciousness: in after-death, 77-78; in after-death and ignorance, 101-102; in after-death, antidote for, 79; due to shock of death, 68; following death, 130-131; following death, length of, 77

Unimpeded manifestation of emptiness, 59. See also Nature of mind

Unimpeded mind: need for direct experience of, 156

Unimpededness: of mind, 7-9, 61, 151

Union of wisdom and means, 90

Upaya. See Means, skillful

Utpattiakrama. See Kyirim

Vajra Pride, 109, 110; stabilizing, 176

Vajradhara, 100, 101, 173; essential tsaway lama, 9. Also see Dorje Chang

Vajrasattva practice: benefits of, 98

Vajrayana, 15-18. See also Mahamudra
— instantaneous liberation through, 15, 105
— methods of: confronting emotionality, 56-57
— path of: defined, 105; recognition of emptiness, 89-90; suitability of path, 105-106; and virtuous actions, 31
— practice: beginning visualization/prayers, 113; commitments to, 111; demonstration of, by Buddha Shakyamuni, 103; given by Buddha Shakyamuni, 110
— sacredness of path: 103-104; reason to practice now, 161; only three historical Buddhas to teach it, 91

Veils of obscuration. See Obscurations, four veils of

Violence, physical, 53, 55

Vipashyana. See Lhatong

Virtuous actions, 11, 158; and
compassion, 3; defined, 32; ten,
12. *See also* Non-virtuous
actions
Visualization. *See also* Meditation
— at beginning of vajrayana
practices, 113
— of Chenrezig: 113-114; during
mantra recitation, 115; practice
of white Chenrezig, 111-117.
(*See also* Chenrezig sadhana
commentary in Appendix B)
— for bodhisattva prayer/vow,
133
— practice of: and interdependent
arising, 97; stabilizing visualization, 143-144; tonglen, 140
— principles of: 109; usefulness
of, 79
— on space: nature of, 7
— on spheres of light, 145
— of Yidam: and clinging, 19;
and vajra pride, 176
Void, consciousness, 16
Void, form, 16, 17; emptiness of,
90
Void: meaning of term, 14
Void of: causal reality. *See*
Skandas; karmic fruition, 17
Void, sound, 16, 17; emptiness of,
90
Voidness, 14; eighteen characteristics of, 155
Voidness, seal of. *See* Mahamudra
Vows. *See also* Samaya
— bodhisattva: 127, 134-135; as
taken in former times, 132;
benefits of, 140; how broken,
139; how to take and maintain,
132-133; keeping and maintaining, 138-139; need to renew,
139-140; in Tibetan transliteration,
136-137; what it means in
everyday life, 138

— choice of: when re-entering
world from retreat, 168-169
— genyen, 12
— monk and nun: full ordination
12; novice 12
— purification of: broken, 98
— of Refuge: 46-48; breaking of,
48
Water: boiling, 65. *See also* Metaphors, using water
Water element, 85; breakdown of,
in dying process, 73-74
Waves: manifestation of ocean, 63
Wealth: attachment to in bardo of
possibilities, 81; benefit of
prostrations, 96; beyond death's
door, 42-43; mantra for, 108. *See
also* Generosity
Weather, control of, 108
Wind element. *See* Air element
Wisdom: accumulation of, 146; co-
emergent, 95; co-emergent, two
methods to recognize, 145-146;
defined, 89; development of,
and liberation, 30; primordial
(or base), 3; and skillful means,
15
Wisdom and means, union of, 15;
defined, 90
Wisdom element, 85-86; flowing
through channels, 106-107
Yanas, three. *See* Triyanas
Yidam. *See also* Vajrayana
— blessing of: 16; as source of
refuge, 46; brings union of
wisdom and means, 91; pure
realm, 102
— Chenrezig, 110
— form union of void and appearance, 15
— Lord of Knowledge, 128
— meditation on: in after-death
bardos, 79
— path of: manifested by Lord

Buddha, 88; why important, 89
— practice of: benefits/obstacles
to, in after-death state, 81; and
interdependent arising, 97;
leads to accomplished
bodhisattva level, 88; three
characteristics of, 109
— root of all accomplishments, 95
— samadhi: realization of, 101
— and tsaway lama: inseparable,
172
— visualization of: and clinging,
144-147; practice of, 101; result
of vajra pride, 176
Yoke. *See* Allegories: tortoise and
yoke
Zhinay, 19, 30-31, 103; darkness
during practice, 152-153; reason
to practice, 11-12; two traditions
of, 19

Prajnaparamita, holding a vajra and the Prajna Paramita Sutra (Pen and ink drawing by unknown artist, 20th century)

AFTERWORD

&

PRAYER FOR THE CONTINUATION OF THE KAGYU TRADITION

Lost in my thoughts while sitting in the shrine room at Sonada in 1983, I had no idea my desire to bring Kalu Rinpoche's words to you, the reader, would require the amount of effort it has (over 4,000 hours to date). Nor was there any anticipation of how the work itself would deeply change my life by changing my understanding concerning the true nature of mind.

Somewhere around 1,800 hours into the work, I was deeply involved in the material contained in Chapters Six, Nine, and Ten. Late one night, the overwhelming message they contained somehow settled into clarity. There arose in me an intensity of devotion that spontaneously manifested itself into the following prayer.

It has frequently been said that the Kagyu lineage will last as long as time (and space) to bring benefit to all sentient beings. Still, because of the unadulterated joy the blessing of the Shangpa Kagyu and Karma Kagyu mothers and fathers has given me, my prayer is for this fruition. Please share in the aspiration as you read this, my offering of the truth of my being as I stand, as ever, poised on the threshold to liberation.

E.S.

Prayer for the Continuation of the Kagyu Tradition

Endlessly turning the vortex
of spacious clarity,
Compassionately taming the psora
of sorrowful delusion,
Mindfully transforming the arising
of salient wisdom,

Kagyu Fathers, hear our prayer!

In the dead of night, the sound of thunder,
the touch of rain,
May transcendent wisdom wash the mind clean,
And, in the light of day, the time of now,
the taste of amrita,
May luminous clarity manifest as enlightened mind,

Kagyu Mothers, pray, heed our plea!

Before you succumb to desolation at my faithless wanderings,
May you outlive my last faltering grasp
of ego's reluctance at true 'self'-acceptance.

Before you succeed in achievement of your faithful goal,
May you witness the complete liberation
of beings, finally tamed in acceptance of 'other'.

Before you pass into the beyondness of the beyond,
  May the last grain of samsaric shores
  be dissolved in your ocean of compassion.

Before you rest your life and love for sentient beings,
  May you succeed in your bodhicitta
  by dispersing innumerable waves of awareness.

Kagyu Mothers, Kagyu Fathers, Kagyu Tulkus,
In all our lifetimes, may we find solace in you!

Kalu Rinpoche and Lama Gyaltsen share the enjoyment of the moment with Sherab Ebin at Sonada in the late 1960s.(Photograph by J.G. Sherab Ebin)

Kalu Rinpoche, together with several other highly respected Rinpoches, has established a non-profit organization intent upon translating Tibetan Dharma texts into several languages. Currently, this project has begun its first work, the translation of the *Treasury of Knowledge* by Jamgon Kongtrul the Great, which will be more than two thousand pages when finished. The construction of a permanent residence for the translators is scheduled to begin soon in Bodh-Gaya, India, and some fifty translators and pandits are to be involved in this on-going effort to enable the wisdom preserved in Tibet to reach the world. It was one of Kalu Rinpoche's last wishes that the work in progress be completed and that the project continue to bring the Dharma into as many languages as possible. Donations for this project, entitled Dragyur Dzamling Kunchab, should be sent in care of Lama Norlha, Kagyu Thubten Chöling, 127 Sheafe Road, Wappingers Falls, New York 12590, USA. Donations may also be sent to Lama Norlha at the same address to help keep Kalu Rinpoche's monastery in Sonada (a small town in the Darjeeling District of West Bengal, India) in good repair and to support the lamas, genyens, monks, and nuns living there.

For a complete list of Karma Kagyu Dharma Centers and Study Groups, please write to Karma Triyana Dharmachakra, 352 Meads Mountain Road, Woodstock, New York 12498, USA.

E.S.

About the Editor

Raised in rural California, Elizabeth Selandia began a long and adventurous search for the teachings concerning the true nature of the mind at the age of seventeen while in the midst of reading haiku and Stendhal. In the seventeen years to follow, she was to travel the world, visiting thirty-seven countries, and taking the time to reside in several places and to deepen her appreciation for other cultures. Returning to her native California, her search eventually led her to vajrayana. She has since attended several important cycles of initiations and teachings in the Shangpa Kagyu, Karma Kagyu, and Nyingma traditions, traveling to Canada, Denmark, Nepal, and India to receive these blessings of insight. She holds a B.A. with honors from the College of Letters and Science, University of California at Berkeley.

A smiling Kalu Rinpoche in the late 1960s in his home at Sonada, India. (Photograph by J.G. Sherab Ebin)